Welcome to Zoom español 2

Abigail Hardwick
Isabel Alonso de Sudea
María Isabel Isern Vivancos

Meet Elena, Juan and Roberto.
Find out more about them in this book
and on the *Zoom español 2* video.

Symbols and headings you will find in the book: what do they mean?

  A video activity

  A listening activity

 A speaking activity

 A reading activity

 A writing activity

 Do this with a partner

 Grammar information

 Think about this!

 Important words or phrases

Challenge A challenge

Extra Star / Plus	Reinforcement and extension activities
Labolengua	Grammar, strategies, pronunciation
Prueba	Test yourself
Vocabulario	Unit vocabulary list
Leer	Reading pages
Gramática	Grammar reference
Glosario	Glossary

OXFORD
UNIVERSITY PRESS

Tabla de materias

0.1 ¡Bienvenido!

- Vocabulary: meet and greet people; talk about a journey
- Grammar: use the imperfect tense; ask questions about someone's journey
- Skills: greet people formally and informally

🎧 **Escucha y pon en orden la conversación.**

Ejemplo: 8, 1 ...

1 Y yo soy Juan.
2 Bienvenido a Segovia.
3 Bien, gracias.
4 ¿Qué tal el viaje?
5 ¡Vamos!
6 ¡Vale!
7 El avión era cómodo y el tren era rápido.
8 ¡Hola! Soy Elena.
9 ¡Gracias!
10 ¡Encantado! Soy Roberto.

Escribe la conversación en el orden correcto.

Ejemplo: 1 ¡Hola! Soy Elena.

Empareja las frases en español con las frases en inglés.

Ejemplo: 1 d

1 How was your journey?
2 I'm ...
3 The train was quick
4 Let's go!
5 OK
6 The plane was comfortable
7 Pleased to meet you
8 Welcome

a El tren era rápido
b Encantado/a
c Bienvenido/a
d ¿Qué tal el viaje?
e El avión era cómodo
f Soy ...
g Vale
h ¡Vamos!

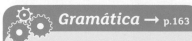

Practica la conversación con tu compañero.

¿Qué tal el viaje?		
El avión El tren El barco El coche	era	cómodo / incómodo rápido ruidoso aburrido
Estoy mareado/a		
Había mucho tráfico		

⚙️ *Gramática* → p.163

The imperfect tense

We use the imperfect to talk about something that carried on for a period of time in the past.

ser: era   *it was*
haber: había   *there was*

5 Escucha. Empareja las conversaciones con los dibujos.

NC 3

Ejemplo: 1 b

6 Escucha otra vez. ¿Qué tipo de transporte era? ¿Qué tal el viaje?

NC 3

Ejemplo: 1 avión – fenomenal, rápido, cómodo

7 ¿Formal o informal? Clasifica las frases.

Ejemplo: 1 informal

1 Hola, José. ¿Cómo estás?
2 Bienvenida a Madrid, señora Luisa.
3 Buenos días, señor García. ¿Cómo está usted?
4 Hola Carlos, ¿qué tal?

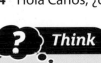 **Think**

Remember that **n** and **ñ** are two different letters in Spanish.

n – n like English, as in *bueno*

ñ – ny, as in *señor* (se**ny**or)

What other words with **ñ** in have you learnt?

8 Escribe y crea un dibujo animado en el aeropuerto o en la estación de tren. Usa las actividades 1 y 6 para ayudarte.

? **Think**

Remember that **r** and **rr** are pronounced differently in Spanish.

r – single r, as in *era*
rr – long, double r, as in *aburrido*

It can change the meaning of the word, so make sure you say it correctly:

pero – but
perro – dog

? **Think**

How does the last person greet the last traveller? Why?

Can you think of any other formal or informal ways of speaking you have learnt before?

Challenge

 With your partner, write and act out a scene where you meet someone at an airport or station. How good or bad was the journey?

NC 3–5

- Vocabulary: say how you feel
- Grammar: use *ser* to describe character and *estar* to describe mood
- Skills: be aware of 'false friends'

1 Estoy triste.

2 Estoy contento.

3 Estamos ilusionados.

4 Estoy furiosa.

5 Estamos aburridos.

6 Estamos decepcionadas.

? Think

Sometimes words that look similar in Spanish and English are not helpful!

Decepcionado looks a little like the English word 'deceive'.

Ilusionado looks a little like the English word 'illusion'.

But this is not what they mean! Use a **dictionary** or the **Vocabulario** section to check what they **really** mean.

LEER 1 Responde a las preguntas.

Ejemplo: 1 La madre de Roberto está triste.

1 ¿Cómo está la madre de Roberto?
2 ¿Cómo están sus amigas María e Isabel?
3 ¿Cómo están sus abuelos?
4 ¿Cómo está su padre?
5 ¿Cómo está su hermana Gabriela?
6 ¿Cómo están sus amigos Ricardo y Rogelio?

ESCUCHAR 2 Escucha. Escoge la palabra correcta de la actividad 1. ¿Por qué están así?

NC 4

Ejemplo: 1 Madre – triste – porque Roberto está en España

HABLAR 3 Habla con tu compañero. ¿Cómo estás? ¿Quién eres?

Ejemplo: **A** Estoy furiosa.
B Eres Gabriela.
A ¡Correcto!

⚙ Gramática → p.162

Estar can be used to say where something is: *Madrid está en España.*

It is also used to say how you are feeling, or what mood you are in **at the moment** (temporary):

Estoy contento – I am happy (at the moment).

estar – *to be*

estoy – *I am*	estamos – *we are*
estás – *you (s) are*	estáis – *you (pl) are*
está – *he/she/it is, you (formal) are*	están – *they/you (pl formal) are*

? Think

*María está content**a***	*Las chicas están content**as***
*Pedro está content**o***	*Los abuelos están content**os***

Why does the ending of *contento* change? Do you know the rule?
Careful! *Triste* is different:
*María está trist**e***
*Pedro está trist**e***
*Los abuelos están trist**es***

Escribe. ¿Cómo están en este momento? ¿Qué dicen?

Ejemplo: 1 Estoy contenta.

 Clasifica los adjetivos en la descripción de la familia de Roberto. ¿Carácter o sentimiento? Busca las palabras que no conoces en un diccionario, o pregunta al profesor o a tu compañero.

Ejemplo: simpática – carácter, triste – sentimiento

 ¿Qué tal tu familia, Roberto? ¿Y cómo es?

Pues, mi madre es muy simpática, pero ahora está triste porque yo estoy aquí en España. Mi papá es muy divertido – ¡está contento porque tiene un coche nuevo! Mi hermana Gabriela es pesada. En este momento está furiosa porque quiere ir a la discoteca pero mamá dice que no puede. Mis amigos Ricardo y Rogelio son un poco testarudos. Hoy están aburridos porque está lloviendo y no pueden jugar al fútbol. Mis abuelos son generosos, y ahora están ilusionados porque van de vacaciones a Méjico. ¡Qué suerte! Mis amigas María e Isabel son inteligentes pero están decepcionadas: no pueden ir al cine porque no tienen bastante dinero. ¡Qué lástima!

 Escribe. Describe a ti mismo. ¿Cómo te llamas? ¿Cómo eres? ¿Cómo estás en este momento?

NC 3–4

Ejemplo: Me llamo Oliver. Soy generoso y divertido, pero hoy estoy furioso porque no puedo jugar al voleibol.

Gramática → p.162

Ser is used to say who you are or what your character is (permanent):
Soy Marcos y soy generoso. – I'm Marcos and I'm generous.

ser – to be
soy – *I am*
eres – *you (s) are*
es – *he/she/it is, you (formal) are*
somos – *we are*
sois – *you (pl) are*
son – *they/you (pl formal) are*

? Think

Be careful!
Ser and *estar* can completely alter the meaning of a word.
Roberto **está** *aburrido* – Roberto is **bored**
but
Roberto **es** *aburrido* – Roberto is **boring**.

Challenge

 Find a photo of your favourite celebrity, a friend or someone in your family. Tell your partner about them, or write a description. Who are they? What are they like? How are they feeling in the picture?

NC 4

- Vocabulary: say if you get on with your friends and family
- Grammar: *me llevo bien con … / me cae mal …*
- Skills: revise opinions

Me llevo bien con mi madre.

Me cae mal mi abuelo.

No soporto a mi hermano.

  Escucha. ¿Qué dice Elena?

NC 3 — *Ejemplo: 2 …*

1 No me llevo bien con mi padre.
2 No me cae bien mi madre.
3 No soporto a mi hermano Juan.
4 Me llevo bien con mi abuelo.
5 No soporto a mi prima Ágata.
6 Mi primo Ramón me cae mal siempre.

+	–
me llevo bien con …	no me llevo bien con …
me cae bien …	no me cae bien …
	no soporto a …

 Escucha otra vez. Empareja las frases.

1	Elena se lleva muy bien con	a	su madre.
2	A Elena no le cae bien	b	su padre.
3	No soporta a	c	su primo Ramón.
4	Le cae bien también	d	su hermano Juan.
5	Se lleva bien con	e	su prima Ágata.
6	Se lleva bastante bien con	f	su abuelo.

 **Think**

Remember that **l** and **ll** are pronounced differently in Spanish.

l – single **l** like the English, as in *familia*

ll – **ly**, as in *llevo* (**ly**evo)

When spoken quickly, **ll** sometimes sounds like a **y** sound – *me llamo* can sound like 'me **y**amo'.

 Gramática → p.165

Llevarse bien con – *to get on with* is a reflexive verb like **levantarse** and **ducharse**.

Caer bien – *to like / get on with* is like the verb **gustar** – an impersonal verb.

Me cae bien Miguel – *I get on well with Miguel.*

¿**Te** cae bien Miguel? – *Do **you** get on well with Miguel?*

Le cae bien su padre – ***She** gets on well with her father.*

Nos ca**en** bien Paco y Pedro – ***We** get on well with Paco and Pedro.*

 Habla con tu compañero. ¿Te llevas bien con tu familia?

NC 3–4 — *Ejemplo: Me llevo bien con mi madre pero me cae muy mal mi …*

4 **Elena habla de los jóvenes de su clase del insti. Lee lo que dice.**

NC 4

Julio

Me llevo muy bien con mi amigo Julio. Es simpático y divertido, y normalmente está contento. Montamos en bici, vamos al cine y a la piscina. ¡Lo pasamos bomba! Me ayuda con los deberes y me escucha cuando tengo problemas. Es un amigo de verdad.

Lucía

No me cae bien Lucía. Está en mi clase, pero es muy antipática. Es testaruda e impaciente, no me habla y siempre está de mal humor. En fin, ¡que es muy pesada! ¡No la soporto!

Pilar y Pepe

Normalmente me llevo muy bien con Pilar y Pepe. Son extrovertidos, inteligentes y divertidos. Cuentan muchos chistes. Pero a veces, cuando están aburridos, son un poco inmaduros, entonces me caen mal.

Mi madre/mi padre Mi hermano/a Mi abuelo/a Mi amigo/a	me ayuda	no me ayuda
	me escucha	no me escucha
	me habla	no me habla
	dice mentiras	no dice mentiras
	cuenta chistes	no cuenta chistes
	es pesado/a	no es pesado/a
	es estricto/a	no es estricto/a
	siempre está de mal humor	nunca está de mal humor

5 **Lee las descripciones otra vez. ¿Quién es?**

NC 4   *Ejemplo: 1 Julio*

1 Normalmente está contento.
2 Siempre está de mal humor.
3 Elena se lleva bien con ellos porque son extrovertidos.
4 Le caen bien porque siempre cuentan chistes.
5 Cuando están aburridos, le caen mal.
6 Le ayuda y le escucha.

6 **Habla con tu compañero. ¿De quién hablas?**

NC 3–4   Ejemplo: A *Elena se lleva bien con ellos normalmente.*
                          B *Pepe y Pilar.*

Challenge

Carry out a survey. Ask your friends who they get on with in their family and why. Present some of your findings to the class and write them up.

NC 3–4

0.4 ¿Vienes conmigo?

- Vocabulary: accept and refuse invitations, buy cinema tickets
- Grammar: understand use of the personal *a*, use *conmigo/contigo*
- Skills: accept and refuse politely

El Video Reto

 Mira el video (primera parte) y completa las frases.

a Roberto se lleva bien con ⬜ cuando está de ⬜ ⬜.

b Elena no se lleva bien con ⬜ porque es ⬜ y dice ⬜.

c A Roberto le cae bien ⬜ porque cuenta ⬜.

 Mira el video y contesta a las preguntas en inglés.

a What do they want to do?
b What's the problem?
c How much money do they have?
d What time must the show be?

 Which of these questions ask about:

a when the film showings are
b how much the tickets cost
c if there is a discount for students

¿A cuánto son las entradas?
¿A qué hora hay sesiones?
¿Cuánto cuestan las entradas?
¿Hay alguna sesión de *Transformers* hoy?
¿Qué precio tienen las entradas?
¿Tienen descuento para estudiantes?

la entrada – *ticket*
la sesión – *showing*
¿cuánto ...? – *how much?*
un descuento – *discount*
palomitas – *popcorn*

 Mira el video y completa la tabla.

	Sesión – hora	Entrada – precio
Elena		
Roberto		
Juan		

 Who do you think won? Watch the video again.

NC 4

🎧 **Lee y escucha las excusas para rechazar las invitaciones. ¿Son rechazos corteses o groseros?**

¿Te gustaría ir al museo de Segovia conmigo?

a

¿El museo? ¡Qué horror! Odio los museos, son aburridos.

b

Lo siento, pero no me gustan mucho los museos.

c

Muchas gracias, pero no puedo ir contigo al museo. Voy al partido de fútbol con Juan.

cortés – *polite*
grosero – *rude*
el rechazo – *refusal*

Invitación				Respuesta		
¿Te gustaría		al cine	conmigo?	Sí, me gustaría mucho	ir	contigo.
¿Quieres	ir	al partido de fútbol		Lo siento, no puedo		
¿Vienes		al museo		¡Qué horror! No quiero		
		al parque				
		a la piscina				

Excusa				
Voy a	visitar	a	mis abuelos.	
	ayudar		mi padre.	

Gramática → p.160

The personal *a* has no real translation in English. You use it with certain verbs (*visitar, ayudar*) when talking about something you are doing with people but **not** things.

Voy a visitar **a** mis abuelos. *I'm going to visit my grandparents. (people)*

But:

Voy a visitar el museo. *I'm going to visit the museum. (thing)*

 7
NC 3–4

Tus amigos te invitan a salir. ¿Cuál es tu respuesta? Puedes ser cortés o grosero.

Ejemplo: Lo siento, no puedo ir contigo. Voy al parque con Andrés.

a

Vamos a la playa. ¿Quieres venir?

b

¿Te gustaría venir al parque con Ana y conmigo?

? **Think**

Remember that **b** and **v** sound the same in Spanish.

b – like the English b, *b*ien

v – like the English b, *v*amos (**b**amos)

Practise saying all the words with **v** on these two pages.

 **Challenge**

Work in groups of three or four. One person is given different invitations by the others, and has to decide to accept or refuse, and how. Act it out to the rest of the class, who will vote for the best group.

NC 3–4

- Vocabulary: make excuses
- Grammar: *conmigo, contigo, con él, con ella* etc.
- Skills: respond politely

Voy al cine para ver la nueva película de ciencia ficción. ¿Quieres venir conmigo?

Lo siento, no puedo ir contigo porque voy de compras con mi mamá.

¡No quiero ir al cine con ella! No me cae bien, y además odio las películas de ciencia ficción.

 LEER 1 Lee la invitación y la respuesta.

 ESCUCHAR 2 🎧 Escucha las tres conversaciones. Empareja las frases con la conversación correcta.

NC 5

Ejemplo: 1 a, ...

- **a** ¡No quiero ir a la piscina con ellas!
- **b** ¿Les gustaría venir con nosotros?
- **c** ¿Quieres venir con nosotras?
- **d** ¿Vienes conmigo?
- **e** Lo siento, no puedo ir con vosotras.
- **f** No podemos ir con ustedes.
- **g** No puedo ir contigo.
- **h** No queremos ir con ellos.
- **i** No quiero ir con ella.

> ⚙️ **Gramática**
>
> On page 11 you learnt that **conmigo** means 'with me', and **contigo** means 'with you'.
>
> Look at activity 2. Can you work out how to say:
>
> with him   with her   with us   with you (plural)
> with them (female)   with them (male)
> with you (plural formal)?

 ESCUCHAR 3 🎧 Escucha otra vez. ¿Cuáles son las excusas, y cuál es la verdad?

Ejemplo: 1 excusa – tengo muchos deberes; verdad – odio nadar

Empareja las excusas con los dibujos.

Ejemplo: **1** f

1 Voy a pasear al perro.
2 Voy a hacer los deberes.
3 Voy a hacer las compras para mi madre.
4 Voy a lavarme el pelo.
5 Voy a ayudar a mi padre en el jardín.
6 Voy a visitar a mis abuelos.

Con tu compañero inventa excusas para rechazar invitaciones. Utiliza las palabras de la casilla.

Ejemplo: No puedo ir al restaurante contigo porque voy al partido de rugby con mi tío.

> tío   acostarme   vacaciones   (el) partido   medio-hermano
> restaurante   cumpleaños   madrastra

? Think

Look back at page 11. Which of the excuses in activity 4 use the personal **a**?

Lee y completa el email con las palabras de la actividad 5.

Hola Sofía

¡Qué desastre! No puedo salir contigo el fin de semana. El sábado voy a ayudar a mi **1** _____. Vamos a hacer las compras para la fiesta de **2** _____ de mi **3** _____. Mi hermano va a un **4** _____ de fútbol con sus amigos, y no va a ayudar. ¡Increíble! Es muy perezoso. El domingo vamos a visitar a mi **5** _____. Está muy ilusionado porque va de **6** _____ la semana que viene. Vamos a comer en un **7** _____.
Por la tarde voy a **8** _____ temprano porque tengo insti el día siguiente.
Lo siento mucho. ¿Quieres venir conmigo al cine el martes por la tarde?
Carlota

⚙ Gramática → p.164

You learnt how to talk about what you are **going to do** in *Zoom 1*.

You use the correct part of the verb *ir* – to go, and the infinitive of the verb you are going to do.

Voy a comer paella – *I'm going to eat paella.*

Vamos a visitar a los abuelos – *We're going to visit the grandparents.*

Can you make up another example?

Escribe la respuesta de Sofía. ¿Acepta o rechaza la invitación?

Challenge
Write text messages inviting your friends to go out, and reply to their messages, making excuses. Think up some outrageous excuses if you can, e.g. *No puedo ir a la discoteca contigo. No tengo zapatos.*

NC 4–5

Comprender – *Ser* and *estar*

A *Ser*

Ser and *estar* both mean 'to be', but they are used in different situations. *Ser* is used for permanent states such as nationality, the time, jobs, descriptions, relationships, what things are made of and, as you have learnt in this unit, character traits.

Soy colombiano. I am Colombian.
Son las ocho y media. It's half past eight.
Mi hermano es actor. My brother's an actor.
Carla es mi prima. Carla is my cousin.
Mi abuela es generosa. My grandmother is generous.

1 Complete the description using the correct part of the verb *ser*.

Me llamo Jorge y **1** ▓▓▓▓ de Méjico, así que **2** ▓▓▓▓ mejicano. Juanita **3** ▓▓▓▓ mi madre y **4** ▓▓▓▓ profesora en mi instituto. Mi instituto **5** ▓▓▓▓ grande, pero las aulas **6** ▓▓▓▓ pequeñas. **7** ▓▓▓▓ 32 alumnos en mi clase. Tengo muchos amigos en el insti – ¡**8** ▓▓▓▓ todos divertidos!

> **ser – *to be***
> soy – *I am*
> eres – *you (s) are*
> es – *he/she/it is, you (formal) are*
> somos – *we are*
> sois – *you (pl) are*
> son – *they/you (pl formal) are*

B *Estar*

Estar is used for temporary states, for moods and for location.

Mis abuelos están enfermos. My grandparents are ill.
Clara está muy ilusionada. Clara is very excited.
Madrid está en el centro de España. Madrid is in the centre of Spain.

> **estar – *to be***
> estoy – *I am*   estamos – *we are*
> estás – *you (s) are*   estáis – *you (pl) are*
> está – *he/she/it is, you (formal) are*   están – *they/you (pl formal) are*

2 Find the mistakes in the following sentences. Say what the problems are, and correct them.

1 Marcos está inteligente pero no es muy contento.
2 Mi casa es en las afueras de la ciudad. Está bonita.
3 Estamos organizados, y ellos son deprimidos.
4 Mi tío está futbolista, y es triste.

3 Write a caption for each picture using the phrases below on the left.

C More phrases using *estar*

Some of these are not what you would expect!
estar casado – *to be married*
estar vivo – *to be alive*
estar divorciado – *to be divorced*
estar muerto – *to be dead*

D The personal *a*

There is no equivalent to the personal *a* in English. It is used before pronouns and nouns when referring to people (and pets!) but not objects. It shows the difference between people and things.

Voy a visitar **a** mis primos. *I'm going to visit my cousins. (people)*
Voy a visitar el castillo. *I'm going to visit the castle. (thing)*

A becomes **al** in front of a masculine noun:
Voy a pasear (a + el) **al** perro. *I'm going to walk the dog.*

4 Should you use the personal *a* in these sentences?

1 Voy a sacar ▭▭▭▭ la basura.
2 Voy a ayudar ▭▭▭▭ mi amigo.
3 Quiero ▭▭▭▭ mis padres.
4 Busco ▭▭▭▭ el cine.

Aprender – Dictionary skills

E Using a dictionary

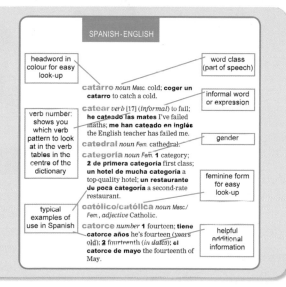

SPANISH-ENGLISH

headword in colour for easy look-up

word class (part of speech)

catarro *noun Masc.* cold; **coger un catarro** to catch a cold.

informal word or expression

verb number: shows you which verb pattern to look at in the verb tables in the centre of the dictionary

catear *verb* [17] (*Informal*) to fail; **he cateado las mates** I've failed maths; **me han cateado en inglés** the English teacher has failed me.

catedral *noun Fem.* cathedral.

gender

categoría *noun Fem.* **1** category; **2 de primera categoría** first class; **un hotel de mucha categoría** a top-quality hotel; **un restaurante de poca categoría** a second-rate restaurant.

feminine form for easy look-up

typical examples of use in Spanish

católico/católica *noun Masc./ Fem., adjective* Catholic.

catorce *number* **1** fourteen; **tiene catorce años** he's fourteen (years old); **2** fourteenth (*in dates*); **el catorce de mayo** the fourteenth of May.

helpful additional information

5 Find these words in a dictionary. What do they mean? What kind of words are they (noun, verb, adjective, adverb)?

> soler polvo crujiente quinto
>   acostarse orillas
>   salado por lo general

6 Write sentences using these words to help you remember them.

Example: La manzana es muy crujiente.

Hablar – Vowel sounds

F Sounding Spanish

It is important to pronounce the vowels correctly when speaking in order to sound Spanish. To remind you:

a [ah] – like apple   i [ee] – like seen   u [oo] – like boot
e [eh] – like pen   o [oh] – like dot

It is especially important to pronounce words that look like English ones in the Spanish way.

7 👥 Practise these words with a partner.

Europa inteligente actividad café tenis fútbol catedral elefante grande televisión transporte vacaciones supermercado

EEEnteligente

8 🎧 Now listen. How Spanish did you sound?

0.7 / Extra Star

- Vocabulary: talk about feelings and character
- Grammar: practise using *ser* and *estar*
- Skills: give invitations

¿Carácter o sentimiento? Elige la palabra correcta.
Character or mood? Choose the correct word.

NC 3

*Ejemplo: Mi mamá **es** muy divertida.*

1 Rodrigo es / está desordenado.
2 Valentín es / está triste.
3 Vicente y Amalia son / están estudiosos.
4 Soledad y Ramona son / están decepcionadas.
5 ¡Somos / estamos extrovertidos!
6 ¿Eres / estás contento?

Empareja las frases de la actividad 1 con los dibujos.
Match the sentences from activity 1 to the pictures.

NC 2

*Ejemplo: **1** d*

Empareja las dos partes de las frases.
Match the two parts of the sentences.

NC 3

*Ejemplo: **1** c*

1 Me llevo bien con Paco
2 No me cae bien el profesor
3 Me cae bien Magdalena
4 No me llevo bien con León

a porque es muy estricto.
b porque es muy simpática.
c porque es divertido.
d porque es muy pesado.

> **Gramática → p.162**
>
> **Remember!**
> *Ser* is used for character (permanent):
> *Soy extrovertido/a.*
>
> *Estar* is used for mood (temporary):
> *Estoy decepcionado/a.*

Invita a tu amigo/a a estos lugares.
Invite your friend to these places.

NC 2–3

*Ejemplo: **1** ¿Vienes al parque conmigo?*

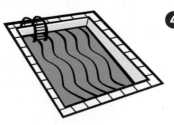

- Vocabulary: say if you get on with someone
- Grammar: practise using *ser* and *estar*
- Skills: respond to invitations

LEER 1

¿Ser o estar? Completa las frases con las palabras de la casilla.

(NC 3–4)

*Ejemplo: Santi **es** muy simpático, pero a veces **está** triste.*

| está | estamos | están |
| estás | sois | son |

1 ¡Feliz cumpleaños! ¿ ilusionada?

2 Pero niños, ¡qué pesados !

3 muy decepcionados porque no vamos de vacaciones.

4 Los chicos aburridos porque no pueden jugar al fútbol.

5 Julia casada con Luis.

6 Mis amigas estudiosas.

LEER 2

Lee lo que opina Rosario. ¿Son las frases verdaderas o falsas?

(NC 4)

No me cae bien mi padre. Es demasiado estricto, y muy testarudo. Pero a veces, cuando está de buen humor, es divertido.
En cambio, me llevo muy bien con mi madre. Es simpática y paciente. A veces está triste, porque mi hermano Pablo vive muy lejos, en Méjico. Me cae muy bien Pablo. Me escucha, me ayuda, y es muy divertido. ¡Qué pena que está en Méjico! También me caen bien mis abuelos, los padres de mi madre. Son generosos e inteligentes, y siempre están contentos. No soporto a mi tío Francisco. Es muy antipático e impaciente. Me caen bastante bien mis primas. Son un poco inmaduras y tímidas, pero no son antipáticas como su padre.

? Think

If *simpático* means nice / friendly, what does *antipálico* mean?

1 El padre de Rosario es estricto.
2 A Rosario no le cae bien su madre.
3 Pablo no ayuda a Rosario.
4 Sus abuelos están contentos.
5 A Rosario no le cae bien su tío.
6 Sus primas son muy maduras.

en cambio – *whereas*

ESCRIBIR 3

Tus amigos te invitan a salir. Acepta o rechaza las invitaciones.

(NC 3)

Ejemplo: Gracias, me gustaría mucho ir con vosotros.

Oye, ¿vienes al cine con nosotros? Dan una nueva película de acción.

Hay un concierto de nuestro grupo favorito en el parque. ¿Vienes?

Vamos al café para comer algo. ¿Quieres venir?

Escuchar

Listen to the three people. Which is speaking? How were their journeys?

Hablar

NC 3

1 Invite your friend to one of these places.
2 Accept or refuse their invitation.

Leer

NC 4

Read the description of Ofelia and decide if the sentences are true or false.

1 Ofelia is 14.
2 Ofelia doesn't listen.
3 She has problems.
4 She is intelligent.
5 She isn't silly.
6 Sometimes she is angry.

> Mi amiga Ofelia tiene catorce años. Es una amiga de verdad. Me escucha, habla conmigo, me ayuda con mis problemas. Es madura, inteligente y extrovertida. No es tímida ni boba. Normalmente está contenta pero a veces está triste. Nunca está furiosa conmigo. Me llevo muy bien con Ofelia.

Escribir

NC 3–4

Describe one of these people. What are they like? How are they feeling?

¡Bienvenido! — *Welcome!*

Bienvenido/a	*Welcome*
Encantado/a	*Pleased to meet you*
¿Qué tal el viaje?	*How was the journey?*
Soy	*I am*
Vale	*OK*
Vamos	*Let's go*
era	*it was*
fatal	*terrible*
largo	*long*
incómodo	*uncomfortable*
Había mucho tráfico	*There was a lot of traffic*

¿Cómo estás? — *How are you?*

aburrido/a	*boring/bored*
contento/a	*happy*
decepcionado/a	*disappointed*
furioso/a	*angry*
ilusionado/a	*excited*
generoso/a	*generous*
pesado/a	*a nuisance*
testarudo/a	*stubborn*
triste	*sad*

Me llevo bien con Elena — *I get on well with Elena*

me ayuda	*he/she helps me*
me habla	*he/she talks to me*
me escucha	*he/she listens to me*
dice mentiras	*he/she tells lies*
es estricto/a	*he/she is strict*
es bobo/a	*he/she is silly*
es testarudo/a	*he/she is stubborn*
cuenta chistes	*he/she tells jokes*
llevarse bien/mal con	*to get on well/badly with*
caer bien/mal	*to get on well/badly with*
estar de mal humor	*to be in a bad mood*
en cambio	*on the other hand/whereas*

¿Vienes conmigo? — *Are you coming with me?*

¿A qué hora hay sesiones?	*What time are the showings?*
¿Hay alguna sesión de … hoy?	*Is there a showing of … today?*
Hoy hay una sesión a las 21 horas.	*There's a showing at 9pm today.*
Tenemos una sesión que empieza a las 21 horas.	*We have a showing that starts at 9pm.*
¿Qué precio tienen las entradas?	*What price are the tickets?*
¿A cuánto son las entradas?	*How much are the tickets?*
¿Cuánto cuestan las entradas?	*How much do the tickets cost?*
Hay entradas a 8.50 euros.	*There are tickets for 8.50 euros.*
Tenemos entradas a 8.50.	*We have tickets for 8.50 euros.*
Las entradas cuestan 8.50 euros.	*The tickets cost 8.50 euros.*
¿Tienen descuento para estudiantes?	*Is there a discount for students?*
Sí, tenemos entradas a 7 euros para estudiantes.	*Yes, we have tickets at 7 euros for students.*
¿Vienes?	*Are you coming?*
Voy a …	*I'm going to …*
Me gustaría ir …	*I would like to go …*
¿Te gustaría venir?	*Would you like to come?*
Sí, me gustaría mucho.	*Yes, I'd like to a lot.*
Lo siento, no puedo.	*I'm sorry, I can't.*
¿Quieres venir conmigo?	*Do you want to come with me?*
el rechazo	*refusal*
la excusa	*excuse*
aceptar	*to accept*
rechazar	*to refuse*
cortés	*polite*
grosero/a	*rude*

I can …

- meet and greet people formally and informally
- talk about a journey
- ask someone about their journey
- say how I feel
- describe character and mood
- say if I get on with someone
- accept and refuse invitations politely
- make excuses politely

- Vocabulary: discuss differences in daily routines
- Grammar: use the verb *soler*; frequency adverbs
- Skills: adapt previously learnt language to revise the present tense

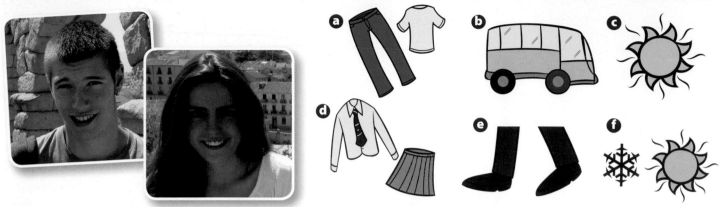

 Lee y empareja las frases con los dibujos.

NC 3

1 **Suelo ir** al insti a pie porque está cerca.
2 **Suelo ir** en el autobús escolar al colegio.
3 **Suelo ponerme** el uniforme.
4 Como no hay que llevar uniforme **suelo ponerme** vaqueros y una camiseta.
5 **Suele hacer** mucho calor en Cartagena.
6 En Segovia **suele hacer** frío en invierno y bastante calor en verano.

? Think

Another way of talking about things you **usually** do is to use the expressions *de costumbre*, *normalmente* and *por lo general*:
De costumbre voy a pie. *I usually go on foot.*
Normalmente me pongo vaqueros. *Normally I wear jeans.*
Por lo general voy en autobús. *I usually go by bus.*

🜂 Gramática → p.166

Soler + verb in the infinitive – I usually ...

To say you usually do something in Spanish you can use the verb *soler* plus the infinitive:

Suelo	levantarme a las siete. *I usually get up at seven o'clock.*
Sueles	ir en coche al colegio. *You (sing.) usually go to school by car.*
Suele	comer a la una en punto. *He/She usually eats at one o'clock on the dot.*
Solemos	hacer deporte los jueves. *We usually do sport on Thursdays.*
Soléis	ver la tele por la noche. *You (pl) usually watch TV in the evening.*
Suelen	visitar a sus abuelos los domingos. *They usually visit their grandparents on Sundays.*

- Verbs like *soler* are called radical or stem-changing verbs.
- Look at how and when *soler* changes. Can you remember other similar verbs that change in the same way?

 Lee las frases de la actividad 1 otra vez. ¿Puedes adivinar quién habla? ¿Roberto o Elena?

? Think

Which words are used for 'school'?

  **Escucha la conversación entre Roberto y Elena y verifica.**

Escucha y lee la conversación entre Roberto y su madre.

NC 4

¡Hola, hijo! ¿Qué tal te va en casa de tus tíos?
Bueno ... pues, la vida es bastante diferente.
¿A qué hora sueles levantarte para ir al colegio?

Normalmente me levanto temprano a las seis y media.

¿Qué hora es ahora en España?
Es la una de la tarde aquí pero son las siete de la mañana en Cartagena, ¿verdad?

Así es; hay seis horas de diferencia. ¿Qué sueles hacer los sábados?

Elena, Juan y yo solemos ir al cine a las cuatro porque mis tíos suelen trabajar.

¿Y los domingos?

Solemos comer en familia, una comida grande a las tres de la tarde.

 Lee otra vez y anota el orden de los relojes.

  Escucha otra conversación entre Roberto y Elena. Anota las diferencias. Copia y completa las fichas.

NC 4

 Escribe cinco frases sobre lo que suele hacer Juan en un día típico. Usa los verbos y las frases de abajo para ayudarte.

NC 3

Ejemplo: Juan suele ir al instituto en autobús.

Juan suele	comer jugar levantarse hablar ir ver	a las siete y media al instituto en autobús al tenis pizza la tele con sus amigos
Normalmente Por lo general De costumbre	come juega etc.	

Roberto
Se levanta a las _____
No come _____
Lleva _____
Vive en _____
Suele volver a casa a las _____
Se acuesta a las _____

Elena
Se levanta a las _____
Suele comer _____
No lleva _____
Vive en _____
Vuelve a las _____
Se acuesta a la _____

 **Elige la ficha de Roberto o la ficha de Elena. Lee la ficha a tu compañero.**

Challenge

Write six sentences in Spanish about what you usually do during the day. Include the time and write two sentences each for the morning, the afternoon and the evening.

Normalmente por la mañana ...
Por la tarde suelo ...
Por lo general por la noche ...

NC 3–4

1A.2 Faenas caseras

- Vocabulary: say what you do and have to do to help at home
- Grammar: use the present continuous
- Skills: hints on how to use a dictionary to look up verbs

LEER 1

Empareja los dibujos con la frase adecuada.

Ejemplo: **1** d

1 Sebas está sacando la basura.
2 Isa está poniendo la mesa.
3 Luchi está escribiendo la lista de la compra.
4 Pablo está recogiendo su dormitorio.
5 Merche está paseando al perro.
6 Toni está haciendo su cama.

ESCUCHAR 2

Escucha e indica quién es.

Ejemplo: **1** Isa

Gramática → p.162

The present continuous

- You use this tense to say what you **are doing** or to describe what **is happening**.
- English and Spanish use the present continuous in the same way. For example:
  What are you doing? *¿Qué estás haciendo?*
  I am washing the dishes. *Estoy fregando los platos.*
- What is the English equivalent of the Spanish *-ando* and *-iendo*?
- Can you make up a rule to guide you about how to form the present continuous?

Use the information below to help you. Check it out on page 31.

estoy...	hablar	comer / escribir
	habl- **ando**	com- **iendo** escrib- **iendo**

- Here are two more examples.
  El gato está **durmiendo** en la silla del abuelo.
  The cat is sleeping in Grandpa's chair.
  La abuela está **leyendo** su revista favorita.
  Grandma is reading her favourite magazine.
- What do you notice about *leyendo* and *durmiendo*? Have they followed the rule?

HABLAR 3

Mira los ejemplos de la actividad 1. Pregunta y contesta con tu compañero.

Ejemplo: **A** *¿En el numero 6, qué estás haciendo?*
B *Estoy haciendo mi cama.*

? Think

Note in the example that *su cama* has changed to *mi cama*: why?

¿Qué está haciendo el robomop? Escribe ocho frases.

Ejemplo: 1 Está fregando los platos.

pasar la aspiradora
limpiar
quitar el polvo
cocinar
fregar los platos
hacer la cama
poner la mesa

La persona A hace la mímica. La persona B adivina lo que está haciendo.

Ejemplo: **A** ¿Qué estoy haciendo?
       B Estás ...

Mira los dibujos de la actividad 1 y escribe lo que tienes que o debes hacer.

Ejemplo: a Tengo que pasear al perro. / Debo pasear al perro.

Gramática → p.167

To say what you **have to do** or **must do** in Spanish you use:
tener que + infinitive
deber + infinitive

Tengo que recoger mis libros.
I have to tidy my books away.
Debo hacer mi cama. *I must make my bed.*

Lee las instrucciones de Juan para Roberto. Completa el texto con uno de los verbos de la casilla.

tocar   recoger   limpiar
comer   hacer   leer

En mi dormitorio y en mi casa

TIENES QUE
1   tus libros
2   tu cama
3   el cuarto de baño

NO DEBES
4   mi guitarra
5   mis revistas
6   mis chocolates

? Think

Remember that when you look up verbs in a dictionary, you must think about the infinitive form. See page 31 for more advice on how to check verbs in a dictionary.

Escucha. Anota todos los verbos.

Ejemplo: estoy recogiendo

Escucha otra vez. ¿Quién ayuda más en casa, Roberto o Elena? Escribe dos listas.

NC 4

Challenge

Quiz: ¿Qué haces o tienes que hacer para ayudar en casa?

With a partner prepare a survey. Choose eight household chores and ask ten people in your class if they have to do each one.
Example: *¿Tienes que fregar los platos?*

Who does the most to help at home? Report back to the class orally or in writing.

 NC 3–4

- Vocabulary: revise mealtimes and say what you prefer to eat
- Grammar: use the present tense of radical-changing verbs
- Skills: practise memorising verb patterns

a el bocadillo

b la mazorca

c la piña

d el arroz con carne

e la tortilla

f la ensalada

g los cereales con tostadas

h el café

LEER 1 Mira los dibujos y decide para qué comida son.

ESCUCHAR 2 🎧 Escucha y verifica.

el desayuno – desayunar
el almuerzo – almorzar
la merienda – merendar
la cena – cenar
la comida – comer

LEER 3 🎧 Lee las frases de abajo y escucha otra vez. ¿Quién dice lo siguiente – Roberto o Elena?

Ejemplo: 1 Elena

1 Me despierto temprano y desayuno enseguida.
2 Normalmente tomo un café con leche y voy al cole.
3 Almuerzo en la casa de mi abuela.
4 Como a la una en casa con mi hermana.
5 Por lo general meriendo sobre las cinco después de clases.
6 Me gusta cenar viendo la tele, a las siete a más tardar.
7 Solemos cenar en familia a las nueve en punto.
8 No puedo comer tan temprano; tiene que ser pasadas las nueve.

ESCRIBIR 4

NC 4

¿Qué diferencias hay entre Roberto y Elena?
Escribe cuatro frases.

Ejemplo: Roberto desayuna a las ... pero Elena desayuna a las ...

? Think

Read sentences 1–8 again and focus on the times.
How do you say ...
at about six o clock?   on the dot of nine thirty?
around four o'clock?   just past midday?

HABLAR 5

NC 3

Sondeo en clase. Pregunta y contesta.

Write ten items of food from memory or using a dictionary.

Ejemplo: **A** *¿Qué prefieres comer para el desayuno / el almuerzo / la merienda / la cena?*

B *Prefiero comer cereales con tostadas y café con leche.*

Escribe los resultados y preséntalos a la clase oralmente.
¿Qué prefieren – el desayuno? el almuerzo? la merienda? la cena?
¿Cuál es el plato favorito? ¿Cuál es el plato menos popular?
¿Cuál es el plato más diferente?

Me gusta comer Prefiero	el arroz la ensalada	porque es	(demasiado) (bastante)	sabroso/a delicioso/a soso/a salado/a picante dulce rico/a

ESCUCHAR 6

NC 4

🎧 **Escucha. ¿Qué prefieren comer? ¿A qué hora?**
¿Qué opinan? Copia y completa la tabla.

	Nombre	Comida	Hora	Opinión
Ejemplo:	Teresa	zumo de naranja	el desayuno	—

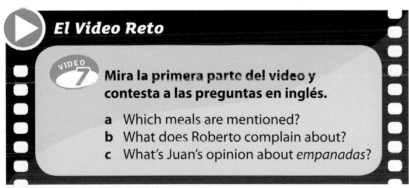

El Video Reto

VIDEO 7

Mira la primera parte del video y contesta a las preguntas en inglés.

a Which meals are mentioned?
b What does Roberto complain about?
c What's Juan's opinion about *empanadas*?

HABLAR 8

NC 4

👥 **Lee el diálogo, luego practícalo.**

Elena: ¿Quieres probar el arroz?
Roberto: Sólo quiero un poco, gracias.
Elena: ¿No sueles comer arroz en Colombia?
Roberto: Sí, pero prefiero el arroz con coco. Es muy sabroso.
Elena: ¿Te gustaría más salsa con la carne?
Roberto: No, gracias, es demasiado picante.
Elena: ¿Quieres más aceitunas?
Roberto: No, gracias, están bastante saladas.

⚙️ *Gramática* → p.162

Think again about the verb *soler* (*ue – suelo*) which you looked at on page 20. Verbs like *soler* are called **radical-changing** or **stem-changing** verbs.

almorzar (ue) – *to have lunch*
alm**ue**rzo
alm**ue**rzas
alm**ue**rza
almorzamos
almorzáis
alm**ue**rzan

merendar (ie) – *to snack*
mer**ie**ndo
mer**ie**ndas
mer**ie**nda
merendamos
merendáis
mer**ie**ndan

The letters in brackets show you the way the stem (the 'o' in *soler*) changes. Always make a note of the change by writing it in brackets after the verb each time you come across a new example.

- Now write down the full pattern for the following verbs:
  preferir (ie) *to prefer*
  querer (ie) *to want*
  comenzar (ie) *to begin*

Challenge

👥 Write an imaginary dialogue at the meal table. Offer, accept, refuse and say why you don't like different foods. Then practise your dialogue with a partner. Use the dialogue in activity 8 to help you.

NC 4

- Vocabulary: discuss recipes, ingredients and local dishes
- Grammar: use quantities and large numbers
- Skills: read a Spanish recipe

Las cantidades

un kilo de

medio kilo de

100 gramos de

medio litro de

media docena de

una lata de

un paquete de

una bolsa de

una botella de

las cebollas – *onions*
el perejil – *parsley*

ESCUCHAR 1 🎧 **Escucha y anota lo que compra Elena.**

ESCUCHAR 2 🎧 **Escucha otra vez y anota las cantidades de cada ingrediente.**

NC 3

⚙ Gramática

Large numbers

The number 100 changes from **ciento** to **cien** before both masculine and feminine nouns:
cien euros = *100 euros*; cien personas = *100 people*
It then continues as **ciento uno**, **ciento dos**, etc.
cien**to** veinte euros = *120 euros*;
cien**to** cincuenta personas = *150 people*

Numbers ending in -**cientos** agree with the noun:
doscientos/as; trescientos/as; cuatrocientos/as

doscient**os** gramos = 200 grammes;
doscient**as** manzanas = 200 apples
Note:
quinientos/as (*500*); **sete**cientos/as (*700*);
novecientos/as (*900*).

- Take turns with a partner to write down a series of high numbers.
  Person A reads out their list in Spanish and person B writes down the numbers.

ESCUCHAR 3 🎧 **Escucha el mensaje de Roberto y escoge la(s) palabra(s) adecuada(s).**

NC 4

1 Es un mensaje para pedir comida / ayuda / empanadas.
2 Mañana va a salir / cocinar / hablar con Elena.
3 Roberto no sabe escribir / preparar / comprar la receta.

4 Quiere saber los platos / ingredientes / vasos que debe comprar.
5 Su madre va a explicar cómo se lavan / se cocinan / se comen las empanadas.

LEER 4

NC 4

Lee el email de la madre de Roberto y empareja los dibujos con las instrucciones. Usa un diccionario.

Ejemplo: **1 b**

Primero tienes que hacer la masa **(1)**; en casa siempre hacemos la masa con maíz fresco pero tú debes comprar harina de maíz en paquete.
Ahora tienes que:
<u>mezclar</u> la harina **(2)** con un poco de sal y agua.
<u>aplastar</u> la masa con un rodillo **(3)** sobre una mesa cubierta de harina.
<u>cortar</u> los redondos con un vaso. **(4)**
<u>poner</u> en aceite bien caliente hasta que se inflen. **(5)**
<u>sacar</u> y <u>abrir</u> con la punta de un cuchillo. **(6)**
<u>rellenar</u> con un poquito del picadillo y un huevo entero sin batir. **(7)**
<u>freír</u> todas las empanadas en el aceite otra vez.

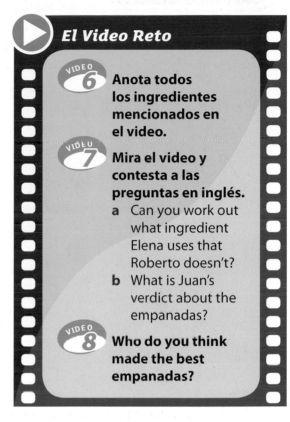

El Video Reto

VIDEO 6 Anota todos los ingredientes mencionados en el video.

VIDEO 7 Mira el video y contesta a las preguntas en inglés.
a Can you work out what ingredient Elena uses that Roberto doesn't?
b What is Juan's verdict about the empanadas?

VIDEO 8 Who do you think made the best empanadas?

a

b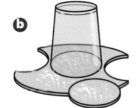

c

d

e

f

g

la masa – *dough*
el rodillo – *rolling pin*
el picadillo – *filling*
el relleno – *filling*

LEER 5

Lee las instrucciones otra vez. Empareja los verbos subrayados con las palabras inglesas abajo.

put into
cut fill
fry take out
mix open up
flatten/roll out

Challenge

Write a brief description of your favourite regional or family dish. Write a list of ingredients and explain how to cook it in five easy steps. Say why you like it. Use a dictionary to help you.

Mi plato favorito es …

Ingredientes: Cantidad:
Primero tienes que … .
Ahora tienes que …

NC 4

- Vocabulary: talk about life in different regions and countries
- Grammar: revise the present tense including *hay* and *no hay*
- Skills: give opinions and descriptions

LEER 1

Empareja las fotos con la palabra adecuada.

a la montaña	**c** el campo	**e** un pueblo
b la costa	**d** la ciudad	**f** una aldea

pequeño/a	grande	bonito/a
aburrido/a	antiguo/a	histórico/a
tranquilo/a	ruidoso/a	industrial

ESCUCHAR 2

🎧 **Escucha y anota dónde viven.**

NC 3

1 Ana		**3** Pedro
2 Isidoro		**4** Maite

ESCUCHAR 3

🎧 **Escucha otra vez y añade una descripción de la casilla.**

HABLAR 4

Habla con tu compañero.

A ¿Dónde vive Ana?
B ...

ESCRIBIR 5

Escribe una frase para cada persona.

NC 2–3

Ejemplo: **1** *Ana vive en el campo en un pueblo bonito.*

LEER 6

Lee. ¿Verdad, mentira o no se menciona?

NC 4

1 Cartagena está en las montañas.
2 Amira vive en una región tranquila.
3 Tiene una abuela.
4 No le gusta levantarse temprano.
5 Va en coche al colegio.
6 Le encanta comer pescado y fruta.

Vivo en una aldea cerca de Cartagena, en la costa norte de Colombia. Me encanta porque es muy tranquila y bonita. Vivo con mis tres hermanos y mi madre. No tengo padre. Tengo que levantarme temprano – a eso de las seis – para ayudar en casa antes de ir al colegio. Suelo ir a pie. Aquí vivimos muy bien porque tenemos comida fresca: pescado del mar y fruta tropical.

Amira

ESCUCHAR 7 Escucha y anota los lugares mencionados.

Ejemplo: 1 h, g ...

ESCUCHAR 8 Escucha otra vez y anota lo que *no* hay en la ciudad.

| Hay | un cine |
| No hay | museo |

LEER 9 Copia y completa la carta ilustrada. Usa el vocabulario de la casilla para ayudarte.

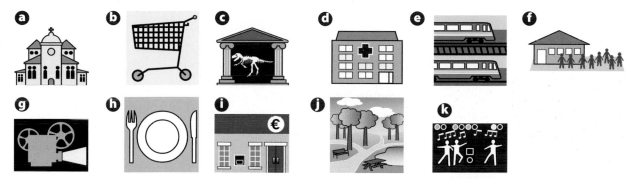

¡Hola, compañeros! Saludos desde el ⊕ de España donde estoy pasando un buen rato en Gaucín, en las ⛰ de la serranía de Ronda. No está lejos del 🌊 y es un pueblo blanco muy atractivo, aunque está un poco aislado. Todos los días me levanto a 🕕 y 🚿 enseguida. No tengo que ponerme 👕 porque hacemos mucho ⚽. Solemos desayunar 🥛 y 🥣 con 🍞 o 🪣 si queremos. Después de 💇 y 🪥 salimos con las mochilas a hacer senderismo.

Miguel

cereales
deporte
las seis
lavarme los dientes
mar
me ducho
montañas
peinarme
sur
tostadas
uniforme
yogur
zumo de naranja

LEER 10 Lee la carta otra vez y contesta a las preguntas.

NC 4 *Ejemplo: 1 He's in the south of Spain.*

1 Where is Miguel?
2 How is the town of Gaucín described?
3 What time does he get up?
4 Why doesn't he have to wear uniform?
5 What does he usually have for breakfast?
6 What does he do before going out?

Challenge Write an extract for a brochure to attract visitors to the area where you live. Describe the region and explain what there is and isn't. You can also include details such as typical regional dishes. Use the present tense.

NC 4

Comprender – The present tense of verbs (revision)

A Regular verbs

When you look up a verb in a dictionary you will find it in the **infinitive** form like this: *hablar* (to speak); *comer* (to eat); *vivir* (to live). Spanish infinitives are made up of a **stem + an ending**: *habl + ar.* All regular verbs in Spanish follow a pattern and fall into three groups, indicated by the last two letters of the infinitive: **-ar**, **-er**, **-ir**.

Subject pronoun (person doing the verb)	Infinitive hablar – to speak	comer – to eat	vivir – to live
yo – *I*	hablo	como	vivo
tú – *you (s)*	hablas	comes	vives
él – *he* / ella – *she* / usted – *you (formal)*	habla	come	vive
nosotros/as – *we*	hablamos	comemos	vivimos
vosotros/as – *you (pl)*	habláis	coméis	vivís
ellos/ellas – *they* / ustedes – *you (pl formal)*	hablan	comen	viven

Remember: the pattern of the verb ending tells you which person is doing the verb so you don't often need to use the personal pronoun in Spanish unless you want to emphasise who it is.

1 **Write out these verbs on to learning cards with the English on one side and the Spanish on the other.**

cantar (to sing)   *aprender* (to learn)   *escribir* (to write)

B Radical or stem-changing verbs

These verbs follow the regular pattern for the endings but change their spelling in the stem of the verb. For example, *u → ue: jugar* (to play); *o → ue: poder* (to be able); *e → ie: preferir* (to prefer). You will find them in the dictionary set out like this:

jugar (ue)	poder (ue)	preferir (ie)	querer (ie)
juego	puedo	prefiero	quiero
juegas	puedes	prefieres	quieres
juega	puede	prefiere	quiere
jugamos	podemos	preferimos	queremos
jugáis	podéis	preferís	queréis
juegan	pueden	prefieren	quieren

2 **Copy these sentences and write the correct form of the verb.**

  1 Elena (preferir) comer un bocadillo con tomate.
  2 Juan no (querer) comer pescado.
  3 Ellos (preferir) la comida española.
  4 Nosotros no (poder) ir al restaurante esta noche.
  5 Roberto (jugar) al baloncesto los jueves.

C Reflexive verbs

These are verbs which have *se* attached to the end of the verb; for example, *levantarse* 'to get up' (i.e. to get **oneself** up). The *se* part is called a reflexive pronoun. This pronoun changes to match the person doing the verb action.

me levanto – *I get (myself) up*
te levantas – *you get (yourself) up*
se levanta – *he / she gets (himself / herself) up*
nos levantamos – *we get (ourselves) up*
os levantáis – *you get (yourselves) up*
se levantan – *they get (themselves) up*

- Some reflexive verbs are also radical-changing, like the verbs in B opposite: *despertarse* (ie) *to wake up*; *acostarse* (ue) *to go to bed*; *vestirse* (i) *to get dressed*

3 **Complete the sentences with the correct form of the verb.**

  1 Roberto _____ (despertarse [ie]) a las seis.
  2 Juan _____ (levantarse) a las diez los sábados.
  3 Elena, ¿tú a qué hora _____? (acostarse [ue])
  4 Yo _____ (lavarse) antes de desayunar.
  5 Nosotros _____ (vestirse [i]) después del desayuno.

D Present continuous

This is used to describe what **is happening** at the time of speaking or writing. It is formed with the present tense of the verb *estar* (to be) plus the verb of action with its ending changed to *-ando* for -ar verbs and *-iendo* for -er and -ir verbs. The endings *-ando* and *-iendo* in Spanish are like the English ending -ing. Can you remember two verbs that break the rule?

E Irregular verbs

Memorise the five main irregular verbs: *tener, hacer, ir, ser, estar.*

4 Add the verb endings.

estoy com	(comer)
estás escrib	(escribir)
está cen	(cenar)
estamos recog	(recoger)
estáis d	(dormir)
están le	(leer)

5 Write out learning cards for irregular verbs with the Spanish on one side and the English on the other. *Estar* is done above. Check the others on page 162.

Aprender – Dictionary work

F Checking verbs

If you can't find the exact word you want in a dictionary, the chances are it is a verb. Look for a word which starts the same way as the one you want to look up but think about the infinitive form, which will end in either *-ar, -er* or *-ir*.

6 See if you can recognise these verbs and think about their infinitive form. Then look them up in a dictionary and write down how they are set out.

beben comiendo vivimos habláis

7 Analyse these radical-changing verbs and think about how they would be set out in a dictionary. Then check them.

quiero pueden prefieres jugamos

8 Don't forget that some verbs are both reflexive and radical-changing. How are these verbs set out in a dictionary?

me acuesto se visten te despiertas

9 If you have learnt the irregular verbs by heart then you should be able to recognise these words. Which verbs do they belong to?

hacemos tengo estáis son voy

Hablar – Pronunciation

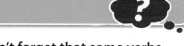

G The sound of the letters c and z

Think about how you form the sound of the letter *c* plus the vowel which follows it. Which part of the mouth does the sound come from?

Which are hard-sounding syllables and which sound soft?

When you see the letter *z* in a word then it is pronounced like *the* in 'theatre' with the tip of the tongue protruding between the front teeth.

However, in Latin America and the very south of Spain they often make this sound like an *s*.

10 Listen and repeat these examples. Make up a rule to remember how to pronounce the sounds *ca, co, cu* then *ce* and *ci*.

Cartagena centro ciudad Colombia Cuba

En el centro de la ciudad de Cartagena en Colombia comen arroz con coco pero en Cuba comen cerdo.

- Vocabulary: talk about chores and meals
- Grammar: revise present tense
- Skills: extending your sentences

1

Empareja la acción con un dibujo adecuado.
Match up the actions with a suitable drawing.

1 Sacar la basura.
2 Escribir la lista de la compra.
3 Pasear al perro.
4 Poner la mesa.
5 Hacer su cama.
6 Recoger su dormitorio.

2

NC 2

Lee. ¿Es para el desayuno, el almuerzo, la merienda o la cena?
Read and decide which meal this is for.

1 un café con leche con tostadas y mermelada
2 un zumo de naranja y un bocadillo de queso
3 pescado frito con arroz y verduras
4 una tortilla con ensalada y un vaso de vino

3

Escoge una hora adecuada para cada comida.
Write down a suitable meal for each time.

 **Think**

If you can add an extra phrase about the time to your answer (such as *en punto*) it will improve the level of your work.

4

NC 3–4

Escribe ocho frases sobre lo que haces cada día y a qué hora.
Write eight sentences to say what you do each day and at what time.

- Vocabulary: talk about daily routine at weekends and after school
- Grammar: use the present tense from memory
- Skills: check and correct work using a dictionary

LEER 1

NC 3–4

Copia y completa el texto con los verbos correctos de la casilla.

Todos los sábados tengo que **1** ▒▒▒▒ en casa. Paso la mañana **2** ▒▒▒▒ mi dormitorio, **3** ▒▒▒▒ mis libros y mi ropa y **4** ▒▒▒▒ mi iPod. Por la tarde me gusta **5** ▒▒▒▒ con mis amigos y **6** ▒▒▒▒ ir al cine. Normalmente tengo que **7** ▒▒▒▒ en casa para cenar en familia. Por lo general **8** ▒▒▒▒ pescado con patatas fritas porque **9** ▒▒▒▒ el plato favorito de mis padres. Después de ver la tele, **10** ▒▒▒▒ a las diez y media.

ayudar	limpiando
comemos	me acuesto
es	recogiendo
escuchando	salir
estar	solemos

ESCRIBIR 2

NC 4

Prepara un párrafo breve. Escribe por lo menos diez frases. Usa un diccionario para ayudarte.

- ¿Qué te gusta hacer los sábados y domingos? ☺
  Ejemplo: Los sábados por la mañana me gusta pasear al perro ...
- ¿Qué te fastidia de los sábados y domingos? ☹
  Ejemplo: Me fastidia almorzar en familia los domingos ...

? Think

Ask yourself why you have used each verb in the place you have chosen in activity 1. How can you tell if it is correct or not? Think about the person doing the verb and what type of verb it is. If you need to, read page 31 again on how to check verbs in a dictionary.

LEER 3

NC 4

Lee los textos de María y Sofía y contesta a las preguntas.

Esta tarde después de clase pienso ir a dar una vuelta por el centro de la ciudad. ¿Quién me acompaña? M

No puedo porque tengo que hacer muchos deberes y más tarde tengo que ayudar a mi madre en casa. S

Puedes decir que vienes a mi casa a comer conmigo. ¿Qué haces para ayudar en casa? M

Siempre paseo a mi perro, pongo la mesa y me encanta cocinar; no voy a decir mentiras a mi madre, ¡siempre se da cuenta y me castiga! S

Voy sola entonces y quedamos mañana en el patio del insti como siempre. M

1 What does María want to do and when?
2 Who is not going with her?
3 What reason is given?
4 What does María ask her to do?

5 What does Sofía like doing?
6 What is she not prepared to do and why?
7 What does María decide to do then?
8 Where do they always meet up?

Escuchar

NC 4

Read sentences 1–8 below then listen and decide which **five** are true.

1 Gabriela is Roberto's sister.
2 She lives in Segovia with Elena.
3 She goes to school every Saturday.
4 She has to cook for her mother each night.
5 She doesn't like Spanish food.
6 She usually goes to the cinema with her friends.
7 She loves to eat pizza.
8 She usually goes to bed at half past ten.

Hablar

NC 3–4

Answer the questions using the illustrations to help you.

- ¿Dónde vives?
- ¿Cómo es?
- ¿Qué sueles hacer los domingos?
- ¿Qué haces para ayudar en casa?
- ¿Qué te gusta comer en el desayuno?
- ¿A qué hora sueles levantarte durante la semana?
- ¿Cuál es tu plato favorito?

Leer

NC 4

Read Gabriela's email and answer the questions.

1 Where is Gabi?
2 What does Roberto want her to send him?
3 What is her opinion of the dish?
4 Why is she pleased Roberto isn't at home?
5 What doesn't she like about the meal?
6 Name three things she does during the week.
7 What does she say is boring?
8 What does she say about the recipe?
9 What problem does she think there might be?
10 What instructions does she give him?

¡Hola, Tico! ¿Cómo te va allí tan lejos en Segovia? Pues estás preguntando por mi vida en Cartagena y pidiendo una receta de un plato típico de la costa colombiana. Para mí no hay plato más típico de aquí que el sancocho de pescado.

Lo bueno es que mamá suele prepararlo todos los domingos porque sabe que me gusta mucho y como ya no estás en casa ¡puedo comerlo todo yo! Lo malo es que tengo que ayudar a fregar los platos después de comer.

La rutina no cambia mucho. Me levanto temprano los días de semana; voy en autobús al colegio; tengo las mismas clases; vuelvo a casa sobre las dos y media. Hago los deberes y escucho mi MP3.

Bueno, si quieres cocinar mi plato preferido primero tienes que comprar un pescado bien fresco. ¿Dónde puedes comprar pescado fresco si vives en Segovia, tan lejos del mar? Llámame a las nueve, hora de España, y hablamos más largo rato – besotes de Gabi

Escribir

NC 3–4

Write a paragraph about your daily life.

Mention:
- where you live and what there is/is not
- what you usually do each day
- what you do at home to help
- what food you like to eat and why
- your favourite typical dish

Primeras impresiones	**First impressions**
soler	to usually do something
a pie	on foot
cerca (de)	near (to)
lejos (de)	far (from)
hace calor	it is hot
hace frío	it is cold
en invierno	in winter
en verano	in summer
el instituto	secondary school
el colegio	school
comer	to eat
la cantina	school canteen
levantarse	to get up
acostarse	to go to bed
vivir	to live
volver	to return
de costumbre	usually
normalmente	normally
por lo general	generally
por la mañana	in the morning
por la tarde	in the afternoon
por la noche	in the evening

Faenas caseras	**Household chores**
sacar la basura	to take the rubbish out
poner la mesa	to lay the table
escribir la lista de la compra	to write a shopping list
recoger el dormitorio	to tidy your room
pasear al perro	to walk the dog
hacer la cama	to make your bed
pasar la aspiradora	to hoover
limpiar	to clean
quitar el polvo	to dust
cocinar	to cook
fregar los platos	to wash the dishes
¿Qué estás haciendo?	What are you doing?
está durmiendo	he/she/it is sleeping
está leyendo	he/she is reading
tener que	to have to
deber	to have to (must)
jugar	to play
dormir	to sleep

¡Buen provecho!	**Enjoy your meal!**
el desayuno	breakfast
desayunar	to have breakfast
el almuerzo	lunch
almorzar	to have lunch
la merienda	tea/afternoon snack
merendar	to have tea/a snack
la cena	supper/evening meal
cenar	to have supper/an evening meal

la comida	food/dinner
el arroz	rice
un bocadillo	sandwich
la carne	meat
la ensalada	salad
el jamón	ham
una mazorca	corn on the cob
una piña	pineapple
una tortilla	omelette
las tostadas	toast
sabroso/a	tasty
salado/a	salty
picante	hot/spicy
crujiente	crunchy
soso/a	bland
dulce	sweet
rico/a	delicious

A cocinar algo típico	**Let's cook something typical**
un kilo de	a kilo of
medio kilo de	500g of
100 gramos de	100g of
medio litro de	half a litre of
media docena de	half a dozen
una lata de	a tin of
un paquete de	a packet of
una bolsa de	a bag of
una botella de	a bottle of
el aceite de oliva	olive oil
un huevo	an egg
la harina (de trigo)	(wheat) flour
la harina de maíz	maize/corn flour
una cebolla	onion
el atún	tuna
la sal	salt
el azúcar	sugar
el agua	water
un pastel	a pie/pastry
las aceitunas	olives
la masa	dough/pastry

◉ I can ...

- ◉ discuss daily routines
- ◉ say what I do/am doing and have to do at home to help
- ◉ talk about meal times
- ◉ recognise quantities and ingredients
- ◉ talk about regional dishes
- ◉ talk about where I live
- ◉ compare life in Segovia and Cartagena
- ◉ use the present tense and large numbers
- ◉ remember some verb patterns

1B.1 ¿Qué opinas de la moda?

- Vocabulary: talk about clothes and give your opinion on them
- Grammar: give your opinion – review of singular and plural
- Skills: transfer previous knowledge to new situations; use cognates

 HABLAR 1

Trabaja con un compañero. ¿Recuerdas las palabras en español para la ropa?

Ejemplo: sweater – un jersey

 LEER 2

Escribe dos listas de palabras. ¿Son positivas o negativas?

Ejemplo: negativo – qué asco
positivo – bonito

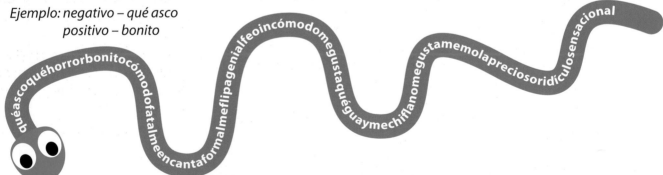

quéascoquéhorrorbonitocómodofatalmeencantaformalmeflipagenialfeoincómodomegustaquéguaymechiflanomegustamemolapreciosoridículosensacional

 ESCUCHAR 3

NC 3

 Mira la ropa de arriba y escucha. ¿Qué opinan?

Ejemplo: 1 los vaqueros – cómodos

 HABLAR 4

NC 3

Habla con tu compañero. ¿Qué opinas de la ropa?

Ejemplo: **A** *Me gusta la falda – es bonita.*
B *No me gusta nada – es formal.*

Gramática → p.168

Remember!
Me gust**a la** camisa (singular – one)
But:
Me gust**an los** vaqueros (plural – more than one)
Which other opinion phrases behave in the same way?

La falda **es** elegant**e** (singular – one)
BUT
Los pantalones **son** elegant**es** (plural – more than one)

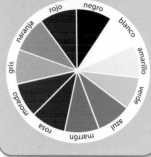

un abrigo
una blusa
unas botas
una camiseta
un paraguas
una rebeca
un sombrero
un traje
un vestido

rojo · negro · blanco · amarillo · verde · azul · marrón · rosa · morado · gris · naranja

LEER 5
NC 4

Lee las descripciones e identifica la ropa. Anota las palabras de opiniones.

Ejemplo: 1 d, me flipan

1 La chica pequeña lleva un bonito pijama rojo con rayas amarillas. Me flipan las zapatillas blancas de conejos, son muy cómicas.
2 El señor americano lleva un traje elegante negro con un abrigo largo y marrón. Lleva un sombrero negro, y botas de vaquero marrones. Me parece muy formal.
3 El chico de pelo rubio lleva unos pantalones cortos azules de flores y una camiseta con un logotipo. Parece ridículo porque también lleva botas de goma con puntos rosas y un anorak rojo. Sin embargo, me encanta el paraguas multicolor, es genial.

ESCRIBIR 6

Completa la descripción del dibujo c. Usa el vocabulario de las actividades 2 y 5.

La chica lleva una **1** b＿＿＿ verde y una minifalda **2** a＿＿＿.
Es **3** g＿＿＿. Lleva también unas **4** b＿＿＿ negras. Son **5** p＿＿＿.
Pero no me gusta el cinturón **6** n＿＿＿. Es **7** f＿＿＿.

ESCRIBIR 7
NC 4

Escribe una descripción para el dibujo b.

Challenge

Produce your own page for a fashion magazine.
Draw your model or use ready-made pictures.
Label it and write about it.
Example: Me encanta el chándal azul con rayas blancas. Es precioso, y muy cómodo.

NC 4

? Think

Look for other words in the Vocabulario section on page 51. Remember to use words you do know to help you work out new ones.

Words that look very similar in two different languages are called **cognates**. How many can you find in activity 5?

Gramática → p.161

el chico llev**a** – *the boy wears*
las chicas llev**an** – *the girls wear*
Remember the ending of the verb changes to match the person.
How would you say:
I wear
we wear?

1B.2 Mi estilo

- Vocabulary: discuss different styles and eras of fashion
- Grammar: use the imperfect tense to say 'used to'
- Skills: work out the meaning of new vocabulary

 1 **Identifica la fecha de la casilla.**

Ejemplo: **a** *el siglo dieciséis*

 2 **Empareja las descripciones y los dibujos.**

NC 5

1. En esta época las chicas llevaban minifaldas y vestidos muy cortos. Llevaban ropa de muchos colores.
2. La mujer llevaba vestidos largos y preciosos con falda cónica. Era difícil moverse. El hombre llevaba chaquetas cortas ¡y medias! Era un poco ridículo.
3. En esta época era muy popular ser hippy. Llevaban pantalones grandes de campana. Era un estilo relajado.
4. Para parecer muy delgadas, las mujeres llevaban un corsé muy estrecho debajo de sus largos vestidos. Era muy incómodo.

 3 **Habla con tu compañero.**

NC 3–5

Ejemplo: **A** *¿Qué llevaban las chicas en los años sesenta?*
B *Llevaban minifaldas.*

 4 **Completa las frases con la parte correcta de *llevar*.**

1. Juan ▒▒▒ pantalones grises al instituto. Ahora lleva pantalones negros.
2. Mi hermana y yo ▒▒▒ vestidos bonitos. Ahora preferimos llevar vaqueros.
3. Chicos, ¿ ▒▒▒ uniforme al instituto en el pasado?
4. Abuela, ¿ ▒▒▒ minifalda en los años sesenta?

---

el siglo dieciséis
el siglo diecinueve

los años sesenta
los años setenta

⚙ *Gramática* → p.163

The imperfect

The **imperfect tense** is a past tense. Here it is used to describe what **used to** happen.

*Las mujeres **llevaban** vestidos largos.*
*Women **used to wear** long dresses.*

llevar – *to wear*
llevaba – *I used to wear*
llevabas – *you (s) used to wear*
llevaba – *he / she / you (formal) used to wear*
llevábamos – *we used to wear*
llevabais – *you (pl) used to wear*
llevaban – *they / you (formal) used to wear*

LEER
5
NC 4

 Trabaja con tu compañero. Identifica las palabras en español de la actividad 2.

> corset   conical   flared trousers   mini skirt

ESCUCHAR
6

🎧 Mira los dibujos de la actividad 1 y escucha a los estudiantes. ¿Qué estilo describen? ¿Qué opinan?

Ejemplo: **1** *el siglo diecinueve – romántico pero incómodo*

LEER
7
NC 5

Mira las fotos y completa el párrafo con las palabras de la derecha.

Ahora Twiggy es una modelo muy famosa. En los años sesenta era una modelo joven, y **1** ▭ un estilo completamente nuevo y moderno – **2** ▭ y **3** ▭ cortos.

John Travolta es un actor muy famoso todavía, pero en los años setenta era un joven actor. En la película *Saturday Night Fever* llevaba **4** ▭ con **5** ▭ y **6** ▭, y **7** ▭.

Hoy en día Kylie es una de las cantantes más famosas del mundo, pero en los años ochenta era una joven actriz de una serie australiana que se llamaba *Neighbours*. Su pelo era largo y rizado, y llevaba **8** ▭.

ESCRIBIR
8

Mira las fotos otra vez. ¿Qué opinas?

Ejemplo: Twiggy llevaba minifaldas.
Me gustan porque son muy modernas.

⚙️ *Gramática* → p.163

The **imperfect** is also used for **descriptions** in the past. This is a very useful verb – learn it!
ser – *to be*
era – *I was*
eras – *you (s) were*
era – *he / she / you (formal) were*
éramos – *we were*
erais – *you (pl) were*
eran – *they / you (formal) were*

---

camisetas muy grandes
llevaba
minifaldas
un chaleco
pantalones de campana
un traje blanco
una camisa elegante
vestidos

❓ **Think**

una campana = a bell, so what are *pantalones de campana*?
If a man's 3-piece suit has *una chaqueta, pantalones y un chaleco*, what is *un chaleco*?

Challenge
Find a picture of a fashion from a previous time or bring in an old item of clothing. Prepare a few sentences and then describe it to the rest of the class. Don't forget to give your opinion. Use at least two tenses.
NC 5

- Vocabulary: try on clothes, talk about sizes and how well clothes fit
- Grammar: use demonstrative adjectives
- Skills: understand Spanish clothes sizes, revise numbers

ESCUCHAR 1 🎧 **Escucha y decide. ¿Este, ese o aquel?**

Ejemplo: **1** *ese*

LEER 2 **Escoge la palabra correcta.**

1 Quiero probarme **esta / esa** camisa. (this)
2 Me gusta mucho **ese / aquel** vestido rojo. (that, close)
3 No me gusta nada **ese / aquel** jersey – ¡qué feo! (that, far)
4 ¿Te gustan **estos / esos** vaqueros? (those, close)

ESCRIBIR 3 **Completa las frases.**

1 ¿Quieres probarte ▭▭ botas? (those, far)
2 Me encantan ▭▭ zapatos. (these)
3 ¡ ▭▭ sombrero es horrible! (this)
4 ▭▭ camiseta es muy bonita. (that, far)

HABLAR 4 👥 **Juega con tu compañero o en grupo. ¿Qué quieres?**

NC 3

Ejemplo: **A** *Quiero ese lápiz.*
B *¿Este lápiz rojo?*
A *No, ese lápiz verde.*

⚙ Gramática → p.158

Demonstrative adjectives

este, ese, aquel – *this, that, that over there*
Where in English we have one way of saying 'that', in Spanish they have two – one for 'that close by', and one for 'that far away / over there'.
Me gusta este vestido – *I like this dress.*
Me gusta ese vestido – *I like that dress.*
Me gusta aquel vestido – *I like that dress over there.*
The endings of demonstrative adjectives must change depending on whether the noun they are with is masculine, feminine or plural:

	this	that (close)	that (far)
ms	este	ese	aquel
fs	esta	esa	aquella
	these	**those (close)**	**those (far)**
mpl	estos	esos	aquellos
fpl	estas	esas	aquellas

LEER 5
NC 3

👥 **Pregunta a tus compañeros. ¿Qué talla usas? ¿Qué número calzas? Elige una talla imaginaria.**

Ejemplo: **A** ¿Qué talla de vestido usas?
B La cuarenta y dos.
A ¿Qué número de zapatos calzas?
B El treinta y nueve.

Zapatos	🇬🇧	4	5	6	7	8	9
	🇪🇸	37	38	39	40	41	42
Vestido (mujer)	🇬🇧	8	10	12	14	16	18
	🇪🇸	34	36	38	40	42	44

① una camiseta <u>holgada</u> de talla extra-grande

② un traje <u>ajustado</u> de talla pequeña

③ un vestido <u>largo</u> de talla grande

④ una falda <u>corta</u> de talla mediana

HABLAR 6 **¿Cómo se dicen en inglés las palabras <u>subrayadas</u>?**

Ejemplo: **1** holgada – baggy

ESCRIBIR 7 **Escribe una frase para cada dibujo de arriba.**

Ejemplo: **1** La camiseta holgada no le queda bien.

Gramática

Me queda bien

This is an impersonal expression. It changes depending on whether you are talking about a singular or plural item:

me queda bien – *it suits* **me**
te queda bien – *it suits* **you**
le queda bien – *it suits* **him** (or **her**)

me qued**an** bien – *they suit* **me**
te qued**an** bien – *they suit* **you**
le qued**an** bien – *they suit* **him** (or **her**)

El Video Reto

VIDEO 8 **Mira el video y contesta a las preguntas.**

a What are Juan, Roberto and Elena doing?
b Write down the words for clothes. What do they mean?
c ¿Qué talla usan? ¿Qué número calzan?

VIDEO 9 **Mira el video otra vez. Completa la conversación.**

Roberto: Yo quería probarme **1** _____ bermudas, **2** _____ camiseta y **3** _____ gorra.
Dependiente: ¿Qué **4** _____ usas?
Roberto: Una "M", creo.

Dependiente: Sí, esta es tu talla.
Roberto: Y quiero probarme **5** _____ playeras.
Dependiente: ¿Qué **6** _____ usas?
Roberto: Un 42.

VIDEO 10 **Whose outfit is best and why?**

Challenge With a friend or a small group, prepare and perform a role play in a clothes shop.
NC 4

1B.4 ¿Dónde comprar?

- Vocabulary: discuss different types of shops
- Grammar: use comparatives and superlatives
- Skills: make choices, evaluate options

el centro comercial

los grandes almacenes

la tienda de una cadena

el mercado

la boutique

la tienda de segunda mano

es anticuado / barato / caro – *it's old fashioned / cheap / expensive*
está en la onda – *it's in fashion*
si tienes suerte ... – *if you're lucky ...*
puedes regatear / encontrar una ganga – *you can haggle / find a bargain*

 Empareja las descripciones y las fotos.

NC 4

a Son muchas tiendas con el mismo nombre, como Zara o Mango. Hay gran variedad de ropa de moda, y es bastante barata.

b Aquí puedes comprar ropa original y diferente. Normalmente es muy barata, y puedes regatear el precio.

c En este lugar hay muchas tiendas, gran variedad de ropa, y variedad de precios. Se puede pasar todo el día aquí con amigos.

d Es una tienda muy grande, con gran variedad de ropa. Puede ser bastante cara. Algunas veces la ropa es un poco anticuada.

e Aquí hay ropa de moda incluso ropa de diseñador. Puede ser ropa que está muy en la onda – y muy cara.

f La ropa aquí es muy barata porque no es nueva. Puede ser anticuada, pero si tienes suerte puedes encontrar una ganga. Además, es muy ecológico comprar aquí.

*La ropa de las cadenas de tiendas es bastante **barata** ...*

... pero la ropa del mercado es más barata ...

*... sin embargo la ropa de las tiendas de segunda mano es **la más barata.** ¡Pero no me gusta!*

LEER 2

NC 3

👥 **Trabaja con tu compañero. ¿Qué tienda es la más barata?**

*Ejemplo: **1** el mercado*

1 Normalmente el mercado es más barato que el centro comercial.
2 El mercado es barato, pero la tienda de segunda mano es más barata.
3 En mi opinión, la ropa de las boutiques no es más barata que la de los grandes almacenes – las boutiques son a veces más caras.
4 El centro comercial es bastante barato, más barato que la boutique.

ESCRIBIR 3

NC 3

Describe la ropa de los dibujos.

*Ejemplo: **1** La falda es más barata y más corta que el vestido.*

❶  €30

❷ €62

❸  €45

❹  €54

❺  €10

❻  €199

ESCUCHAR 4

NC 4

🎧 **Escucha las conversaciones. ¿Qué deciden?**

*Ejemplo: **1** la boutique*

Which shop:
1 is the most expensive
2 is the cheapest
3 is the trendiest
4 has the greatest choice
5 has the most unusual clothing
6 is the most environmentally friendly option?

⚙️ *Gramática* → p.169

Comparatives and superlatives

How to compare things:
barato – *cheap*
más barato (que) – *cheaper (than)*
el más barato – *the cheapest*
un jersey barato – *a cheap jumper*
una falda barata – *a cheap skirt*
- How would you say: *cheap jeans? cheap sandals?*
  las botas caras – *expensive boots*
- How would you say: *more expensive boots? the most expensive boots?*

menos caro – *less expensive*
La falda es **menos cara que** el vestido – *The skirt is **less expensive than** the dress.*

🎯 **Challenge**

Compare different places for buying clothes in your town for a Spanish visitor. Take photos and write a short description of each one.

NC 4

- Vocabulary: describe clothes for different activities and occasions
- Grammar: revise singular and plural verb forms
- Skills: understand and produce descriptions

La ropa especializada

Los deportes acuáticos.
Esta gente lleva un traje de neopreno, y muchas veces zapatos de neopreno. Es muy cómodo y protege del agua fría.

El esquí.
Para este deporte de invierno se necesitan pantalones de esquí y una chaqueta acolchada, o para los niños un traje de nieve. La gente también lleva botas de esquí y bastones. Normalmente lleva gafas de sol.

El baile.
Hay muchos tipos de baile – el ballet, el jazz, el hip hop, el bollywood, la danza folklórica etc. Normalmente la gente lleva un tipo de malla y zapatillas de ballet cuando entrenan. Para el ballet las chicas muchas veces llevan un tutú.

La ropa especializada

El fútbol.
Para este deporte se necesita una camiseta especial en el color del equipo con un número y el nombre del jugador en la espalda, unos pantalones cortos y botas. La tela sintética es muy importante para la ropa de deporte hoy en día.

Los carnavales.
Todo el mundo lleva disfraces de colores muy vivos, y baila en la calle toda la noche con mucha música.

El senderismo.
La gente que practica este deporte lleva ropa que abriga mucho, como un forro polar, pantalones impermeables, y botas de senderismo. Normalmente lleva una mochila y a veces también usan bastones para caminar.

> algún tipo – *some kind*
> entrenar – *to train/practise*
> los disfraces – *costumes*

 LEER 1 **Empareja las fotos con las descripciones.**

 NC 4 *Ejemplo: 1 Los carnavales*

 ESCUCHAR 2  **Escucha. Verifica tus respuestas.**

LEER 3 **Busca la expresión en español para las palabras y frases.**

NC 4

> ballet shoes   colourful   fleece   padded jacket   rucksack
> snow suit   waterproof trousers   wet suit   poles   synthetic

 ESCUCHAR 4 **Escucha: ¿Dónde está? ¿Qué hace? ¿Qué ropa se menciona? Anota en inglés.**

NC 4

Ejemplo: 1 playing football, black and yellow shirt ...

 HABLAR 5 **Habla con tu compañero: ¿qué describe?**

NC 4 *Ejemplo:* **A** *Para este deporte la gente lleva una camiseta en el color del equipo, con el número, y pantalones cortos y botas.*
B *El fútbol.*

 ESCRIBIR 6 **Escribe. ¿Qué te gusta llevar? ¿Cuándo? ¿Por qué?**

 NC 4 *Ejemplo: En el invierno me gusta llevar ropa de esquí porque abriga mucho.*

 **Challenge**
Design an outfit for a special event or your favourite activity. What items do you need? What colours? Are any particular materials necessary? Is it comfortable / practical / beautiful? Present your design.

NC 4

? Think

abriga mucho – *it's very warm (about clothes)*
Which word (item of clothing) does this phrase come from?
How would you say *the trousers are very warm*?

se necesita(n) – *you / we / they need*
This is an **impersonal** expression, and can be used in any situation to say that any person needs something.

Para esquiar, se necesitan esquís. *For skiing, you need skis (= skis are needed).*

⚙ Gramática → p.161

Can you remember how to talk about what people wear?
la gente lleva – *people wear*
las personas llevan – *people wear*
Remember that with a plural subject, you need a plural verb.

How would you say:
*the team (**el equipo**) wears?*
*the team members (**los miembros del equipo**) wear?*

Comprender – The imperfect tense, comparatives and superlatives

A The imperfect tense – 'used to'

This past tense is used to talk about what you **used to** do. It is also used to say what **was happening** in the past – you will learn more about this in Unit 2A.

Llevaba vaqueros, pero ahora llevo un traje.
I used to wear jeans, but now I wear a suit.

-ar verbs	-er and -ir verbs
llevar – *to wear*	**parecer** – *to seem / look like*
llev**aba**	parec**ía**
llev**abas**	parec**ías**
llev**aba**	parec**ía**
llev**ábamos**	parec**íamos**
llev**abais**	parec**íais**
llev**aban**	parec**ían**

There are two irregular verbs:
ser: era, eras, era, éramos, erais, eran (*I was / used to be* etc.)
ir: iba, ibas, iba, íbamos, ibais, iban (*I used to go* etc.)

1 Complete these sentences with the correct part of the verb:

1 Mi madre _____ un abrigo azul pero ahora lleva uno negro. (llevar)
2 Mis amigos y yo _____ al centro comercial pero ahora vamos al mercado. (ir)
3 Rosa y Ana _____ modelos con los vestidos elegantes. (parecer)
4 El actor _____ famoso en el pasado. (ser)

B Comparatives and superlatives – cheap, cheaper, cheapest!

In *Zoom 1* you learned how to compare things:
El centro comercial es *barato* pero el mercado es *más barato*.
The shopping centre is *cheap* but the market is *cheaper*.
In English some adjectives add -est to show 'the most' of something, e.g. *cheapest, shortest, funniest*. In Spanish you just use **el más**.

El más must change and agree with the thing it is describing depending on whether it is masculine, feminine, singular or plural, as must the adjective it uses:

Masculine singular: **El** estilo de los años setenta es **el** más ridícul**o**.
The style from the seventies is the most ridiculous.
Feminine singular: **La** tienda de segunda mano es **la** más barat**a**.
The charity shop is the cheapest.
Masculine plural: **Los** grandes almacenes son **los** más anticuad**os**.
The department store is the most old-fashioned.
Feminine plural: **Las** botas negras son **las** más car**as**.
The black boots are the most expensive.

Superlatives

	the most / -est
ms	el más
fs	la más
mpl	los más
fpl	las más

Don't forget!
good – **bueno**
better – **mejor**
best – **el/la mejor**

2 Complete these sentences:

El jersey marrón es _____ . (ugliest)

Los pantalones amarillos son _____ . (most ridiculous)

Aprender – Learning to listen

C Listening to long texts

Sometimes listening to a foreign language can be like picture 1.
Don't panic – there are ways to make it easier.

3 🎧 Listen to this conversation between six friends. Don't try to take any notes, just sit back, maybe close your eyes if it helps you concentrate, and listen. What do you think they are talking about?

4 This time, before you listen, write down the names of any shops you heard. Listen again. Were you right? Do you need to change anything?
- *Did you try to write while you were listening? Did that stop you listening? Or is it harder to just remember what you heard and write at the end?*

5 Listen again. This time, near the bottom of your page, write down any opinions you hear, either during or after listening. Compare what you have written with someone else. Did they hear anything different?

6 Listen again. Can you match any of your opinions to the shops?
- *Hopefully by now, what you are listening to is more like picture 2!*

7 Last job. Listen again. <u>Underline</u> any opinions expressed by a boy. ⟨Circle⟩ any opinions expressed by a girl.
- *It might not sound quite like picture 3 yet, but by now what you are hearing should be closer to that than to picture 1!*

Why is listening so hard? Is it easier to 'listen' to a video? Why? Which of the techniques on the right help you listen?

- Listen many times.
- Listen to short pieces of a long text.
- Listen and take notes.
- Just listen, and take notes at the end.
- Listen for one piece of information.
- Listen for anything you understand.

Hablar – Speaking in real situations

D Speaking Spanish in shops

Speaking Spanish in the classroom is quite easy – you can prepare what you want to say and practise it before you have to say it. But what if you're on holiday and want to buy a souvenir? Do you know how to say 'Excuse me please, I think I'd quite like that blue china elephant over there in the corner'? Probably not, but you know 'please', 'blue' and 'that over there' (and you probably know 'elephant' if you think about it):
– ***Aquel elefante azul, por favor.*** It might not be the best sentence ever in Spanish, but it gets your message across reasonably correctly.

Ese vestido, por favor.

8 Can you remember how to say: thank you, I would like, I'm interested in?

9 Without looking anything up, how would you ask for:
- **a** this white T-shirt with the pink flowers
- **b** that funny red and yellow straw hat
- **c** that really strange orange stripy dress hanging up over there

- Vocabulary: practise describing clothes
- Grammar: use the impersonal expression *me queda bien*
- Skills: give an opinion on whether something suits you

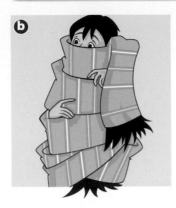

LEER 1 · NC 3

Empareja las frases con los dibujos.
Match the sentences and the pictures.

Ejemplo: 1 c

1 ¡Qué horror! No me gustan los zapatos – son muy feos.
2 ¡Qué guay! Me gusta mucho la camiseta. ¡Es genial!
3 No me gusta la bufanda – es demasiado larga.
4 ¡Perfecto! Me gustan mucho los vaqueros, son muy cómodos.

es genial / cómodo / largo / feo

Gramática

Remember!
me qued**a** bien – *it* suits me
me qued**an** bien – *they* suit me
How would you say *it* **doesn't**
suit me?
Look back at page 41.

ESCRIBIR 2 · NC 2

¿Me queda bien? Completa las frases.
Does it suit me? Complete the sentences.

*Ejemplo: 1 La camiseta **me queda bien**.*

1 La camiseta ▒▒▒ ▒▒▒ ▒▒▒.
2 La bufanda ▒▒▒ ▒▒▒ ▒▒▒ ▒▒▒.

3 Los zapatos ▒▒▒ ▒▒▒ ▒▒▒ ▒▒▒.
4 Los vaqueros ▒▒▒ ▒▒▒ ▒▒▒.

ESCRIBIR 3 · NC 2–3

Escribe frases para los dibujos. ¿Qué opinas?
Write sentences for these pictures. What's your opinion of them?

Ejemplo: 1 Me gustan los zapatos. ¡Qué elegantes!

ESCRIBIR 4 · NC 3

Escribe más frases para la ropa de la actividad 3. ¿Te queda bien?
Write some more sentences about the clothes in activity 3. Do they suit you?

Ejemplo: 1 Me quedan bien los zapatos.

- Vocabulary: practise saying what suits you and others
- Grammar: use the impersonal expression *me / te / le queda bien*
- Skills: give opinions politely

1 **Completa las frases y emparéjalas con los dibujos.**

NC 3

1 Le queda muy bien la chaqueta: ¡está muy ░░░░░ !

2 Me queda muy bien el traje: es muy ░░░░░ .

3 No te queda bien el sombrero: ¡es demasiado ░░░░░ !

4 Te queda muy bien el vestido: ¡es ░░░░░ !

en la onda   elegante   grande   precioso

Gramática

me queda bien – *it suits* **me**
te queda bien – *it suits* **you**
le queda bien – *it suits* **him / her**
Can you remember how to say *it doesn't suit me*?
How do you say *they suit me*?
Look back at page 41.

a

b

c

d

2 **Empareja las dos partes de las frases.**

NC 3

1 ¡Qué lástima, María! El pijama es muy bonito, pero es demasiado holgado

2 Ese vestido largo es precioso y

3 Aquella camiseta es demasiado ajustada para Juan y

4 No estoy segura. El color de la falda está bien, pero es demasiado corta:

a no le queda bien.
b creo que no me queda bien.
c y no te queda bien.
d ¡te queda perfecto!

3 **Escribe una descripción para cada dibujo. ¿Le queda bien?**

NC 3–4

a

b

c

4 **Busca una foto de una persona famosa. Describe su ropa. ¿Qué opinas?**

NC 3–4

? Think

Look back at pages 36 and 37 for ways of describing clothing.

Escuchar
NC 3–4

Listen to the two conversations in the shop.

a What item do they want?
b What size?
c What colour?
d Is it near to the customer?

Hablar
NC 3–4

Have a conversation with a friend. One plays the shop assistant, and one the customer.

Customer: Ask to try on this/that (T-shirt).
Shop assistant: Ask what size.
Customer: State size.
Shop assistant: Say it suits the customer.
Customer: Say you think it is too small / big / tight / baggy / short / long and want to try that (T-shirt) over there instead.

Leer
NC 4

Read the descriptions and match them to the pictures.

1 En el pasado, las mujeres llevaban vestidos largos. Estaban muy elegantes pero también incómodas porque llevaban corsés muy estrechos.

2 En esta época las chicas llevaban minifaldas o vestidos muy cortos. Era un estilo completamente nuevo.

3 Chicos y chicas llevaban ropa al estilo hippy, con pantalones muy grandes de campana. Estaba de moda llevar camisas de muchos colores.

Escribir
NC 4

Write a description of this boy's style and clothes. Do you think they suit him?

¿Qué opinas de la moda? — *What do you think of fashion?*

un abrigo	*a coat*
un anorak	*an anorak*
una blusa	*a blouse*
unas botas	*boots*
unas botas de goma	*wellies*
una bufanda	*a scarf*
unos calcetines	*socks*
una camisa	*a shirt*
una camiseta	*a T-shirt*
una chaqueta	*a jacket*
un cinturón	*a belt*
un jersey	*a sweater*
unos pantalones cortos/ shorts	*shorts*
un paraguas	*an umbrella*
un pijama	*pyjamas*
una rebeca	*a cardigan*
unas sandalias	*sandals*
un sombrero	*a hat*
un traje	*a suit*
un vestido	*a dress*
unas zapatillas	*trainers/slippers*
una manga	*sleeve*
llevar	*to wear*
bonito/a	*pretty*
cómodo/a	*comfortable*
feo/a	*ugly*
incómodo	*uncomfortable*

Mi estilo — *My style*

los años sesenta/setenta	*the sixties/seventies*
el siglo diecinueve	*the 19th century*
el siglo dieciséis	*the 16th century*
un chaleco	*a waistcoat*
un corsé	*a corset*
las medias	*tights*
los pantalones de campana	*flared trousers*
cónico/a	*cone-shaped*
corto/a	*short*
elegante	*smart*
formal	*formal*

¿Me queda bien? — *Does it suit me?*

¿Qué talla usas?	*What size (clothes) are you?*
¿Qué número calzas?	*What size (shoes) do you take?*
ajustado/a	*tight*
holgado/a	*baggy*
largo/a	*long*
Quiero probarme	*I want to try on*
los probadores	*changing rooms*

quedar bien	*to suit someone*
las playeras	*canvas shoes*
las bermudas	*bermuda shorts*

¿Dónde comprar? — *Where shall we go shopping?*

los grandes almacenes	*department store*
la boutique	*boutique*
el centro comercial	*shopping centre*
el mercado	*market*
la tienda de una cadena	*chain store*
la tienda de segunda mano	*charity shop*
anticuado/a	*old-fashioned*
barato/a	*cheap*
caro/a	*expensive*
está de moda	*it's in fashion*
una ganga	*a bargain*
regatear	*to haggle*
tener suerte	*to be lucky*

La ropa especializada — *Specialist clothing*

un bastón (de senderismo/ de esquí)	*a walking pole/ski stick*
una chaqueta acolchada	*a padded jacket*
de colores muy vivos	*colourful*
los disfraces	*costumes*
un forro polar	*a fleece*
una mochila	*a rucksack*
una malla	*a leotard*
los pantalones impermeables	*waterproof trousers*
la tela sintética	*synthetic fabric*
un traje de nieve	*a snow suit*
un traje de neopreno	*a wet suit*
las zapatillas de ballet	*ballet shoes*
los zapatos de neopreno	*wet shoes*
algún tipo	*some type*
entrenar	*to train*

◉ I can ...

- ◉ talk about clothes
- ◉ discuss different styles and eras of fashion
- ◉ buy clothes, say what size I am and how well clothes fit
- ◉ discuss different types of shops
- ◉ describe the clothes I wear for special occasions and different activities

- Vocabulary: talk about what you like doing in your free time; talk about music you like/don't like
- Grammar: use *gustar* and similar verbs with nouns and verbs
- Skills: justify opinions

  Escucha y anota los pasatiempos.

*Ejemplo: **1 a** – salir con mis amigos ...*

 Gramática → p.168

Gustar (to like) and similar verbs

Remember!

Verbs like *gustar* can be used either with another verb or a noun. For example:

Me gusta ir al cine or **Me gusta el cine**
I like to go to the cinema or *I like the cinema.*

Remember, if the noun is plural you need to say:
Me gust**an** las películas. *I like films.*

You use the following verbs in the same way.

A mí ...	me encanta – *I really like* me apasiona – *I love* me interesa – *it interests me* me flipa / me mola – *it's great / ace* (less formal)	me fastidia – *it annoys me* me aburre – *it bores me* no me interesa – *it doesn't interest me*

 Escucha otra vez e indica la opinión.

interesante   aburrido/a   divertido/a
creativo/a   competitivo/a   emocionante
fenomenal   guay   genial

cool

great   exciting

  Pregunta y contesta usando expresiones diferentes.

Ejemplo: **A** ¿Qué *te gusta* hacer?   **A** *¿Te gustan* los videojuegos?
             B *Me encanta* ir al cine.   **B** Sí, *me apasionan* porque
                                                  son muy divertidos.

 Escribe cinco frases sobre lo que te gusta o no te gusta hacer. Justifica tu opinión.

NC 3

LE E R
5

Lee el mensaje de Ana Luisa y contesta a las preguntas.

NC 4

1 ¿Cómo pasa su tiempo libre?
2 ¿Adónde va con sus amigos?
3 ¿Qué no le gusta mucho?
4 ¿Qué va a hacer esta noche?

¡Hola gente! Busco amigos de mi edad; tengo quince años y vivo en Gijón, Asturias. Me interesa la música de Shakira y de Lady Gaga y paso horas escuchando mi MP3. Además me encanta salir con mis amigos y vamos bastante al cine. No me gusta mucho el deporte, sobre todo si es un deporte competitivo. Paso horas haciendo sudoku porque me flipan los números. Esta noche tengo que hacer los deberes y después voy a ver la tele. Tú, ¿qué prefieres hacer en tu tiempo libre? ¿Por qué? ¿Cómo pasas los sábados y domingos normalmente? ¿Adónde sueles ir? ¿Qué vas a hacer el fin de semana que viene?

ESCUCHAR 6

NC 4

🎧 **Escucha y lee.**

A mí me apasiona la música. Paso horas escuchando mi MP3 y descargando música de internet. Prefiero la música con un ritmo fuerte porque me encanta tocar los tambores tradicionales de Colombia. También toco la batería en un grupo de rock. Ahora me mola la fusión de la música típica española con los ritmos de rock y de salsa.

Claro que me gusta pero prefiero la música suave y lírica. Paso horas tocando la guitarra e inventando mis propias canciones. Cuando era pequeña siempre cantaba cancioncillas infantiles*. Me encantan las baladas antiguas; me parecen muy agradables. No me gusta la música estrepitosa como el grunge; está fatal y es muy ruidosa.

(A mí) Me gusta(n) / me apasiona(n) Prefiero Odio	la música las canciones	pop / rock / ska / hip hop / clásica / heavy metal / indie / grunge / de los años setenta/noventa
porque	es ...	rítmico/a nulo/a suave chulo ruidoso/a estrepitoso/a emocionante sensacional creativo/a
	tiene ritmo / no tiene sentido	

* cancioncillas infantiles –
nursery rhymes

LEER 7

Lee los textos otra vez. ¿Verdad, mentira o no se menciona?

1 A los dos les gusta la música.
2 A Roberto no le interesa la música española.
3 Roberto prefiere la música tradicional.
4 Elena pasa su tiempo libre tocando la batería.
5 A Elena le apasiona la música infantil.
6 Los dos tienen gustos de música diferentes.

? Think

Where did you meet terms such as *los años setenta / noventa* recently?

ESCUCHAR 8

🎧 **Escucha y anota el tipo de música y la opinión.**

NC 3

*Ejemplo: **1** la música rock – tiene ritmo*

⚙ Gramática → p.162

Remember! You use the *-ando* or *-iendo* endings to say what you are **doing**.
Paso horas escuch**ando** mi MP3 –
I spend hours listening to my MP3.
Paso mi tiempo libre hac**iendo** sudoku – *I spend my free time doing sudoku.*

• Follow the examples and write three sentences about what you spend your free time doing.

Challenge

Write a reply to Ana Luisa's message (activity 5). Make sure you answer all the questions and include as much detail as possible about your hobbies, what you do in your free time and what kind of music you like. Make sure you give your opinion as well.

To reach level 5 you would need to use two tenses. Which two tenses does Ana Luisa use? Follow her example!

NC 4–5

2A.2 De compras

- Vocabulary: talk about going shopping
- Grammar: use direct object pronouns (for things/objects)
- Skills: adapt previously learnt language in a new context

1 la frutería

2 la carnicería

3 la charcutería

4 la pescadería

5 la tienda de comestibles

LEER 1 **Empareja las compras con la palabra adecuada de la casilla.**

Ejemplo: **a** *manzanas*

aceite de oliva   aceitunas
chorizo   limones   manzanas
patatas fritas   pescado   pollo

 a
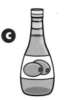 **b**
 c
d

 e
 **f**
 **g**
h

ESCUCHAR 2 **NC 3** 🎧 **Escucha la conversación e indica en qué tienda están.**

Ejemplo: **1** *en la frutería*

ESCUCHAR 3 🎧 **Escucha otra vez y anota lo que compra cada persona.**

Ejemplo: **1** *un kilo de manzanas amarillas*

⚙ Gramática → p.167

Direct object pronouns – replacing things/objects

Pronouns are words we use to avoid repeating words for things we have already mentioned:

el melón	aquí **lo** tienes – *the melon, here it is*
la piña	aquí **la** tienes – *the pineapple, here it is*
los tomates	aquí **los** tienes – *the tomatoes, here they are*
las manzanas	aquí **las** tienes – *the apples, here they are*

Can you work out a rule about which pronoun to use for each word?

? Think

Can you remember all the quantities and high numbers you learnt on page 26? If not then look back and revise them. Can you remember how to say *this, these, that* and *those* (page 40)?

HABLAR 4

NC 3–4

 Practica los diálogos. Usa los dibujos para ayudarte.

a
Quiero ⬤ , por favor.

¿Lo necesita para hoy o para mañana?

Lo quiero para hoy y lo quiero dulce.

b
Estoy buscando

.

¿La quiere fresca o en lata?

La quiero fresca, madura y grande.

c
Quiero 🍅🍅 :
los compro en el mercado, ¿verdad?

¿Los quiere usted grandes o pequeños? ¿Son para cocinar o para la ensalada?

Los quiero grandes para la ensalada.

d
Quiero un kilo de

, por favor.

Las tengo rojas, verdes o amarillas. ¿Cuáles quiere usted?

Las quiero rojas – son más sabrosas.

 HABLAR 5 Inventa otros diálogos usando los dibujos de la actividad 1.

NC 4

 ESCRIBIR 6 Escribe tus diálogos de la actividad 5.

 LEER 7 Lee la lista de la compra.

un paquete de galletas
tres latas de maíz
seis botellas de limonada
medio kilo de azúcar
una bolsa grande de patatas fritas
cien gramos de jamón

 ESCUCHAR 8 Escucha y escribe lo que falta de la lista.

 ESCUCHAR 9 Escucha la discusión y contesta a las preguntas.

NC 4–5

1 Why are Elena and Juan arguing?
2 Where do they decide to go in the end?
3 Why?
4 What present is Elena going to buy?
5 What does Juan want to do afterwards?

? Think

How do the ordinal numbers (first, second, third etc.) correspond to the numbers you have learnt? Can you work out which floors would be called *Planta baja* and *Sótano*?

primero/a; segundo/a; tercero/a; cuarto/a; quinto/a; sexto/a; séptimo/a; octavo/a; noveno/a; décimo/a

Challenge

With a partner play a shopping game. You are in a large department store. Write out a shopping list of ten items either from memory or with the help of a dictionary. Then ask your partner where each item is to be found in the store.

Example: **A** *Quiero comprar <u>una raqueta de tenis</u>.*
B *La sección de <u>deportes</u> está en la <u>primera planta</u>.*

5A Planta	Informática y electrodomésticos
4A Planta	Hogar, muebles y cafetería
3A Planta	Caballeros: ropa y zapatos
2A Planta	Señoras: ropa y peluquería
1A Planta	Niños: juguetes y ropa
0 Planta	Perfumes, cosméticos e información
–1 Sótano	Deportes y floristería

NC 3

2A.3 De vacaciones

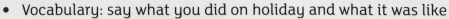

- Vocabulary: say what you did on holiday and what it was like
- Grammar: revise the preterite tense (regular and some irregular verbs)
- Skills: respond to open-ended questions, e.g. *¿Adónde fuiste?*

a   b   c   d   e   f

LEER 1 Empareja las frases con las fotos.

Ejemplo: **1** c

1 **Ayer** fuiste de compras al nuevo centro comercial, ¿verdad?

2 Juan fue a la feria **el sábado pasado**.

3 **La semana pasada** fuimos a la playa en coche.

4 **El verano pasado** fui de camping con el instituto.

5 **Anoche** todos fueron a la disco.

6 ¿**Anteayer** vosotros fuisteis al parque de atracciones?

ESCUCHAR 2
NC 3

 Escucha y anota el orden de las frases de la actividad 1.

ESCUCHAR 3
NC 4–5

 Empareja las preguntas con las respuestas. Luego escucha y verifica. Añade la persona.

Ejemplo: **1** a Enrique

1 ¿A qué hora saliste?
2 ¿Qué cosas de interés viste?
3 ¿Qué comiste?
4 ¿Adónde fuiste?
5 ¿Cómo fuiste?

a Salí a las seis de la mañana.
b Fuimos en taxi.
c Comí un helado de pistacho.
d Fui de camping.
e Vi el acueducto de Segovia.

Gramática → p.163

The preterite tense or simple past tense

Remember!
You use this tense to say what you **did** and to describe events which began and ended in the past:
Yesterday I went to the funfair. *Ayer fui al parque de atracciones.*
Last year we went to Cuba on holiday. *El año pasado fuimos a Cuba de vacaciones.*

ir – *to go* (irregular)

fui	*we went*
fuiste	*you (s.) went*
fue	*I went*
fuimos	*they went*
fuisteis	*he / she went*
fueron	*you (pl.) went*

- Match up each part of the verb to the English. Then go back and translate the sentences in activity 1.

Me encantó (No) me gustó mucho (No) me interesó Lo detesté	porque	fue (muy)	increíble emocionante fatal aburrido/a divertido/a mal
		fue un desastre	
Lo pasé fatal / bomba			

Gramática → p.163

Remember!
The verb *hacer* (to do or to make) is irregular. In the preterite tense it follows this pattern:

hice – *I did / made*	**hicimos**
hiciste	**hicisteis**
hizo	**hicieron**

- Notice there are no written accents on this verb.
- Why do you think the *c* changes to a *z* in *hizo*?

4 **Practica el diálogo. Luego inventa otros diálogos (ver la actividad 3).**

NC 4–5

A María, ¿adónde fuiste?   **B** Fui a Mallorca.
A ¿Qué tal lo pasaste?   **B** Lo pasé bomba.
A ¿Qué hiciste?   **B** Comí helados.

5 🎧 **Escucha otra vez y completa una tabla así:**

NC 4–5

Nombre	¿Adónde?	☺	☹
María	Mallorca	✓	

6 **Lee la tarjeta postal y empareja las traducciones 1–6 con las palabras en negrita.**

Londres   Madrid   Mallorca
Los Picos de Europa   Segovia
en casa

> ¡Llegué tarde después de **un viaje desastroso**! El avión salió con retraso y el viaje fue horrible. El hotel **donde nos alojamos** era muy pequeño y no me gustó. Visitamos los monumentos más importantes pero **todo resultó ser** muy aburrido y cuando **empezó a llover** decidimos ir a un restaurante. Cenamos y nos acostamos **temprano**. No compré nada y no me divertí mucho. Mañana va a ser **un día mejor**.
>
> Ana María

? **Think**

What would happen to the sound if you didn't put a *u* next to the *g* in *llegué*?

 salió con retraso – *was delayed*

1	it began to rain	**4**	a better day
2	where we stayed	**5**	a disastrous journey
3	early	**6**	it all turned out to be

7  **Contesta a las preguntas en inglés.**

NC 5

1. Why does Ana María say it was a disastrous journey?
2. Why didn't she like the hotel?
3. How was the visit to the monuments?
4. What did they do when it started to rain?
5. What did she buy?

Challenge
Write no more than 100 words on what you did during your last holidays. It can be a true account or an imaginary one. Use the verbs from the lists on these pages to help you. Make sure you include some opinions.

NC 5

8 **Ahora escribe un breve párrafo en español sobre el viaje de Ana María.**

NC 4–5

- Vocabulary: describe past events
- Grammar: use a mix of preterite (some irregular) and imperfect verbs
- Skills: summarise and recount what happened

LEER 1

NC 5

Empareja las preguntas con las respuestas.

1 ¿Qué tal pasaste tu cumpleaños, Roberto?
2 ¿Qué recibiste de regalo?
3 ¿Dónde te alojaste?
4 ¿Tuviste que visitar algún monumento?
5 ¿Qué tiempo hizo?
6 ¿Cuánto tiempo estuviste allí?
7 ¿Hiciste algo interesante?
8 ¿Cómo fue?

a Hizo buen tiempo durante toda la visita.
b Nos alojamos en la casa de unos amigos a las afueras.
c Fue inolvidable, sobre todo los fuegos artificiales al final.
d Lo pasé bomba en la fiesta de San Isidro en Madrid.
e Nos vestimos de castizo – el traje típico de los madrileños.
f Recibí un regalo interesante: una entrada para una corrida en Las Ventas.
g Estuvimos allí unos cuatro días.
h Tuvimos que visitar el Rastro para hacer compras, nada más.

Gramática → p.163

Here are three more irregular verbs in the preterite tense.

estar – *to be*	ser – *to be*	tener (que) – *to have (to)*
estuve – *I was*	fui – *I was*	tuve (que) – *I had (to)*
estuviste	fuiste	tuviste
estuvo	fue	tuvo
estuvimos	fuimos	tuvimos
estuvisteis	fuisteis	tuvisteis
estuvieron	fueron	tuvieron

- Note: these verbs do not have a written accent.
- What do you notice about the verb *ser* in the preterite tense? Clue: the verb *ir* (to go).

HABLAR 2

NC 5

 Con tu compañero, practica las preguntas y respuestas (actividad 1).

ESCUCHAR 3

NC 5

 Escucha. ¿Qué imagen se describe?

ESCUCHAR 4

 Escucha otra vez y pon las frases en el orden correcto.

1 Vimos las procesiones de los gigantes y cabezudos.
2 Hizo mucho calor.
3 Nos alojamos en un hotel pequeño.
4 Fuimos a Sitges.
5 Comimos pescado frito y bebimos sangría.
6 Vimos unos fuegos artificiales maravillosos.
7 Estuvimos allí durante cinco días.
8 Hicimos una fiesta.

LEER 5

NC 5

Empareja las preguntas con las respuestas (actividad 4).

a ¿Cuánto tiempo estuviste allí?
b ¿Dónde te alojaste?
c ¿Qué comiste y bebiste?
d ¿Qué hiciste la última noche?
e ¿Qué viste de interés?
f ¿Adónde fuiste?
g ¿Qué tiempo hizo?

Gramática → p.164

To describe an event in the past you need to be able to use both the imperfect and the preterite tenses. For example, in the video, Juan tells Roberto:
'Esta vez el último tiene que contar **lo que hacía** durante el recorrido y **cómo le fue**.'
'This time the last one has to tell **what they were doing** and **what happened**.'

● Complete the following sentence.
We use the ⬚⬚⬚ tense to say what used to happen or was happening over a period of time in the past and the ⬚⬚⬚ tense to describe something which happened – began and ended – in the past.

▶ **El Video Reto**

VIDEO 6

Mira el video (primera parte) y contesta a las preguntas.

a Write down three opinion words or phrases you hear that you have learnt so far in this unit.
b Why wouldn't you want to lose?

VIDEO 7

Watch the second part of the video (as many times as you need to) and note down when a preterite tense is used and when an imperfect tense is used.

VIDEO 8

Lee y completa el texto con un verbo adecuado de la casilla.

Ejemplo: 1 hicimos

Primero **1** la formación **2** muy interesante, pero cuando **3** a los árboles, **4** fatal. Nada más subir a los árboles **5** un ataque de vértigo. Elena y Juan lo **6** sin miedo, **7** de un árbol a otro como monos pero a mí me **8** las piernas. **9** de un árbol a otro atado con una cuerda. **10** con un arnés de una plataforma a otra y lo **11** mal. Me **12** allí suspendido en el aire. ¡Lo pasé mal pero supermal! **13** el último.

hice   hicimos   subimos
Fue   fue   tuve   saltaban
temblaban   Salté   quedé
hacían   Terminé   Caminé

ESCRIBIR 9

NC 5

Escribe sobre una aventura (como el "pino a pino"). Usa el texto de Roberto para ayudarte.

Challenge

Write no more than 100 words about an event you went to last year. Try to use both the preterite and the imperfect tenses.
For help on the imperfect tense, look back at page 46.
To achieve level 6 you would need to say what you are going to do next year as well.

NC 5–6

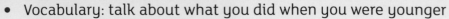

- Vocabulary: talk about what you did when you were younger
- Grammar: use a mix of preterite and imperfect tenses
- Skills: adapt previously learnt language and give opinions

Empareja las frases con los dibujos.

NC 5

Ejemplo: 1 c

1 Cuando tenía tres años me gustaba ir al parque. Jugaba en los columpios y toboganes.
2 Cuando tenía cinco años me regalaron un muñeco de acción. Jugaba con mi muñeco todos los días, lo adoraba.
3 Me encantaba pintar con colores vivos y pintaba con los dedos; me fascinaba.

4 Cuando era pequeño no veía mucho la tele. Lo que sí me gustaba eran los programas infantiles como *Barrio Sésamo*.
5 Durante las vacaciones iba con mis padres a la Costa Brava. Me encantaba hacer castillos de arena en la playa.
6 Cuando tenía cuatro años iba a la piscina y allí es donde aprendí a nadar. Me gustaba mucho nadar.

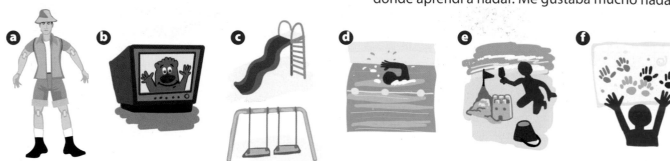

(a) (b) (c) (d) (e) (f)

🎧 **Escucha y anota quién ...**

Ejemplo: 1 Pablo

1 pintaba con los dedos.
2 aprendió a nadar cuando tenía cuatro años.
3 veía programas infantiles en la tele.
4 hacía castillos de arena en la Costa Brava.
5 adoraba a un muñeco.
6 iba al parque.

Escribe lo que hacía cada persona.

Ejemplo: Isabel iba ... / hacía ...

Copia y completa el texto con las palabras de la casilla.

NC 5

Cuando **1** ▨▨▨ diez años **2** ▨▨▨ los sábados porque siempre **3** ▨▨▨ con mi madre a hacer las compras. Primero **4** ▨▨▨ al mercado donde **5** ▨▨▨ cantidad de fruta y verdura. Un día mi madre **6** ▨▨▨ unas uvas deliciosas y las **7** ▨▨▨ en la bolsa. Una hora más tarde **8** ▨▨▨ hambre y **9** ▨▨▨ comer unas uvas. Poco a poco las **10** ▨▨▨ todas y cuando **11** ▨▨▨ a casa ya no **12** ▨▨▨ ni una. ¡Por supuesto, mi madre se enfadó conmigo!

| comí compró decidí había |
| iba íbamos llegamos puso |
| me encantaban quedaba |
| tenía tuve |

🎧 **Escucha y verifica.**

6

NC 5

Lee el blog de Juan. ¿Tiene una opinión positiva o negativa de su visita?

Cuando tenía diez años fui con un grupo de mi colegio a la Costa del Sol.

Viajamos en tren hasta Málaga y llegamos tarde, a las diez de la noche. Nos alojamos en un hotel moderno y estuvimos allí cuatro días.

El primer día visitamos el museo Picasso y unas ruinas antiguas de la ciudad. No me gustó mucho porque no me interesaba ni el arte ni la historia. Pero el segundo día lo pasamos bomba en el parque Selwo. Vimos muchos animales salvajes. Comimos un pollo asado muy rico y bebimos cantidad de limonada porque hacía mucho calor. Al día siguiente montamos en dromedario. Fue una aventura maravillosa y todo me encantó.

 7

NC 5

Haz una lista de todos los verbos en el blog. Decide si están en el tiempo pretérito o en imperfecto. Traduce las frases al inglés.

Ejemplo: tenía = imperfecto
*Cuando **tenía** diez años = when I was ten years old*

 8

NC 5

Imagina que vas a entrevistarle a Juan. Prepara una lista de preguntas. Pregunta y contesta con tu compañero.

Ejemplo: **A** *Juan, ¿adónde fuiste cuando tenías diez años?*
B *Fui a la Costa del Sol / a Málaga.*

 **Challenge**

Write a blog of no more than 100 words about an imaginary or real visit you made to somewhere special when you were younger. Set the scene and describe when it was, where you went, what you did and what it was like.

NC 5–6

 **Think**

What do you have to include to write at level 6?

Comprender – Direct object pronouns, preterite tense

A Direct object pronouns

These are words like **it** or **me** which we use to avoid having to repeat the name of a person or thing that has already been mentioned. They usually go in front of the verb.

¿Tienes **las llaves**? Sí, **las** tengo.
*Have you got **the keys**? Yes, I've got **them**.*

lo *it (masc. thing)*   los *them (masc. things)*
la *it (fem. thing)*   las *them (fem. things)*

1 Answer these questions. Use direct object pronouns.

   1 ¿Compraste las sandalias? Sí, …
   2 ¿Vas a comprar helados? Sí, …
   3 ¿Estás limpiando el coche? No, …
   4 ¿Ves aquella casa? No, …

2 Completa y practica los diálogos.

   1 A ¿Tienes mis gafas de sol?
      B No, no ▨▨▨▨ tengo, ▨▨▨▨ tienes tú en tu bolso.

   2 A ¿Dónde están mis vaqueros?
      B Creo que ▨▨▨▨ pusiste en la maleta.

   3 A ¿Vas a llevar esa camisa?
      B Sí, voy a poner ▨▨▨▨ en la maleta también.

B Preterite tense

The preterite tense or simple past tense is used to refer to an action that began and ended in the past. To form the preterite of regular verbs:

	viajar	comer	salir
take the infinitive	viajar	comer	salir
remove the ending	viaj-	com-	sal-
and add the following endings: yo	viaj**é**	com**í**	sal**í**
tú	viaj**aste**	com**iste**	sal**iste**
él/ella/usted	viaj**ó**	com**ió**	sal**ió**
nosotros/as	viaj**amos**	com**imos**	sal**imos**
vosotros/as	viaj**asteis**	com**isteis**	sal**isteis**
ellos/ellas/ustedes	viaj**aron**	com**ieron**	sal**ieron**

● Reflexive verbs follow the same pattern as regular -ar verbs **but** remember to place the pronoun in front of the verb:
  me levanté, te levantaste, se levantó etc.

Now complete the verb *alojarse* (to stay) in the same way.

● Here are some common verbs that have irregular preterites. Check them. Note that they have no accents when written in the preterite.

  estar (to be)   *hacer* (to do)   *tener* (to have)   *ir* (to go)   *ser* (to be)

Ser and *ir* have the same form in the preterite tense, so *fui* can mean 'I went' or 'I was'. The context should make the meaning clear.

3 Write out the verbs *viajar*, *comer* and *salir* on learning cards with the Spanish on one side and the English on the other. Learn them by heart.

4 Complete these sentences with the preterite of the verb in brackets.

   1 El invierno pasado mi hermano y yo ▨▨▨▨ a esquiar. (ir)
   2 Ayer yo ▨▨▨▨ la trompeta en la orquesta. (tocar)
   3 Ana y Pedro ▨▨▨▨ a casa en taxi. (volver)
   4 Mi padre ▨▨▨▨ una paella deliciosa. (hacer)
   5 Mi hermano ▨▨▨▨ al fútbol pero yo ▨▨▨▨ al tenis. (jugar)

Aprender – Recounting events and answering questions

C Recounting and summarising a past event

This requires a great deal of practice so start with simple sentences to build up your confidence.

Remember, if you are recounting actions that began and ended in the past you need to use the preterite tense.
Hizo buen tiempo así que jugamos al fútbol. The weather was fine so we played football.

If you want to say what you used to do or describe a scene or recount an event which went on over a longer period of time then you can use the imperfect tense.
Cuando hacía buen tiempo jugábamos al fútbol. When the weather was fine we used to play football.

D Responding to open-ended questions

When answering most questions you usually listen first for the question word: *¿Dónde?* (Where?), *¿Cómo?* (How?), *¿Quién?* (Who?), for example. This helps you to pinpoint the information required. Then you listen for the tense of the verb and any extras required such as adjectives or adverbs.

When you answer an open-ended question it is up to you to supply the information.

¿Adónde fuiste? (Where did you go?), *¿Qué hiciste?* (What did you do?), *¿Qué tal lo pasaste?* (How did you get on?) are some of the most commonly used questions so far.

5 Read these examples and write down the verb and the tense used. Think about why each tense has been used.

1 El verano pasado fuimos a Sitges.
2 La semana pasada hizo buen tiempo pero ayer llovió e hizo mal tiempo.
3 Cuando tenía diez años iba al colegio infantil.
4 Mi padre se puso el abrigo porque hacía frío.
5 Salimos a la calle porque queríamos comprar revistas.

6 Now think back to last summer and write five sentences about what you did.

Example:

1 Fui …
2 Comí …
3 Jugué …
4 Salí …
5 Lo pasé …

Hablar – Pronunciation

E Intonation in questions

How is a statement made into a question?

When writing you use punctuation: ¿ … ?

When speaking you use your voice:

Hoy es sábado.

¿Hoy es sábado?

7 Listen. What difference can you hear in the way each of these sentences is spoken?

A Mañana vas a ir con tus amigos al cine.
B ¿Mañana vas a ir con tus amigos al cine?
C Estás comiendo un bocadillo de jamón.
D ¿Estás comiendo un bocadillo de jamón?

- Vocabulary: read and write more about hobbies and past events
- Grammar: use the preterite, imperfect and present tenses
- Skills: write a few simple opinions in the past

LEER 1 NC 3

Empareja las preguntas con las respuestas. Mira los dibujos.
Match the questions to the answers. Use the illustrations to help you.

1 ¿Adónde fuiste?

2 ¿Cómo viajaste?

3 ¿Dónde te alojaste?

4 ¿Qué tiempo hizo?

5 ¿Qué comiste?

6 ¿Qué visitaste?

7 ¿Qué tal lo pasaste?

a Hizo sol y calor.
b Lo pasé bomba / fatal.
c Viajamos en tren.
d Comí un pescado delicioso.
e Nos alojamos en un hotel pequeño.
f Fui a Benidorm.
g Visité un parque de atracciones.

ESCRIBIR 2 NC 4–5

Contesta a las preguntas de la actividad 1. Escribe sobre tus últimas vacaciones.
Answer the questions in activity 1 about your last holiday.

LEER 3 NC 3–4

Lee el anuncio e identifica a la persona: Xavi o Maite.
Read the advert and identify the person: Xavi or Maite.

Hola, me interesa tener amigos de todas las partes del mundo. Me apasiona toda clase de música. Cuando tenía cinco años empecé a tocar la guitarra pero ahora no me gusta tanto. Prefiero tocar la batería. También me encanta jugar al ajedrez porque tienes que pensar bastante para ser un buen jugador. Paso horas chateando con amigos por internet y cada tarde, después del insti, salgo a pasear con mi perro.

Xavi

Maite

ESCRIBIR 4 NC 3–4

Escribe un anuncio similar. Usa las palabras de la actividad 3 para ayudarte.
Write a similar advert. Use the words in activity 3 to help you.

- Vocabulary: read and understand an account in the past
- Grammar: use past, present and immediate future tenses
- Skills: respond to a variety of questions

LEER 1

NC 5

Lee el texto y contesta a las preguntas.

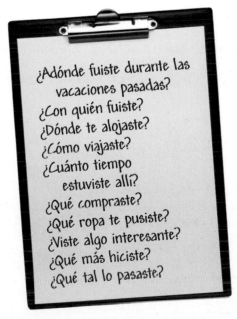

El ocho de mayo de 1975 nació en Madrid el tercer hijo de Julio Iglesias y le llamaron Enrique. Su madre es filipina. A los trece años sus padres se divorciaron y Enrique se fue a vivir a Miami con su padre. Estudió Administración de Empresas (Business) en la Universidad de esa misma ciudad pero su primer amor era la música y por eso dejó de estudiar.
Decidió grabar un disco del que vendió medio millón de copias en la primera semana. Durante su carrera ha sido cantante, actor, modelo y productor. Su estilo de música es pop latino con un poco de R & B.

1 ¿De quién trata el artículo?
2 ¿Cuándo es su cumpleaños?
3 ¿Qué pasó cuando tenía trece años?
4 ¿Adónde se fue?
5 ¿Por qué?

6 ¿Qué estudió?
7 ¿Por qué no continuó con sus estudios?
8 ¿Qué decidió hacer?
9 ¿Qué tal resultó?
10 ¿Qué otras profesiones tiene?

ESCRIBIR 2

NC 5

Escribe un párrafo sobre unas vacaciones verdaderas o imaginarias. Contesta a las preguntas.

¿Adónde fuiste durante las vacaciones pasadas?
¿Con quién fuiste?
¿Dónde te alojaste?
¿Cómo viajaste?
¿Cuánto tiempo estuviste allí?
¿Qué compraste?
¿Qué ropa te pusiste?
¿Viste algo interesante?
¿Qué más hiciste?
¿Qué tal lo pasaste?

ESCRIBIR 3

NC 5

Ahora escribe lo que vas a hacer durante el próximo verano. Basa tus ideas en la actividad 2.

Ejemplo. El próximo verano voy a visitar a mi amigo en Barcelona ...

Escuchar

Listen and answer the questions with a single word or a short phrase.

1 ¿Adónde fue Roberto?
2 ¿Con quién fue?
3 ¿Cómo viajó?
4 ¿Qué tiempo hacía?
5 ¿Qué ropa llevaba?

6 ¿Qué visitó?
7 ¿Vio algo interesante?
8 ¿A qué hora llegó a casa?
9 ¿Qué hizo después?
10 ¿Qué tal lo pasó?

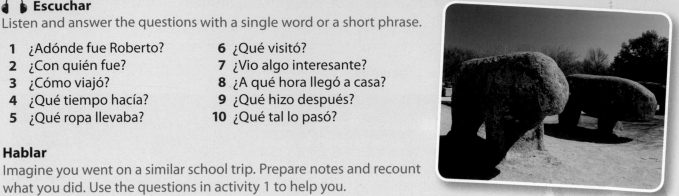

Hablar

Imagine you went on a similar school trip. Prepare notes and recount what you did. Use the questions in activity 1 to help you.

Leer

Read the text and write ten facts about Santi's shopping trip in English.

¡Hola! Me llamo Santi y vivo en Segovia, no muy lejos de Madrid. El otro día fui de compras con mi hermano menor, Miguelito, porque queríamos comprar un regalo para mi padre que va a cumplir años el próximo sábado. Decidimos ir a El Corte Inglés porque suele ser más fácil encontrar regalos interesantes allí. Primero fuimos a la sección de librería pero no tenían el libro que pensábamos comprarle. Entonces decidimos ir a la sección de hombres para comprarle una corbata, pero no la tenían en su color preferido. Después subimos al tercer piso, a la sección de música, y pasamos dos horas escuchando CDs de los años setenta porque es la música de cuando mi padre era joven. Cuando por fin decidí lo que comprar, Miguelito no estaba. Busqué por todas partes pero no apareció. Al final le encontré – dormido y escuchando música en su MP3.

Escribir

Write no more than 100 words about what you did one weekend in the past.

Use the questions in activity 1 and the bullet points below to help you. Remember that to achieve a level 5 you must use two different tenses. You could mention:

- where you went
- why you went there (because of a hobby/interest?)
- who you went with
- how you travelled
- what you did there
- what you saw
- what you ate
- what you bought
- what you are going to do next weekend (to achieve a level 6!)

Vocabulario

Mi tiempo libre	My free time
la canción	song
los pasatiempos	hobbies
me aburre	It bores me
me apasiona	I love
me encanta	I like a lot
me fastidia	It annoys me
me interesa	It interests me
aburrido/a	boring
creativo/a	creative
divertido/a	amusing
emocionante	exciting
estrepitoso/a	rowdy
fatal	awful
genial	great
ruidoso/a	noisy
descargar	to download
leer revistas	to read magazines
pintar	to paint
salir con amigos	to go out with friends

De compras	Going shopping
la carnicería	butcher's
la charcutería	delicatessen
la frutería	fruit shop/greengrocer's
la pescadería	fishmonger's
la tienda de comestibles	general foodstore
el aceite de oliva	olive oil
las aceitunas	olives
los caramelos	sweets
un helado	ice cream
el jamón	ham
la leche	milk
una lechuga	lettuce
los limones	lemons
las manzanas	apples
las patatas fritas	crisps/chips
el pescado	fish
el pollo	chicken
las sardinas	sardines
las truchas	trout
¿Qué falta?	What's missing?
un regalo	a present
la planta baja	ground floor
el sótano	basement

De vacaciones	On holiday
¿Adónde fuiste?	Where did you go?
¿Qué tal lo pasaste?	How did you get on?
acostarse	to go to bed
alojarse en	to stay in
comer	to eat
Ir de camping	to go camping

ir (fui)	to go (I went)
salir	to go out
empezó a llover	it began to rain
lo pasé / pasamos bomba	I / We had a great time
anoche	last night
anteayer	the day before yesterday
ayer	yesterday
el sábado pasado	last saturday
el avión	aeroplane
desastroso/a	disastrous
increíble	incredible
una feria	a fair
el parque de atracciones	fun fair
un viaje	a journey

¡Lo pasamos bomba!	We had a great time
¿Cuánto tiempo?	How long?
¿Qué tiempo hizo?	What was the weather like?
estar (estuve)	to be (I was)
ganar	to win
ser (fui)	to be (I was)
tener (tuve)	to have (I had)
fatal	dreadful
madrileño/a	person from Madrid
la corrida (de toros)	bullfight
los fuegos artificiales	fireworks
un regalo	a present
un traje típico	typical/traditional costume/ dress

I can ...

- talk about what I like doing in my free time
- talk about what music I like
- talk about going shopping
- use direct object pronouns
- say what I did on holiday
- respond to open-ended questions
- describe past events
- summarise and recount what happened
- use the preterite and imperfect tenses

- Vocabulary: talk about different means of transport
- Grammar: use *a* (preposition) and *que* (relative pronoun)
- Skills: tackle an unfamiliar text

ESCUCHAR 1

🎧 **Escucha. ¿En qué orden se mencionan?**

Ejemplo: **1** c

el tren

el tranvía

el metro

ir a pie

los taxis

el autobús

ESCUCHAR 2

NC 3–4

🎧 **Escucha otra vez. Toma notas en inglés sobre la información adicional.**

Ejemplo: **1** c *flexible, cheap*

ESCRIBIR 3

NC 3

Escribe cinco frases. ¿Cómo vas a los lugares de abajo? ¿Por qué?

Ejemplo: **Voy a** *casa de mis abuelos en tren* **porque** *está lejos.*

casa de mis abuelos	en coche		es barato
Londres	en avión		es gratis
el instituto	en autobús		es cómodo
el cine	en autocar		es rápido
el polideportivo	en barco	porque	es directo
el centro	en tren		es moderno
	en metro		es limpio
	a pie		está cerca
			está lejos

⚙️ *Gramática* → p.160

To say 'to' and 'to the':

a	Voy **a** casa de mis amigos. Voy **a** Madrid.
a + el = al	el mercado → Voy **al** mercado.
a + la = a la	la panadería → Voy **a la** panadería.
a + los = a los	los grandes almacenes → Voy **a los** grandes almacenes.
a + las = a las	las tiendas → Voy **a las** tiendas.

Hola Sofía,

¿Qué tal estás? El fin de semana llegué a Madrid que es una ciudad **bonita** y muy interesante. Ayer lo pasé fenomenal y visité la ciudad en bici. ¡Sí! ¡En bici!

Es una nueva manera muy popular de hacer turismo aquí en Madrid **que** transforma el alquiler de bicicletas convencional. Alquilamos una bicicleta e hicimos el tour "Madrid en un día" **que** realiza un recorrido completo por los lugares más importantes de la capital: monumentos, calles, museos, plazas, parques ... La ruta es autoguiada, **lo que significa** que tienes todo lo que necesitas incluido en el precio: un mapa detallado de la ruta y un dossier informativo de cada punto de interés **que** contiene descripciones, horarios, precios etc.

Lo que más me gustó fue ir a mi propio ritmo y poder sacar fotos cuando quería.

¡Un abrazo!

Elena

 Think

Don't be put off by an unfamiliar longer text. The information you need to answer the questions is often in the right order in the text.

 Lee el email. Identifica las cuatro frases correctas.

NC 5   *Ejemplo: 2,*

1 Elena está en Segovia.
2 Ayer lo pasó muy bien.
3 Visitó la ciudad en el autobús turístico.
4 Muchos turistas visitan Madrid en bicicleta.
5 No tuvo que comprar un mapa.
6 Hizo fotos.

 ¿Cómo se dice en español ...? Elige una frase de color rojo.

Ejemplo: 1 que es una ciudad bonita

1 which is a beautiful city
2 that has descriptions
3 which means that
4 what I liked most

 Hablar en equipo. ¡Preparados, listos, ya!

NC 3   In teams of 3–5 make an extended sentence (see below).

Each member can only say one block at a time. Be careful! Places, means of transport and adjectives cannot be repeated.

Voy a + place in town	means of transport	*porque*	*es/está* + adjective or reason

Ejemplo: Voy al restaurante / en coche / porque / está lejos.

Keep practising until you get it down to one minute or less.

 *Gramática* → p.160

Relative pronouns *que* and *lo que*

The relative pronouns in English are *which, that, who, whom* and *whose*. The most common relative pronoun in Spanish is **que**. You can use it for people and things:

El museo **que** está en el centro de Madrid se llama El Prado.

*The museum **that** is in the centre of Madrid is called El Prado.*

When you are referring to a concept or idea, use **lo que**:

Lo que más me gustó fue el museo.

***What** I liked most was the museum.*

 Challenge

Using the grid in activity 6, write down the places where you go and how you get there for each day of the week.

Example: El sábado voy al supermercado en coche porque está lejos.

NC 4

- Vocabulary: recognise some tourist attractions in Madrid
- Grammar: use the immediate future to talk about plans
- Skills: transform level 4 speaking or writing into level 5

① el Museo del Prado

② el Palacio Real

③ la Puerta del Sol

④ la Plaza de Toros de las Ventas

⑤ el Parque del Retiro

⑥ el Estadio Santiago Bernabéu

LEER 1

Lee las descripciones. ¿Qué foto es?

NC 4   *Ejemplo: 1 d*

a Es la plaza de toros más famosa de España con capacidad para 25.000 espectadores, lo que significa que también se utiliza frecuentemente para conciertos.

b Es la residencia oficial de la Familia Real española aunque no vive aquí porque prefiere el Palacio de la Zarzuela que es más modesto y acogedor. Se utiliza para las ceremonias de Estado.

c Inaugurado en 1947, es el hogar de uno de los equipos de fútbol más conocidos de España. Tiene una capacidad de más de 80.000 espectadores.

d Su obra más conocida es *Las Meninas* de Velázquez. Tiene una de las mejores colecciones europeas de arte del siglo XII al siglo XIX.

e Está lleno de esculturas y monumentos preciosos. Hay un lago muy tranquilo y una variedad de eventos. Está en el centro, rodeado por la ciudad.

f Es una plaza enorme que es muy concurrida y popular. Es el centro de España, donde está el "kilómetro cero".

> concurrida – *with lots of people, busy*

ESCUCHAR 2 🎧 **Escucha. ¿Qué sitio les recomiendas?**

NC 3–4   *Ejemplo: 1 el Museo del Prado*

ESCUCHAR 3 🎧 **Escucha otra vez. ¿Qué palabras te ayudaron a encontrar las respuestas de la actividad 2?**

? Think

In a matching activity like the one above, often just one or two words per text will give the answer away.

ESCRIBIR 4

NC 5

Copia los párrafos y escribe los verbos (que están en la casilla). ¿Qué van a hacer? ¿Cuándo?

Mañana por la mañana *(to go)* voy a ir al Museo del Prado porque me interesa el arte. Después *(to eat)* ⬚ en un restaurante típico y por la tarde *(to hire)* ⬚ una bicicleta y *(to do)* ⬚ un tour autoguiado del Parque del Retiro. Por la noche no *(to go out)* ⬚ , *(to return)* ⬚ al hotel pronto para descansar.

Helena

alquilar comer comprar hacer
ir salir ver visitar volver

⚙ *Gramática* → p.164

The immediate future

To talk about what you are going to do, use:

present tense of verb **ir** (to go) + **a** + infinitive

Example: **Voy a visitar** el estadio.

? *Think*

Both these paragraphs are writing at level 5. Can you work out why? How do you get a level 5?

El próximo martes *(to go)* vamos a ir ⬚ al Parque Warner Bros porque nos gustan las emociones fuertes. El miércoles por la mañana *(to go)* ⬚ a El Corte Inglés donde *(to buy)* ⬚ regalos para la familia y *(to visit)* ⬚ la Plaza Cibeles. Por la tarde *(to see)* ⬚ un partido de fútbol en el estadio Santiago Bernabéu porque nos encanta el fútbol.

Atsu y Bujune

LEER 5

Lee las frases. ¿Verdad o mentira?

Ejemplo: **1** *mentira*

1 A Helena le interesa el arte.
2 Helena va a comer antes de ir al Museo del Prado.
3 Helena va a visitar el Parque del Retiro a pie.
4 Atsu y Bujune van a ir a un parque de atracciones el martes.
5 Atsu y Bujune quieren comprar regalos para sus amigos.
6 A Atsu y Bujune les gusta el fútbol.

HABLAR 6

👥 **Estás en Madrid. Habla con tu compañero. ¿Adónde vas a ir? ¿Por qué?**

Ejemplo: Mañana voy a ir al Museo del Prado porque me interesa el arte.

Challenge

Imagine you are spending a week in Madrid. Write about your plans. Aim to produce a level 5 piece.

NC 5

- Vocabulary: buy travel tickets
- Grammar: ask questions
- Skills: identify key vocabulary from context

LEER 1 **Lee la conversación. ¿Cómo se dice en español?**

Ejemplo: 1 un billete

1 a ticket (for travel)	**5** second class (train)
2 single (travel)	**6** What time does it leave?
3 return (travel)	**7** platform
4 first class (train)	**8** What time does it arrive?

Hola, ¿Qué desea?
Un billete a Segovia, por favor.
¿De ida o de ida y vuelta?
De ida y vuelta.

¿Clase preferente?
No gracias, clase turista.
¿A qué hora sale el próximo?
Sale a las tres treinta del andén número ocho.

¿A qué hora llega?
A las quince cincuenta y siete.
¿Cuánto es?
Son doce euros.

Aquí tiene, gracias. Adiós.
Adiós.

Gramática → p.168

Question words

Remember!

- Statements and questions in Spanish can look the same; you need to put an upside down question mark at the beginning if it's a question:

  Quiere un billete a León. *He/She wants a ticket to León.*
  ¿Quiere un billete a León? *Does he/she want a ticket to León?*

- All question words have accents:

  ¿Qué? *What?*, ¿Cuándo? *When?*, ¿Cuánto/a/s? *How much/many?*, ¿Cómo? *How?*, ¿Quién? *Who?*, ¿Dónde? *Where?*, ¿Adónde? *Where to?* and ¿Por qué? *Why?*

ESCUCHAR 2 **Escucha y rellena la tabla.**

NC 4

	1	2	3	4
Destino	Albacete			
Tipo de billete	ida y vuelta			
Clase	preferente			
Hora de salida	18:18			
Hora de llegada	21:06			
Andén	4			
Precio	56,75			

HABLAR 3 **Practica la conversación de la actividad 1 con tu compañero. Cambia los elementos subrayados.**

NC 3–4

Tipo de billete	Clase	Hora de salida
ida ida y vuelta	turista preferente	08:10 09:52 11:22 13:44
Andén	**Hora de llegada**	**Precio**
1, 2, 3, 4, 5, 6, 7, 8, 9, 10	08:16 10:04 14:26 16:30	8,10€ 11,50€ 10,25€ 15,90€

 **Think**

Remember to pronounce words that look like English in Spanish!
euros: [you-ros] ✗ [eh-oo-ros] ✓

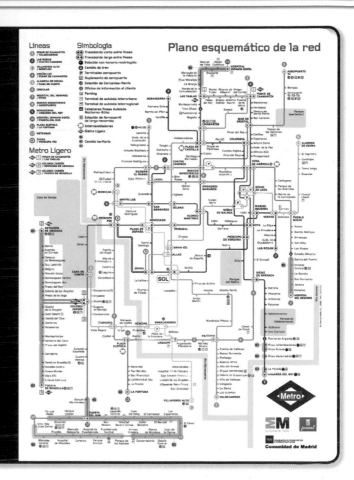

Metro Madrid

El metro de Madrid es una forma cómoda, rápida y segura de viajar por la ciudad, por una red que tiene 283 kilómetros con 293 estaciones. Tiene trece líneas más tres líneas de tranvía o metro ligero. Se pueden comprar varios tipos de billetes:

Billete Sencillo: 1€
Abono 10 viajes para una zona específica (metrobus, metrosur, metronorte ... etc): 9,30€
Abono 10 viajes para toda la red: 15€

Los horarios habituales son desde las 06:00 hasta las 02:00.

Los niños sólo pagan después de cumplir los cuatro años.

Lee y contesta a las preguntas.

NC 4

Ejemplo: 1 293

1 How many stops does the Madrid metro have?
2 How many lines?
3 How much would you pay for a single-journey ticket?

4 What would you get for 15€?
5 At what time does the last train depart?
6 Until what age can children travel free?

Copia y completa la conversación con las palabras de la casilla.

NC 4

Un ____ sencillo a Las Ventas, por favor.
Aquí tiene, es un ____.
¿Qué ____ es?
Es la línea ____, dirección Moncloa.
¿Tengo que ____?
Sí, tiene que cambiar en la próxima ____ y coger la línea dos con ____ Las Rosas.
Gracias.
Adiós.

> línea   tres   parada   billete   dirección
> euro   cambiar

Challenge

Your friend who doesn't speak Spanish has asked you to buy him a first class 7-day return ticket for next Thursday morning from Madrid to Bilbao. Write out the conversation you would have at the ticket office. Check your times and prices at www.renfe.es.

NC 3–4

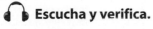 **Escucha y verifica.**

- Vocabulary: talk about what you did on a day out in the past
- Grammar: use the preterite of common irregular verbs; adverbs
- Skills: extend your work to achieve a higher level

 LEER 1 **Empareja los dibujos con las frases.**

1 Fui en el teleférico.
2 Hice ciclismo.
3 Vi leones en el zoo.
4 Pude tocar un delfín en el acuario.
5 Comí en el Paseo de la Gastronomía.
6 Di un paseo cerca del lago.
7 Tuve miedo en el parque de atracciones.
8 Fue fabuloso.

> **Gramática →** p.163
>
> **The preterite**
> What do the sentences in activity 1 mean?
> Match them to the infinitive of their verb:
>
> ser hacer comer tener ver ir dar poder
>
> Are they all irregular?

 LEER 2 **Lee las frases de la derecha. Busca las palabras que no conozcas en un diccionario.**

 LEER 3 **Elige una pregunta (1–4) para cada sección (A–D).**

Ejemplo: 1 B

1 ¿Qué hiciste?
2 ¿En qué orden?
3 ¿Cómo lo pasaste?
4 ¿Qué tiempo hizo?

> **?** **Think**
>
> What other information could you add when producing a piece of extended writing?

 ESCRIBIR 4 **Describe tu día en Casa de Campo, u otro parque de atracciones. Usa las frases A–D.**

 NC 4–5

A
Primero
Después
Luego
Más tarde
Antes de
Después de
Finalmente

B
Hice ciclismo
Jugué al tenis
Vi leones
Comí en el restaurante
Saqué fotos
Monté a caballo
Visité el museo

Mi día en Casa de Campo

C
(No) Hizo calor
(No) Hizo frío
(No) Hizo sol
(No) Hizo viento
(No) Hizo buen tiempo
(No) Llovió

D
Lo pasé bomba
Lo pasé fenomenal
Me encantó
(No) Me gustó mucho
(No) Fue divertido
Fue emocionante
Fue un desastre

El Video Reto

Mira el video. ¿Es Roberto o Elena?

Ejemplo: 1 Roberto

a Hizo un tour en monopatín.
b Vio el Palacio Real y la Catedral de la Almudena.
c Fue a la Plaza Mayor y al Templo de Debod.

d Fue a la Plaza del Sol y a Gran Vía.
e Fue de compras.
f Visitó el Estadio Santiago Bernabéu.
g Fue al Museo Reina Sofía.
h Fue al Museo del Prado.

In your opinion, who had the best day out in Madrid? Why?

el monopatín – *skateboard*

Lee el email e identifica:

NC 6

- 2 present tense verbs
- 2 past tense verbs
- 2 future tense verbs
- 2 adverbs that tell us **how**
- 2 adverbs that tell us **when**
- 2 connectives
- 2 opinions
- 2 reasons

Hola Sebastián,

Como sabes, normalmente en Colombia los domingos me gusta relajarme, sin embargo en España es diferente porque quiero ver muchas cosas antes de volver. Ayer fui a Madrid con Elena: primero hice un tour en monopatín. ¡Fue muy guay! Durante el tour visité rápidamente muchos monumentos y lugares famosos como por ejemplo el Palacio Real que me gustó muchísimo porque es muy impresionante.

Después visité tranquilamente el Templo de Debod y por la tarde fui al Bernabéu y también visité el Museo del Prado aunque un poco apresuradamente. Me encantó el estadio porque soy un fan del Real Madrid pero me gustaría volver al Prado para visitarlo más lentamente.

Esta noche voy a ir a cenar con Elena a un restaurante típico y vamos a hacer planes para el próximo fin de semana.

¿Y tú? ¿Qué hiciste el fin de semana?

Roberto

Gramática → p.169

Adverbs

Use adverbs to describe actions: quickly, softly, slowly etc.

The majority of English adverbs end in -ly. This has an equivalent ending in Spanish: *-mente*.

Salió de casa apresurada**mente**.
He/She left the house hastily.

How many adverbs can you find in Roberto's email?

Think

What level is this passage?

Did you know that it is precisely the elements listed in activity 7 that make it a level 6 or above? Keep them in mind when you do your own speaking or writing work!

Prepare a presentation about an imaginary recent day out. Be as creative as possible. Use activities 2 and 7 for ideas and structures.

Challenge

NC 5 6

- Vocabulary: recognise names of shops and give directions
- Grammar: use simple imperatives and prepositions
- Skills: sound Spanish when pronouncing words with *z*, *ce* or *ci*

LEER 1 — Lee. ¿Verdad o mentira?

Ejemplo: 1 mentira

1. La panadería está al lado del hotel.
2. La floristería está delante de la cervecería.
3. La tienda de electrodomésticos está enfrente de la carnicería.
4. La frutería está entre el supermercado y la carnicería.
5. La carnicería está detrás de la tienda de ropa.
6. Don Quijote está delante de la panadería.

ESCUCHAR 2 — 🎧 Escucha. ¿Qué tienda es?

NC 3

Ejemplo: 1 la pescadería

HABLAR 3 — 👥👥 Mira el barrio La Latina. ¿Dónde están las tiendas para comprar estos artículos?

NC 3

Ejemplo: 1 La tienda de ropa está al lado de la tienda de electrodomésticos.

1. pantalones
2. flores
3. zapatos de flamenco
4. chorizo
5. ensalada
6. arroz

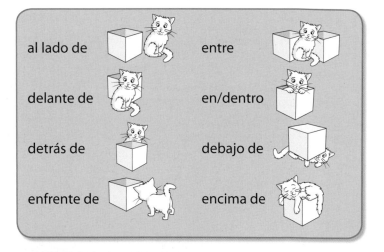

al lado de	entre
delante de	en/dentro
detrás de	debajo de
enfrente de	encima de

⚙️ Gramática → p.160

Remember!

de + el = del: al lado **del** mercado – *next to the market*

de + la = de la: enfrente **de la** panadería – *facing the bakery*

de + los = de los: detrás **de los** grandes almacenes – *behind the department store*

de + las = de las: delante **de las** tiendas – *in front of the shops*

Empareja 1–6 con a–f.

Ejemplo: 1 d

1 Cruza la calle.
2 Toma la primera a la derecha.
3 Sigue todo recto.
4 Tuerce a la derecha.
5 Tuerce a la izquierda.
6 Toma la segunda calle a la izquierda.

Gramática → p.166

The imperative

Use the imperative when you are telling someone what to do.

	Familiar form		Polite form	
	-ar verbs	-er and -ir verbs	-ar verbs	-er and -ir verbs
Singular	-a ¡Habla!	-e ¡Come!	-e ¡Hable!	-a ¡Coma!
Plural	-ad ¡Hablad!	-ed/-id ¡Comed! ¡Escribid!	-en ¡Hablen!	-an ¡Coman! ¡Escriban!

? Think

Remember the Spanish **z**, **ce** and **ci** sound like the **th** in the**atre** or tee**th**.

🎧 Practise with these: *izquierda, zagal, zamparse, Cecilia, cencerro, cizaña, cincel, zodíaco, zorro, zueco, zumbado, azucena,* then listen to check your pronunciation.

Lee y mira el mapa. ¿Adónde van?

NC 3

1 Sigue todo recto, está a la derecha después de cruzar la calle Jorge Juan.
2 Sigue todo recto y toma la tercera a la derecha. Está a la izquierda después de la calle Núñez de Balboa.
3 Tuerce a la izquierda y después a la derecha, luego sigue todo recto y va a estar enfrente.
4 Tuerce a la derecha y está a la derecha.

👥 Don Quijote needs to do the following errands in Madrid. With a partner prepare a list of directions he should follow.
- have breakfast in restaurant
- buy new pyjamas
- cut hair
- collect Sancho from Cibeles

(NC 3–4)

Comprender – The preterite tense and adverbs

A The preterite tense of irregular verbs

Regular verbs are so called because they follow a clear pattern. Irregular verbs don't follow a pattern at all and so you will need to memorise them. These are the most common irregular verbs you are likely to need.

ser to be (permanent & description)	estar to be (temporary & location)	hacer to do/to make	tener to have	ir to go	dar to give	poder to be able to/to be allowed
fui	estuve	hice	tuve	fui	di	pude
fuiste	estuviste	hiciste	tuviste	fuiste	diste	pudiste
fue	estuvo	hizo	tuvo	fue	dio	pudo
fuimos	estuvimos	hicimos	tuvimos	fuimos	dimos	pudimos
fuisteis	estuvisteis	hicisteis	tuvisteis	fuisteis	disteis	pudisteis
fueron	estuvieron	hicieron	tuvieron	fueron	dieron	pudieron

B Adverbs

Adverbs modify or give additional information about the verb in your sentence. There are several kinds of adverbs, telling you:

How?	When?	How often?	How much?
rápidamente alegremente ruidosamente cuidadosamente	temprano después recientemente ayer	siempre a menudo a veces una vez al mes	demasiado muy/mucho bastante totalmente

Mostly, when in English an adverb ends in -ly, in Spanish it will end in -mente. Where an adjective has masculine and feminine forms, add -mente to the feminine form.

noisily: comes from **noisy** → *ruidoso/ruidosa* → *ruidosamente*

---

1 Complete the sentences with the preterite tense of the verb in brackets. Not all the verbs are irregular.

1 Ayer yo _fui_ (ir) a una fiesta con mi hermana Pepa y ▨▨▨ (comer) muchos caramelos.

2 La semana pasada Elisa no ▨▨▨ (hacer) los deberes de matemáticas así que el profesor ▨▨▨ (llamar) a su casa, y por eso ella no ▨▨▨ (poder) salir con nosotros el fin de semana.

3 Roberto y Elena ▨▨▨ (estar) en Madrid el fin de semana pasado donde ▨▨▨ (hacer) muchas cosas. El Museo del Prado ▨▨▨ (ser) muy interesante y los dos lo ▨▨▨ (pasar) muy bien.

4 Ayer por la tarde yo ▨▨▨ (dar) una vuelta por la Gran Vía: ▨▨▨ (ir) de tiendas y me ▨▨▨ (comprar) un vestido nuevo.

2 Work out how to say these adverbs in Spanish. Look up the adjectives if necessary.

Example: rarely – rare – *raro* – *rara* – *raramente*

1 politely   **3** calmly
2 frequently   **4** sadly

Aprender – Improving your work

C Climbing levels

To improve your work and achieve a higher level may seem tedious but it is not difficult!

Start with simple sentences and build on them. If you are asked *¿Qué haces después del instituto?* you might answer: *Hago los deberes, navego por internet y veo la tele.* (Level 3)

To improve on this you could do the following.

1 Extend:

  a Where? *Hago los deberes **en la cocina**, navego por internet y veo la tele **en el salón**.*

  b When? ***Siempre** hago los deberes ...*

  c Who with? *Siempre hago los deberes ... **con mi hermano** en el salón.*

2 Add opinions and justify them: *Siempre hago los deberes ... **¡Odio hacer los deberes porque es aburrido! Me gusta navegar por internet porque es divertido.***

3 Add connectives and/or sequencing words: ***Primero**, siempre hago los deberes en la cocina, **después** navego por internet y **finalmente** veo la tele con mi hermano en el salón. Odio ...* (level 4)

4 Create an opportunity to introduce a different tense: *Primero, siempre hago los deberes en la cocina **aunque ayer estudié para mi examen en mi dormitorio**. Después navego por internet ...* (level 5)

5 Create an opportunity for the missing timeframe. It needs to fit in nicely and be extended as the rest of your piece: *Primero, siempre hago los deberes ... **esta tarde vamos a ver** Glee **porque es mi programa favorito**. Odio ...*

6 Add more detail and description: *Primero, siempre hago los deberes en la cocina aunque ayer estudié para mi examen **de historia** en mi dormitorio. Después navego por internet **en mi ordenador portátil durante una o dos horas** y finalmente veo la tele con mi hermano **pequeño** en el salón ...* (level 6)

3 Imagine last weekend you went to a theme park. You are asked ...
¿Qué hiciste el fin de semana?

Start with a simple answer and use section C to help you build on it.

Hablar – Pronunciation

D Words spelt the same as English

Be careful with words that are spelt similarly or the same as in English:

- Pronounce every letter: *chocolate* [cho- koh- lat- teh]
- Use the Spanish sound of vowels: *Irene* [ee- reh- neh]
- Pay attention to **g**s and **j**s. They sound a little like: ham, hen, his, hose and hood: *generoso* [hen- eh- ros- soh]
- Beware of **ce** and **ci**. They are meant to sound like <u>the</u>ft and <u>thi</u>ef: *cima* [thi(ee)- mah]
- **H** is always silent (except as part of ch): *horrible* [oh- rree- blay]

4 Practise pronouncing these 20 words out loud.

aeropuerto, autobús, dialecto, edificio, esencial, fascinar, gigante, ideal, injusto, horrendo, justicia, nacional, necesario, ocurrir, paciencia, recientemente, seducir, tragedia, urgencia, velocidad

5 🎧 Listen to the recording and check your pronunciation is accurate.

- Vocabulary: revise travel and getting around
- Grammar: practise the preterite of the verb *ir*
- Skills: use common sense and cognates to rewrite a conversation

1 Busca el intruso. ¿Por qué es intruso?
Find the odd one out. Why is it so?

*Ejemplo: **1** museo – all others are means of transport*

1 coche	metro	avión	museo
2 comer	plaza	alquilar	ir
3 barato	cómodo	estadio	directo
4 ida	ida y vuelta	20€	primera clase

2 ¿Adónde fuiste? ¿Cómo fuiste? Escribe las frases.
Where did you go? How did you get there? Write out the sentences using the places in the box.

NC 2–3

Casa de Campo   Museo del Prado
Plaza de Toros   Estadio Santiago Bernabéu
Parque Warner Bros

*Ejemplo: **1** Fui al Estadio Santiago Bernabéu. Fui a pie.*

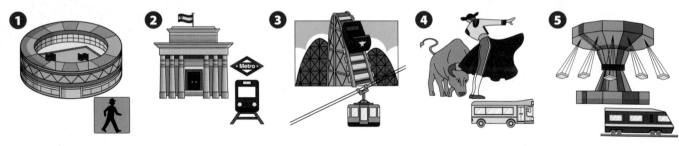

3 Ordena la conversación.
Reorder the conversation so that it makes sense.

NC 3–4

a Sí, ida y vuelta.

b ¿Clase preferente?

c Aquí tiene, gracias. Adiós.

d No gracias, clase turista. ¿A qué hora sale el próximo?

e ¿De ida y vuelta?

f Hola, ¿Qué desea?

g Adiós.

h Ahora mismo ha salido uno, el próximo es a las 11:35 del andén número 6.

i ¿A qué hora llega?

j Un billete a Pontevedra, por favor.

k Llega a las 14:07.

l ¿Cuánto es?

m Son 20,40 euros.

4 Investiga una de las principales atracciones de Madrid. Crea un poster con información para los visitantes.

NC 2–4

Research one of Madrid's main attractions. Create an information poster containing key information visitors may like to know.

- Vocabulary: buy travel tickets
- Grammar: enhance sentences with adverbs
- Skills: invent conversations and role play

LEER 1

NC 4

Lee las conversaciones. Copia y rellena la tabla.

	Destination	Type of ticket	Class of ticket	Departure time	Platform	Arrival time	Price
1							

1

Hola, ¿Qué desea?

Un billete a Figueres, clase preferente, por favor.

¿De ida y vuelta?

No, sólo ida, por favor.

Aquí tiene. Sale a las veintidós cincuenta del andén número trece.

¿A qué hora llega?

Llega a las diez veinte.

¿Cuánto es?

Son sesenta y cuatro euros con sesenta.

Aquí tiene, gracias. Adiós.

Adiós.

2

Buenos días, ¿Qué desea?

Un billete a Huelva, por favor.

¿De ida o de ida y vuelta?

De ida y vuelta.

¿De qué clase lo quiere?

Clase turista. ¿A qué hora sale el próximo?

Sale a las dieciocho cero cinco horas del andén once.

¿A qué hora llega?

A las veintiuna cincuenta y dos.

Vale, gracias. ¿Cuánto es?

Ochenta y cuatro euros con ochenta.

Tome, gracias.

Adiós.

ESCRIBIR 2

Escribe las conversaciones.

NC 4

Destination	Type of ticket	Class of ticket	Departure time	Platform	Arrival time	Price
Tarragona	single	first class	22:50	8	06:33	54.30€
Vigo	return	tourist	14:20	4	21:44	96.50€

LEER 3

Complete these sentences using an appropriate adverb.

completamente   tristemente
tranquilamente   tarde

1 Tenía tiempo así que visité el museo _____ .

2 Salí de casa _____ y perdí el avión.

3 _____ llovió todos los días.

4 Los turistas estuvieron _____ satisfechos con su hotel.

Escuchar

NC 4–5

Listen to the three speakers. True or false?

1 The first speaker loves art.
2 She used the metro to get to the museum.
3 It is the first time the second speaker has visited El Prado.
4 He found the visit educational.
5 The third speaker prefers sculpture to paintings.
6 She says the museum is quiet.

 Hablar

NC 4–5

Imagine last Saturday you went to Madrid. The pictures on the right represent a snapshot of your day in the city. Tell your teacher about your weekend. Speak for as long as you can, trying to mention all the pictures featured.

Example: El fin de semana pasado fui a Madrid. El sábado visité …

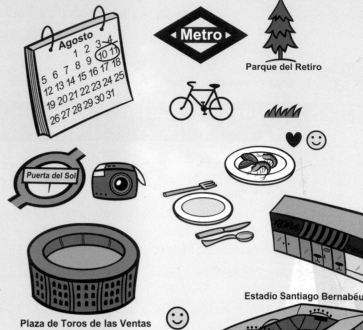

Agosto

Metro

Parque del Retiro

Puerta del Sol

Plaza de Toros de las Ventas

Estadio Santiago Bernabéu

 Leer

NC 4–5

Read and answer the questions.

1 Where exactly is El Rastro market?
2 What does the market offer?
3 Why is the underground the best way to get there?
4 Which metro station is closest to the market? Why?
5 Name three shops you can find there.

"El Rastro"

Cada domingo, a las 9 de la mañana entre las calles Toledo, Embajadores y Ronda de Toledo aparece el mercado del Rastro de Madrid. El Rastro, con sus cientos de tiendas que venden artículos nuevos y de segunda mano, atrae a 100.000 visitantes cada semana: madrileños y turistas. Este mercado ofrece un paseo entretenido y una sorpresa a cada paso.

Si vas a ir al Rastro, el metro es el método más rápido y conveniente de llegar. Está justo delante de la estación "La Latina" y muy cerca de "Puerta de Toledo".

Zapaterías, floristerías, tiendas de ropa nueva o usada, tiendas de electrodomésticos … puedes encontrar de todo en el Rastro.

 Escribir

NC 4–5

Imagine you are on holiday in a foreign country. Write a blog entry about what you did yesterday. You may want to mention:

- Where you went and how
- What you visited
- What the weather was like
- If you enjoyed it
- If you would like to return or would recommend it to a friend.

Example: ¡Hola, amigos! Estoy de vacaciones en Málaga. Ayer por la mañana fui a la piscina …

¿Vamos en bici? — *Shall we go by bike?*

en avión	*by plane*
en barco	*by boat*
en bici	*by bike*
en coche	*by car*
en metro	*by underground*
en tranvía	*by tram*
a pie	*on foot*
es barato	*it's cheap*
es gratis	*it's free*
es cómodo	*it's comfortable*
está cerca	*it's close by*
está lejos	*it's far*
es rápido	*it's fast*

Planes para mañana — *Plans for tomorrow*

el museo	*the museum*
el palacio	*the palace*
el parque de atracciones	*the theme park*
la plaza	*the square*
la puerta	*the door/gate*
alquilar	*to rent/hire*
comer	*to eat*
ir	*to go*
jugar	*to play*
salir	*to go out*
viajar	*to travel*

Billetes de viaje — *Travel tickets*

un billete	*a ticket*
de ida	*single*
de ida y vuelta	*return*
clase preferente	*first class*
clase turista	*second class*
¿A qué hora sale?	*What time does it leave?*
el andén	*platform*
¿A qué hora llega?	*What time does it arrive?*
un abono	*season ticket*

¿Qué hiciste? — *What did you do?*

fui en el teleférico	*I went in the cable car*
hice ciclismo	*I went cycling*
vi leones	*I saw lions*
pude tocar un delfín	*I was allowed to touch a dolphin*
di un paseo	*I went for a walk*
tuve miedo	*I was scared*
fue fabuloso	*It was fabulous*
primero	*first*
después	*afterwards*
luego	*then*
más tarde	*later*
antes de	*before*
después de	*after*

hizo calor	*it was hot*
hizo frío	*it was cold*
llovió	*it rained*
hizo sol	*it was sunny*
hizo viento	*it was windy*
hizo buen tiempo	*the weather was nice*
lo pasé bomba	*I had a great time*
lo pasé fenomenal	*I had a brilliant time*
me encantó	*I loved it*
me gustó mucho	*I liked it a lot*
fue divertido	*it was fun*
fue emocionante	*it was exciting*
fue un desastre	*it was a disaster*

¿Dónde está? — *Where is it?*

la carnicería	*butcher's*
la floristería	*florist's*
la panadería	*bakery*
la pescadería	*fishmonger's*
la tienda de electrodomésticos	*electrical items shop/stall*
la tienda de ropa	*clothes shop/stall*
la frutería	*greengrocer's*
la zapatería	*shoe shop*
al lado de	*next to*
debajo de	*under*
delante de	*in front of*
dentro de	*in/inside*
detrás de	*behind*
enfrente de	*facing/opposite*
encima de	*on/above*
entre	*between*
Cruza el puente/la calle	*Cross the bridge/street*
Sigue todo recto	*Continue straight on*
Tuerce a la derecha	*Turn right*
Tuerce a la izquierda	*Turn left*
Toma la primera/segunda (calle) a la derecha	*Take the first/second (street) on the right*

◉ I can …

- ◉ talk about means of transport
- ◉ talk about plans for visiting a place
- ◉ give directions
- ◉ talk about a day out
- ◉ buy travel tickets
- ◉ use the immediate future
- ◉ use the preterite
- ◉ improve my writing with adverbs

- Vocabulary: talk about what you have to/must do to maintain a healthy lifestyle
- Grammar: revise question words and frequency words
- Skills: practise memorising skills

1 Busca las palabras en inglés en la culebra. Emparéjalas con las palabras en español a–h.

Ejemplo: how – g

howwherewhenwhatwhowhichhowmanywhattime

a ¿Cuándo?
b ¿Cuántos/as?
c ¿Qué?
d ¿Cuál?
e ¿Dónde?
f ¿A qué hora?
g ¿Cómo?
h ¿Quién?

? Think

Learn these words by heart. What do you need to remember when you write a question word in Spanish? As soon as you see a question mark in Spanish you need to think about the intonation of your voice. Look back at page 63.

2 🎧 Escucha y escribe las palabras interrogativas en orden.

Ejemplo: 1 ¿Cuándo? ...

3 🎧 Escucha la entrevista otra vez y pon las preguntas en orden.

NC 4

Ejemplo: 3 ...

1 ¿Qué comes para llevar una vida sana?
2 ¿Cuántas horas pasas delante de la tele?
3 ¿Cuándo tienes clases de deporte?
4 ¿A quién admiras como deportista?
5 ¿A qué hora te acuestas?
6 ¿Qué deporte practicas?

4 Lee las respuestas de abajo y emparéjalas con una pregunta de la actividad 3. ¿Es una vida sana?

NC 3–4

a Nunca admiro a los deportistas. Prefiero las estrellas de cine.
b A menudo paso tres horas en el sofá viendo la tele o escuchando música.
c Rara vez practico deporte.
d Cada semana tenemos deporte en el insti pero a menudo le digo al profe que estoy enfermo.
e Todos los días como chucherías. No me interesa la comida sana.
f Cada día me acuesto muy tarde, pasada la medianoche.

5 Ahora contesta tú a las preguntas.

NC 3–4

siempre	a veces
cada día / semana	todos los días
a menudo	casi nunca
rara vez	nunca
dos veces a la semana / por semana	

6 👥 Practica el diálogo con un compañero.

Gramática → p.167

Remember!

You met the expressions for saying what you must do on page 23, when you talked about what jobs you do at home to help.

You can also use these to talk about healthy lifestyles:

Debes comer fruta todos los días – *You must eat fruit every day.*

Tienes que hacer ejercicio dos veces a la semana – *You have to take exercise twice a week.*

You can use the verb **necesitar** in the same way to say what you need to do.

Necesitas perder peso – *You need to lose weight.*

Hay que – 'it is necessary to' is a more impersonal way of telling someone to do something:

Hay que hacer ejercicio. – *It is necessary to exercise.*

Debes Tienes que Necesitas Hay que	comer comida sana comer menos comida grasa comer ensaladas y fruta seguir una dieta acostarte más temprano hacer más ejercicio pasar menos tiempo viendo la tele y escuchando música perder peso

ESCUCHAR 7

NC 4–5

 Lee las respuestas. Luego escucha y decide quién, Roberto o Elena, dice:

1. Llevo una vida saludable.
2. Estoy más sano que tú.
3. Quiero perder peso.
4. Comí fruta ayer.
5. Fui al gimnasio.
6. Jugué al baloncesto.
7. Jugué durante dos horas.
8. No me gusta el baloncesto.
9. Me levanté temprano.
10. Me acosté con hambre.

ESCUCHAR 8

 Escucha otra vez y verifica.

LEER 9

NC 3

Lee el quiz y contesta a las preguntas.

¿Sana o malsana?

1 ¿Desayunas ...
- **a** café o té? (2)
- **b** nada? (3)
- **c** cereales? (1)

2 ¿Comes fruta
- **a** rara vez? (3)
- **b** todos los días? (1)
- **c** de vez en cuando? (2)

3 ¿Almuerzas
- **a** cosas fritas? (2)
- **b** ensalada? (1)
- **c** chucherías? (3)

5 ¿Bebes
- **a** agua? (1)
- **b** limonada? (3)
- **c** zumo? (2)

5 ¿Meriendas
- **a** unos caramelos? (3)
- **b** pan con chocolate? (2)
- **c** una manzana? (1)

6 ¿Haces ejercicio
- **a** a menudo? (1)
- **b** rara vez? (2)
- **c** de vez en cuando? (3)

1–6 = sobresaliente: llevas una vida muy sana. ¡Enhorabuena!
7–12 = regular: debes hacer más ejercicio y comer más fruta.
13–18 = insuficiente: tienes que cambiar tu rutina y tu dieta por completo. Eres muy vago y necesitas ponerte en forma.

Challenge

Write five pieces of advice for people who get between 13 and 18 points in the quiz.

Example: Debes / Tienes que hacer más ejercicio.

NC 4

- Vocabulary: identify parts of the body and discuss keeping fit
- Grammar: use reflexives in past and present tenses
- Skills: adapt previously learnt language in a new context

ESCUCHAR 1

🎧 **Escucha la clase de yoga. Repite e indica la parte del cuerpo mencionada.**

Ejemplo: la cabeza ...

el corazón

Think

When the instructor mentioned parts of the body, did she use the word for 'your' (head, hands etc.) or 'the'? What rule can you work out from this?

encima de – *on top of*
por delante – *in front of*
por detrás – *behind*

la ... izquierda/derecha – *the left/right ...*

❶	los ojos	❼	los brazos	⓭	el dedo gordo
❷	los dientes	❽	la espalda	⓮	las rodillas
❸	la cabeza	❾	las piernas	⓯	el ombligo
❹	la nariz	❿	los pies	⓰	el estómago
❺	las orejas	⓫	las manos	⓱	los dedos
❻	el corazón	⓬	el tobillo		

ESCUCHAR 2

NC 3

🎧 **Escucha otra vez. ¿Cuáles no se mencionan?**

HABLAR 3

👥 **¡Contrarreloj! A jugar por turnos.**

La persona A se toca cinco partes del cuerpo. La persona B tiene que nombrarlas. ¿Quién contesta más rápido?

ESCRIBIR 4

👥 **Escribe una "sopa de letras" con diez partes del cuerpo – 10 letras por 10 letras. Cámbiala con un compañero.**

¡Contrarreloj! A ver quién puede encontrar las palabras correctas más rápido.

Gramática → p.165

Reflexive verbs

You first met reflexive verbs in Unit 2A of *Zoom 1*. Remember:

When you look them up in a dictionary you will find the pronoun attached to the end of the infinitive.

Example: levantarse – *to get up*

Present	Preterite	Imperfect
me levanto – *I get up*	me levanté – *I got up*	me levantaba – *I used to get up*
te levantas	te levantaste	te levantabas
se levanta	se levantó	se levantaba
nos levantamos	nos levantamos	nos levantábamos
os levantáis	os levantasteis	os levantabais
se levantan	se levantaron	se levantaban

What do you notice about the *nosotros* form in the present and preterite tenses?

¿Qué haces para mantenerte en forma? ✓	¿Qué no haces? ✗
Voy al polideportivo	No fumo
Levanto pesas	No bebo alcohol
Nado en la piscina	No como chucherías
Corro en el parque	
Me relajo haciendo yoga	
Me levanto temprano	
Duermo ocho horas	

ESCUCHAR 5 NC 3

 Escucha la entrevista y anota las partes del cuerpo mencionadas.

? **Think**

Is the older person speaking about the past or the present? Can you recognise which tense is being used?

ESCUCHAR 6 NC 5

 Escucha otra vez. Copia y completa la tabla.

¿Qué hacía?	¿Dónde?	¿Cada cuánto?
Ejemplo: ejercicio	en el polideportivo	todos los días

ESCUCHAR 7 NC 5

 Escucha la parte final de la entrevista. Anota los cinco consejos en inglés.

Ejemplo: **1** Don't smoke.

LEER 8 NC 4

Lee el texto y anota los nueve verbos reflexivos.

Ejemplo: me levanto

Me levanto temprano a eso de las seis y media. Me pongo los pantalones cortos en seguida y me voy a hacer footing al parque. De regreso a casa, me ducho y me lavo el pelo. Me pongo la ropa para ir al instituto y desayuno rápido.

Después de clases me relajo charlando con mis amigos mientras vamos a pie a casa. Me acuesto sobre las diez y normalmente me duermo sin problemas.

ESCRIBIR 9 NC 4–5

Escribe los verbos en pasado para explicar lo que hiciste.

Ejemplo: Me levanté temprano ...

 **Challenge**

Write a paragraph about how you keep fit. Say what you did in the last week. Include healthy and unhealthy things!

NC 4–5

- Vocabulary: talk about illnesses and injuries
- Grammar: use the verb *doler*
- Skills: understand instructions

ESCUCHAR 1

🎧 **Escucha. Empareja lo que dice cada persona con un dibujo adecuado. No se necesitan todos los dibujos.**

Ejemplo: **1** c

1 Me duelen los dientes.
2 Me duele mucho el tobillo.
3 Me duele mucho el dedo.

4 Tengo el brazo roto.
5 Tengo fiebre y me duele la garganta.
6 La espalda me duele bastante.

a  **b** 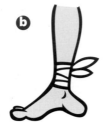 **c**  **d**

e  **f**  **g**  **h**

⚙️ Gramática

The verb *doler*

When you want to say something hurts you can say:
Tengo dolor de cabeza – *I have a headache.*

Or you can use the verb *doler* – to hurt / ache:
Me duele la cabeza – *I have a headache.*

Remember to make the verb plural when you are using a plural word like *dientes*.
Me duelen los dientes – *My teeth hurt / I have toothache.*

I twisted my ankle.
I strained my back.
I ate too many sweets.
I cut my finger.
I fell over.
I spent too much time in the sun.

ESCUCHAR 2

NC 4–5

🎧 **Escucha otra vez e indica por qué tiene el problema. Luego busca las frases en inglés de la casilla.**

Ejemplo: **1** d

a Me doblé la espalda.
b Tomé demasiado sol.
c Me caí.

d Comí demasiados caramelos.
e Me corté el dedo.
f Me torcí el tobillo.

3 **Roberto está en la farmacia. Escucha y lee la conversación.**

Buenos días. ¿En qué puedo ayudarte?

Es que tengo mucha fiebre y me duele la cabeza.

¿Qué hiciste ayer?

Ayer pasamos horas en la piscina. Hizo mucho sol.

Me parece que tienes una insolación grave.

¿Qué debo hacer entonces? ¿Qué me recomienda usted?

Tienes que quedarte en casa y beber mucha agua. También puedes tomar estas pastillas tres veces al día.

Gracias – le agradezco mucho.

De nada. ¡Hay que tener más cuidado con el sol!

4 **Contesta a las preguntas.**

NC 4–5

1 What happened to Roberto?
2 What does the chemist tell Roberto is wrong with him?
3 What instructions does he give him?
4 What advice does the chemist give him?

5 **Practica la conversación de la actividad 3.**

NC 4

Tengo	fiebre / un dolor horrible una insolación / un brazo roto	
Me duele Me duelen	la cabeza el estómago los dientes	
Tienes que	tomar estas pastillas / este jarabe – *take these pills / this medicine* ponerte esta crema / una tirita / venda – *use this cream / a plaster / bandage*	tres veces al día una vez a la semana
	quedarte en la cama descansar pasar el día en casa	

6 **Escucha las instrucciones y copia y completa la tabla.**

¿Qué pasa?	¿Qué tienes que hacer/tomar?	¿Cada cuánto?
Me duele la garganta	*jarabe*	*tres veces al día*

7 **Escribe una conversación en la farmacia. Usa las frases de la actividad 6.**

NC 4

Challenge

Make up a new conversation in a pharmacy. Use the past tense to get a higher level (say what happened to you). Use the Immediate future to get an even higher level (say what you are not going to do in the future – perhaps, for Roberto, not stay in the sun so long!)

NC 4–6

- Vocabulary: discuss sports and how you play them
- Grammar: the impersonal *se (se juega, se necesita, se puede)*
- Skills: listen for detail

LEER 1

Empareja los dibujos con las palabras de la casilla.

Ejemplo: c, la natación

ESCUCHAR 2

NC 4

 Escucha y copia y completa la tabla.

Deporte	Cuándo	Hora	Veces
Ejemplo: la natación	lunes/jueves	2/10h	dos

el baloncesto   el cross   el fútbol
el judo   el skate
la escalada   la natación

ESCRIBIR 3

NC 3–4

Inventa información para tres clases más. Usa tus apuntes de la actividad 2 para ayudarte.

Gramática → p.167

In English we use phrases with 'you' when explaining how to do a sport ('you play ...', 'you need ...', etc.). Spanish prefers to use an impersonal construction with the pronoun *se*:

se necesita – *you / one need(s)*
se juega – *you / one play(s)*
se puede – *you / one can*

Example:
Se necesita una raqueta para jugar al tenis – **You / one need(s)** *a racket to play tennis.*

El tenis **se juega** con una raqueta y pelotas – **You / one play(s)** *tennis with a racket and balls.*

Se puede practicar el fútbol en el parque – **You / one can** *play football in the park.*

▶ El Video Reto

VIDEO 4

Mira el video (primera parte) y contesta a las preguntas en inglés.

- **a** Which two sports are mentioned?
- **b** Who does which sport and how often?
- **c** According to Roberto, which sport is better and why?

LEER 5

Empareja los dibujos con la palabra adecuada de la casilla.

un casco   una tabla   un equipo
unas zapatillas   unas ruedas

6 **Lee las descripciones y emparéjalas con una foto.**

NC 4

❶
Se puede practicar este deporte en un polideportivo o al aire libre, sobre dos ruedas. Normalmente se necesita un casco, una camiseta y pantalones cortos. También se pueden usar guantes y zapatos especiales. ¡Y se necesita una bici!

❷
Es un deporte que es viejo y nuevo a la vez. No se necesita un equipo demasiado grande: sólo una buena tabla, un traje de baño y olas grandes. Hace tiempo lo practicaban en Hawai y ahora se puede hacer en muchas partes del mundo.

❸
Este deporte se juega en equipo y se necesita cuatro personas. Suelen practicarlo en la playa, por ejemplo en Copacabana, Brasil. Se juega con una pelota: hay que pegarla con la mano.

7 **Anota todas las expresiones impersonales.**

Ejemplo: se puede practicar

8 **Sigue los ejemplos de la actividad 6 y escribe un párrafo para la foto que sobra.**

NC 4

▶ **El Video Reto**

9 **Mira el video (segunda parte) y escoge la respuesta adecuada.**

   a Javier tiene 29 / 28 / 27 años.
   b Lleva 10 / 11 / 15 años practicando el cross.
   c Practica todos los días / de lunes a viernes / tres veces a la semana.
   d Es campeón mundial / nacional / regional de cross.

10 **Write down in English three pieces of advice Javier gives about keeping fit.**

11 **What is his ambition?**

Challenge

Choose an unusual sport and write a brief paragraph about it. Explain how, where, and when (how often) it is played; what equipment you need; why you think it is interesting or different. Use words such as *muy, bastante, un poco* and *demasiado* to add emphasis to your writing.

NC 4

3A.5 ⟫ Deporte y salud ⟫

- Vocabulary: talk more about sport and sporting accidents
- Grammar: use the imperfect
- Skills: revise and extend language already covered

ESCUCHAR 1

🎧 **Escucha y anota lo que hacía la persona y la parte del cuerpo que le duele.**

Ejemplo: 1 4, d

ESCRIBIR 2

Inventa una parte del cuerpo que te duele para la acción que sobra.

HABLAR 3

👥 **Por turnos con un compañero pregunta y contesta. Usa los dibujos de la actividad 1.**

Ejemplo: **A** ¿Qué hacías?
B Jugaba al baloncesto.
A ¿Qué te pasa?
B Me duele la rodilla.

ESCRIBIR 4

Escribe una frase para cada respuesta de la actividad 3.

Ejemplo: Jugaba al baloncesto y me duele la rodilla.

LEER 5

Lee el texto de Manuel y contesta a las preguntas.

NC 5

1 ¿Cuál es su deporte preferido?
2 ¿Cuándo lo practica?
3 ¿Dónde hace judo? ¿Cuántas veces a la semana?
4 ¿Con quién lo hace?
5 ¿Qué piensa hacer el próximo año?

HABLAR 6

👥 **Sondeo en clase: El deporte preferido.**

Presenta los resultados oralmente o por escrito.

Manuel – 14 años

¡Hola! Me encanta hacer ciclismo y soy miembro de un equipo local. Nos encontramos los sábados por la mañana pero practico todos los días si no llueve. Además hago judo en un club los jueves por la noche con un grupo de amigos. El año que viene me gustaría aprender a boxear.

¿Qué deporte prefieres practicar?
¿Qué deporte te gusta ver en la tele?

🎧 **Escucha y completa las respuestas de Julio.**

NC 6

1 ¿Cuál es tu deporte preferido?
Prefiero ...

2 ¿Qué otros deportes practicas?
Me gusta ... y también practico ...

3 ¿Cuándo haces deporte?
Hago ... y ...

4 ¿Qué partes del cuerpo se usan para el baloncesto?
Se usa ...

5 ¿Te gusta ver deporte en la tele?
Veo ...

6 ¿A qué hora sueles levantarte?
Normalmente ...

7 ¿Qué desayunas?
Me gusta ...

8 ¿A qué hora te acuestas?
Me acuesto ...

9 ¿Qué hiciste ayer por la tarde?
Bueno, ... pasé ...

10 ¿Qué vas a hacer el fin de semana que viene?
El sábado ... y el domingo ...

 ESCRIBIR 8

Ahora contesta tú a las preguntas.

NC 6

 HABLAR 9

👥 **Practica la entrevista con un compañero.**

NC 6

 LEER 10

Lee y anota en inglés cinco cosas sanas y cinco malsanas.

NC 5

Ejemplo: went to bed early ✓ *ate an unhealthy breakfast* ✗

Me llamo Teresa y llevo una vida bastante equilibrada: ni demasiado sana ni demasiado malsana. Por ejemplo, ayer me acosté a las diez y dormí bien, unas nueve horas, porque me desperté a las siete en punto. Tenía hambre así que tomé un desayuno bastante grande – dos huevos fritos y tres tostadas con mantequilla y mermelada. Además bebí dos tazas de café fuerte. Mi padre me llevó al insti en el coche porque no quería ir a pie. No comí nada al mediodía porque todavía estaba llena pero después de clase fui a comer helados con limonada. Por la noche decidí ir al parque a jugar al voleibol con mis amigos y antes de acostarme bebí un vaso de leche.

ESCRIBIR 11

Escribe en tu agenda una lista de actividades sanas para la semana que viene.

NC 4–5

Escribe siete frases explicando lo que vas a hacer, cuándo y cuántas veces a la semana.

 **Challenge**

👥 Write a brief description of a famous sports personality, their sport and one or two more details about them. Include two or more tenses. Read out what you have written to a partner and see if they can guess who it is you are describing.

NC 5

Comprender – *Doler* and past tenses

A How to use the verb *doler (ue)* to say what hurts

Some verbs are commonly used in the third person only. You have already met the verbs *gustar* – to like something, *encantar* – to like something a lot, and *interesar* – to be interested in something, which are used in this way.

1 Translate these examples:

1 Me gusta la música.
2 Me encanta el arte.
3 Me interesa el cine.
4 Me gustan las ciencias.
5 Me encantan los caramelos.
6 Me interesan las películas sobre naturaleza.

Now you can use the verb *doler (ue)* in the same way to say what hurts.
Me duele la cabeza. My head hurts. (I've got a headache.)
Me duelen los oídos. My ears hurt. (I've got earache.)

Explain the rule about singular and plural to a partner. Do you say '**my** head' in Spanish?

B Past tenses: using a mix of preterite and imperfect

Re-read the section on recounting past events on page 63.

Remember, if you want to say what you did or what happened – when the action began and ended in the past – you need to use the **preterite** tense.

But:

If you want to say what you used to do or describe something that went on over a longer period of time, then you use the **imperfect** tense.

In the sentence below you need to use the **imperfect** to say how old you were but the **preterite** tense to say you began to play.

*¿Cuántos años **tenías** cuando **empezaste** a jugar con el equipo nacional?*
How old were you when you started to play for the national team?

2 How do you say the following in Spanish?

1 My feet hurt.
2 I have a sore throat.
3 I have toothache.
4 My knee hurts.
5 I have a stomach ache.

3 Read these examples and write down the verb and the tense used. Think about why each tense has been used. Which of the sentences is illustrated below on the left?

1 Cuando tenía diez años me gustaba jugar en el parque.
2 Ayer quise practicar en el polideportivo pero no pude porque estaba cerrado.
3 Esquiaba mucho durante el invierno pero el invierno pasado me caí y me rompí la pierna y me quedé en casa durante tres meses.
4 Mi padre era muy estricto y teníamos que acostarnos temprano cuando éramos niños.
5 Antes comía muchas chucherías pero un día decidí cambiar mi rutina y comencé a comer ensaladas y fruta.

Aprender – Listening skills

C Listening for detail

Read the question carefully to make sure you understand what you have to do. Learn the question words by heart so you are sure what each one is referring to; go back to page 84 and try to memorise them.

Think about the tone of voice used; it helps to identify the emotion and tells you if the person is asking a question or giving an answer. Look back at page 63 to remind yourself about intonation in questions.

Think about the general context or situation first. For example, if the person is in the market what are they likely to be buying?

4 Write out a shopping list of as many items as you can think of.

> Next think about the detail of what the person could be asking for.

5 Write down the different quantities people might ask for in the market.

> If the person is talking about school, what vocabulary should you be expecting to hear?

6 Write down school subjects and a list of areas in school.

7 Think about the opinions you might express about school and subjects studied.

> When asked about time, always listen out for the detail.

8 How do you say the following in Spanish?

at about; just past; on the dot

> When listening to instructions the most important thing is to understand the detail.
>
> These are all strategies you should practise because they will help you check your answers carefully in a listening task.

Hablar – Pronunciation

D j/g sounds, plus how to memorise

🎧 Listen to and memorise the caption for the picture on the right to help you remember that the vowels **a o u** make a hard sound with the letter **g**, and **e** and **i** make soft sounds.
This follows the same rule as for the letter **c** (see page 31).
ga go gu   ge gi
The letter **j** always makes a soft sound in Spanish.
ja je ji jo ju

9 👥 Work with a partner and write down two more ways you find helpful when you need to remember things – for example, writing learning cards for vocabulary and verbs.

Jorge Jiménez el gigante gulo jugaba al ajedrez mientras comía jamón y jugo.

- Vocabulary: talk about sports and healthy living
- Grammar: use past and present tenses
- Skills: practise memory games

1

NC 2

Mira la foto y escribe en español las partes del cuerpo de memoria. ¿Cuántas escribiste correctamente?
Look at the photo and label the parts of the body in Spanish from memory. How many did you get right?

Ejemplo: **1** *la cabeza*

2

Escribe correctamente los nombres de los deportes.
Write out the names of the sports correctly.

1 lonbatseco
2 canitanó
3 rateka
4 goya
5 liscomic
6 lobilove

1 head
2 eyes
3 hands
4 teeth
5 stomach
6 legs
7 feet
8 back
9 arms
10 ears

3

NC 3–4

Completa el texto con los verbos adecuados de la casilla.
Complete the text with the appropriate verbs from the box.

Todos los días **1** ▭ (levantarme) temprano y **2** ▭ (vestirme) en seguida pero ayer **3** ▭ (despertarme) muy temprano y **4** ▭ (ir) al jardín porque **5** ▭ (hacer) sol. **6** ▭ (leer) una revista y **7** ▭ (beber) un zumo de naranja. Mi hermana **8** ▭ (llegar) y juntos **9** ▭ (ir) al parque porque **10** ▭ (querer) jugar al tenis.

bebí   fui   fuimos   hacía   leí
llegó   me desperté   me levanto
me visto   queríamos

4

NC 4

Escribe por lo menos cinco cosas que haces para mantenerte en forma.
Write at least five things you do to keep fit and healthy. Say where, when and how often you do them.

Ejemplo: Hago judo todos los jueves en el club del instituto.

5

NC 4–5

Escribe cinco preguntas que quieres hacer a tu deportista preferido/a.
Write down five questions you would like to ask your favourite sportsperson.

? Think

What do you need to include in activity 5 to be sure that your questions reach level 5 or even level 6?

- Vocabulary: talk about sport
- Grammar: use a variety of tenses
- Skills: practise memory games

1
NC 2

De memoria, ¿cuántos deportes puedes nombrar que se juegan …

1 con una raqueta?
2 sobre ruedas?
3 en el agua?
4 con los pies?
5 con un palo?

2
NC 5

Lee el texto y contesta a las preguntas en inglés.

1 How old is Lionel Messi?
2 Where is he from?
3 What happened when he was eleven years old?
4 How did Barcelona help him?
5 What is special about the Fundación Leo Messi?

Lionel Andrés Messi – *el mejor futbolista del mundo*

<u>Nació</u> en Rosario, Argentina el 24 de junio de 1987. A los cinco años <u>empezó</u> a jugar al fútbol con un equipo local llamado Grandoli. Su padre dirigía el equipo. Luego se fue a jugar en otro equipo y comenzó a mostrar su habilidad como delantero.

Cuando <u>tenía</u> once años un médico le diagnosticó con una deficiencia que significaba que no iba a crecer mucho más. Significaba también el final de una carrera en el fútbol. Su familia no podía pagar el tratamiento porque era demasiado caro.

Por fortuna el club de fútbol de Barcelona <u>quería</u> contratarle y <u>decidieron</u> pagar su costoso tratamiento. Así que en el año dos mil la familia <u>se fue</u> a vivir a Barcelona. A los dieciséis años debutó con el equipo de menores y desde 2005 <u>juega</u> con los mayores. Hoy mide 1m 69 y su número de camiseta <u>es</u> el número diez. <u>Tiene</u> dos hermanos mayores, Rodrigo y Matías, y una hermana Marisol. Hasta ahora ha ganado cinco títulos de la Liga y es mundialmente reconocido. Es embajador para la UNICEF y lleva la Fundación Leo Messi que <u>se dedica</u> a ayudar a niños necesitados tanto en Argentina como en el resto del mundo.

3
NC 5

Prepara diez preguntas para hacer una entrevista a Lionel Messi.

Usa los verbos subrayados del texto para ayudarte.

Ejemplo: <u>Nació</u> en Rosario, Argentina = ¿Dónde **naciste**?

4
NC 5

Escribe un artículo similar sobre tu deportista preferido/a.

Escuchar

NC 4

Listen to the interview and choose a, b or c to complete the sentence.

		a	**b**	**c**
1	Leonor does	a lot of sport	not very much sport	no sport at all
2	She goes to the sports centre	every day	once a week	three times a week
3	She goes there to	see her teacher	meet up with her friends	play in the team
4	Her friends usually play	basketball	table tennis	chess
5	Leonor prefers to	referee	take part	watch them
6	She prefers to do	rock climbing	gymnastics	cross country running
7	She has to go with	her brother	her father	her instructor
8	She only does this	on Mondays	at weekends	in the holidays

Hablar

NC 4

Prepare the answers to the questions below.

Normalmente ...

1 ¿Qué deporte haces?

2 ¿Cuántas veces a la semana?   1 / 2

3 ¿Qué haces para relajarte?

4 ¿Qué desayunas?

5 ¿A qué hora te acuestas?   10 / 11.30

6 ¿Cuántas horas sueles dormir?   8 / 9

7 ¿Qué comes en la cantina del insti?

8 ¿Cuál es tu plato preferido?

Leer

NC 4

Read the text and answer the questions.

1 What comment is made about basketball?
2 Why does the writer prefer skateboarding?
3 Where can you practise it?
4 When did it become fashionable?
5 What uniform do skateboarders wear?
6 Explain the moves.

Escribir

NC 3

Reorder the fridge magnets to make complete sentences.

1 | saludable | La | es | el | deporte | más |
  | todos | de | natación |

2 | importante | muy | saber | Es | nadar |

3 | partes | cuando | muchas | Usas | cuerpo |
  | nadas | del |

DEPORTE A LA MODA

El baloncesto es un deporte que está bastante de moda pero tienes que medir 1m 80 por lo menos para jugar en un equipo.

Yo prefiero los deportes que puedes practicar tú solo y por eso me encanta el "street"; patinar en la calle o en las rampas del parque. Se puso de moda en los años noventa y tiene sus normas y su uniforme.

Los aficionados llevan casco, protectores para las rodillas y los codos y todos llevan pantalones anchos. En su lengua un "half pipe" es cuando se sube una rampa en forma de U, ¡y un "Mactwist" es un salto mortal de 360 grados!

Vocabulario

Vida sana	*Healthy living*
en forma	*in shape*
vago/a	*lazy*
gordo/a	*fat*
la rutina	*routine*
cambiar	*to change*
sano/a	*healthy*
malsano/a	*unhealthy*
el polideportivo	*sports/leisure centre*
acostarse (ue)	*to go to bed*
las chucherías	*sweets*
siempre	*always*
a veces	*sometimes*
cada	*each/every*
a menudo	*often*
casi nunca	*hardly ever*
rara vez	*rarely*
nunca	*never*
seguir	*to follow*
dormir	*to sleep*
perder peso	*to lose weight*
saludable	*healthy*

Cuerpo sano	*Healthy body*
la cabeza	*head*
el corazón	*heart*
el cuerpo	*body*
la mano	*hand*
el brazo	*arm*
el dedo	*finger*
el dedo gordo	*big toe*
la espalda	*back*
el estómago	*stomach*
el ojo	*eye*
el ombligo	*belly button*
la oreja	*ear*
la nariz	*nose*
el pie	*foot*
la pierna	*leg*
la rodilla	*knee*
el tobillo	*ankle*
encima de	*on top of*
por delante	*forwards*
por detrás	*backwards*
doblar	*to bend*
poner	*to put*
fumar	*to smoke*
beber	*to drink*

Malestar	*Feeling unwell*
doler (ue)	*to hurt*
un dolor	*pain*
los dientes	*teeth*
la fiebre	*fever/temperature*
la garganta	*throat*
romper (roto)	*to break (broken)*
torcer (torcido)	*to twist (twisted)*
sentirse mal	*to feel unwell*
caer(se)	*to fall*
hacer (hecho)	*to do (done) / make (made)*
una crema	*cream*
una pastilla	*pill*
un jarabe	*syrup/cough mixture*
una tirita	*plaster*
la farmacia	*chemist's*

Nos encanta el deporte	*We love sport*
el baloncesto	*basketball*
el cross	*cross country running*
la escalada	*rock climbing*
la gimnasia	*gymnastics*
la natación	*swimming*
el skate	*skateboarding*
el voleibol	*volleyball*
excepto	*except for*
incluso	*including*
patinar	*to skate*
un casco	*helmet*
un equipo	*team/equipment*
unos guantes	*gloves*
un palo	*stick/club*
una pelota	*ball*
una raqueta	*racket*
las ruedas	*wheels*
una tabla	*surfboard*
unas zapatillas	*trainers*

I can ...

- use question words and frequency words
- use the preterite and imperfect tenses
- talk about sport and a healthy lifestyle
- explain what hurts and why
- understand instructions
- listen for detail
- memorise some things

- Vocabulary: talk about what you will do in the future
- Grammar: use the future tense
- Skills: differentiate between the future and the immediate future

¿Qué harás el año que viene, Roberto?

Pues, primero, **el mes que viene 1** ___ a Colombia.

2 ___ muy contento de ver a mi familia otra vez.

Luego, **el año que viene 3** ___ en el colegio con mis amigos.

Más tarde **4** ___ un buen trabajo.

Y claro, **5** ___ mucho dinero.

Naturalmente **6** ___ muy, muy famoso ...

Vaya, Roberto, ¡qué egoísta eres!

 Escucha y completa las frases de arriba.

NC 3 *Ejemplo:* **1** *volveré*

> estaré estudiaré ganaré seré
> tendré volveré

 Empareja los dibujos de la actividad 1 con las frases en inglés.

Ejemplo: **1** *I will return to Colombia.*

> I will be very famous I will be very happy
> I will study I will earn a lot of money
> I will have a good job

Gramática → p.165

You use the **future tense** to talk about **what will happen** in the future, and your hopes and plans.

Iré a Londres – *I will go to London.*
Estudiaré en la universidad – *I will study at university.*

Add the following endings to the infinitive:

volver – *to return*
volver**é** – **I** *will return*
volver**ás** – *you (s) (formal) will return*
volver**á** – *he/she/you will return*
volver**emos** – *we will return*
volver**éis** – *you (pl) will return*
volver**án** – *they/you (formal) will return*

Completa las frases con los verbos de la casilla. Identifica el tiempo del verbo.

1 Hoy ▢▢▢ al cine con mis amigos.
2 Mañana ▢▢▢ un vestido nuevo.
3 El año que viene ▢▢▢ a Nueva York.
4 Después del instituto, ▢▢▢ en una oficina.
5 La semana que viene ▢▢▢ de vacaciones.

> iré   trabajaré   voy a comprar   voy a ir (x2)

 Gramática → p.165

There are two irregular verbs on page 100:
tener – *to have*   tendré – *I will have*
hacer – *to do*   haré – *I will do*
In what way are their future forms different from those of other verbs? They use the same endings as all future verbs.

 Gramática → p.165

The **immediate future** is used to talk about **what you are going to do quite soon**, and when what you are going to do is **definite**:

Hoy **voy a jugar** al fútbol –
*Today **I'm going to play** football.*

The **future tense** is used to talk about things **further off which may not be completely certain**:

En el futuro **jugaré** en un buen equipo – *In the future **I will play** in a good team.*

Challenge

In a group, work out your plans for next year. How imaginative can you be?

NC 5

Completa las frases con el verbo correcto en el futuro.

NC 5

1 En el futuro, mis amigos y yo ▢▢▢ mucho dinero. (ganar – nosotros)

2 Luisa ▢▢▢ muy contenta de ver a su abuela en el verano. (estar – ella)

3 El año que viene, Ricardo y Rogelio ▢▢▢ ciencias, porque les interesan mucho. (estudiar – ellos)

4 María, ¿▢▢▢ a Perú de vacaciones? (volver – tú)

5 Chicas, ¡▢▢▢ muy famosas en el futuro! (ser – vosotros)

6 Juan ▢▢▢ un buen trabajo. (tener – él)

> iré Jugaré visitaré
> estaré escucharé
> compraré estudiaré

 Habla con tu compañero. ¿Qué harás el año que viene?

NC 5

- Vocabulary: talk about what job you will, would like to, or hope to do in the future
- Grammar: practise using the future tense including irregular verbs
- Skills: understand what qualities are necessary for different jobs

 Escucha y escoge la letra correcta.

Ejemplo: 1 d

 Escucha otra vez. Anota las cualidades personales de cada persona.

Ejemplo: 1 inteligente y serio

inteligente extrovertido/a tímido/a
paciente creativo/a ambicioso/a
comunicativo/a organizado/a serio/a
trabajador(a)

 Gramática

There are various ways of talking about what you want to do in the future.

En el futuro – *In the future*	trabajaré como – *I will work as*		piloto – *a pilot.*
	espero – *I hope* me gustaría – *I would like*	trabajar como – *to work as*	
	espero – *I hope* quiero – *I want*	ser – *to be*	

How would you say these?
- I will work as an IT specialist.
- I hope to work as a reporter.
- I would like to be an actor.
- I hope to be a tour guide.
- I want to be a singer.

 NC 4–5

👥 **Con un compañero, juega a tres en raya con los dibujos de arriba. Tienes que decir lo que harás en el futuro.**

Ejemplo: En el futuro trabajaré como director de empresa.

actor cantante deportista
director de empresa
diseñador de videojuegos
guía turístico informático
periodista piloto

 NC 5

Lee los textos de la página 103. Who ...?

Example: 1 Miguel

1. wants a stimulating job?
2. likes helping people?
3. will have their own company in the future?
4. is very organised?
5. hopes to earn a lot of money?
6. will go to university?
7. doesn't like working with other people?
8. wants a job both in an office and outside?

Quiero ser periodista porque soy ambicioso y comunicativo. Me gustaría trabajar con el público y tener un trabajo estimulante. ¡Tendré que trabajar en una oficina y al aire libre! Así que iré a la universidad y estudiaré mucho.

Miguel

Espero ser informática porque soy trabajadora y seria. Me gustaría mucho trabajar con ordenadores. Espero ganar mucho dinero. Podré trabajar sola. Prefiero eso, no me gusta mucho trabajar con otra gente.

Sofía

Mi padre es director de empresa, así que quiero ser director como él. En el futuro querré tener mi propia compañía y ganaré mucho dinero, porque soy organizado, paciente y trabajador. Me gustaría mucho ser mi propio jefe.

Pepe

Espero trabajar como guía turística. Me encanta ayudar a la gente y viajar. Tienes que trabajar mucho y atender a los viajeros, pero como soy bastante paciente y divertida, creo que me gustaría mucho.

Alicia

 5

NC 5

Lee y completa los planes de Elena. Elige la forma correcta del verbo.

En el futuro, bueno, no sé todavía lo que **1** _____ (hacer / haré). En el insti, me encantan las mátematicas y las ciencias, y me **2** _____ (gustar / gustaría) mucho trabajar como científica, o quizás informática porque me interesan mucho los ordenadores. Espero **3** _____ (viajar / viajaré) por el mundo porque tengo curiosidad por otros países y culturas. Creo que **4** _____ (vivir / viviré) en los Estados Unidos. No quiero **5** _____ (ser / seré) famosa – no me interesa eso. ¿Sabes cuál es mi sueño de verdad? ¡Ser astronauta! Si soy astronauta **6** _____ (poder / podré) trabajar para la NASA, **7** _____ (viajar / viajaré) en una nave espacial y **8** _____ (volar / volaré) hasta las estrellas …

Challenge

What will you do in the future? Write a short paragraph about your future job and hopes.

(**NC 5**)

Gramática → p.165

You have already met *tendré* and *haré*. Here are some other useful verbs that are irregular in the future.
How many of them can you find in the texts above?
decir – **diré** – *I will tell / say*
haber – **habrá** – *there will be*
poder – **podré** – *I will be able*
poner – **pondré** – *I will put*
querer – **querré** – *I will want*
salir – **saldré** – *I will go out*
venir – **vendré** – *I will come*
Can you write short sentences for the others?
Example: Diré al profe que no puedo hacer los deberes.

3B.3 ¿Cómo ganar dinero ahora?

- Vocabulary: talk about how you earn pocket money now
- Grammar: say who gives you money
- Skills: think of unusual ways to earn pocket money

 Roberto

 Pilar

 Ben

 Elena

1
¿Cuánto dinero te dan?	○ 15€ cada semana.
¿Tienes un trabajo?	○ No. **Mi madre me da dinero.**
¿Cuántas horas trabajas?	○ ¡Ninguna!
¿Qué opinas?	○ Necesito más …

2
¿Cuánto dinero te dan?	○ Mis padres me dan 40€ mensualmente.
¿Tienes un trabajo?	○ **Ayudo en casa**, hago las compras, preparo la cena, recojo mi dormitorio …
¿Cuántas horas trabajas?	○ ¡Muchas!
¿Qué opinas?	○ Soy una esclava del hogar.

3
¿Cuánto dinero te dan?	○ Gano £15 semanalmente.
¿Tienes un trabajo?	○ **Reparto periódicos**.
¿Cuántas horas trabajas?	○ De 6h a 7h cada mañana, de lunes a sábado.
¿Qué opinas?	○ Dinero está bien, trabajo duro.

4
¿Cuánto dinero te dan?	○ Gano 65€ cada mes.
¿Tienes un trabajo?	○ **Soy canguro**.
¿Cuántas horas trabajas?	○ Tardes y fines de semanas.
¿Qué opinas?	○ Depende de la familia.

 LEER 1 | **NC 4**

Empareja los dibujos a–d con los textos 1–4.

 ESCUCHAR 2 | **NC 4**

🎧 **Escucha y empareja a los jóvenes con la información de la actividad 1.**

Ejemplo: **1** Roberto

 HABLAR 3 | **NC 3–4**

👥 **Habla con tu compañero. ¿Quién eres?**

Ejemplo: **A** ¿Cuánto dinero te dan?
B Mis padres me dan 40€ mensualmente.
A ¿Tienes un trabajo?
B Ayudo en casa.
A Eres Elena.
B Correcto.

Mi madre/mi padre	me da	5€ 20€	cada semana semanalmente cada mes mensualmente
Mis padres/mis abuelos	me dan		
Gano			
Trabajo		de 3h a 6h / por la tarde	
		el fin de semana / cada día	

4 **Lee el chat y empareja a las personas con los dibujos.**

NC 5

Mensajes	|Q

Juanjo	Hola a todos. Necesito dinero. ¿Cómo ganarlo? ¿Tenéis ideas nuevas?
Carlota23	Saludos, Juanjo. Paseo a los perros de mis vecinos, porque trabajan hasta muy tarde y no están en casa durante el día. ¡A veces paseo a cuatro o cinco perros al día! Gano 8€ por cada perro. No está mal, y es divertido.
PacoX	Trabajo en el jardín de mi abuelo, porque ya está viejo. Me da 5€ por hora. Es un trabajo duro, pero me gusta estar fuera de la casa. La semana que viene también trabajaré en el jardín de su vecino.

| **Ángel** | Yo ayudo a mi abuela y a mi tía. Hago las compras porque son viejas, y mi abuela está bastante enferma. No es fácil para ellas salir de casa. Me dan 10€ cada semana. |
| **Ricky** | Soy inglés, y en Inglaterra se puede trabajar como actor de teatro desde los doce años. Cada invierno actúo en una *pantomime* durante unas semanas, y gano £70 semanalmente. Fenomenal, ¿no? |

5 **Escucha la entrevista.**

6 **Escucha otra vez y completa el texto siguiente.**

NC 5

Ejemplo: 1 mes

Me llamo Gema y tengo 16 años. Mis padres me dan 30€ cada
1 _____ . Tengo que ayudar en casa. **2** _____ al perro cada día,
recojo mi **3** _____ , y pongo la **4** _____ . No me gusta mucho ayudar
en casa – es muy **5** _____ , pero mamá dice que toda la familia
tiene que hacer algo. Papá prepara la cena muchas veces, y hasta
mis hermanos pequeños sacan la **6** _____ y hacen sus camas.
Mamá les da 3€ cada **7** _____ . También trabajo como camarera en
el restaurante cerca de mi casa. Trabajo los sábados por la **8** _____ ,
de 4h a **9** _____ . Gano 25€ semanalmente – no está mal. Mi amiga
inglesa reparte periódicos a las 6h de la mañana: ¡qué horror!
Después de mis estudios **10** _____ un trabajo muy bueno y **11**
_____ muchísimo dinero.

Challenge

Imagine you have a surprising way of earning extra pocket money. Write a paragraph about it. Try to include two tenses (for example, say how much you earned last month or will earn next month).

NC 4–5

3B.4 Lo que estudiaré

- Vocabulary: talk about choosing options/subjects
- Grammar: recognise some phrases in the conditional
- Skills: give reasons for your choices

ESCUCHAR 1 🎧 **Escucha. Anota la asignatura y la opinión.**

Ejemplo: 1 matemáticas – interesantes

ESCUCHAR 2 🎧 **Escucha a los jóvenes y anota las letras correctas.**

NC 5 *Ejemplo: 1 f, d*

Es mi asignatura preferida.

Soy bueno/a en ...

Me interesa.

Mi padre dice que es importante.

Mis amigos lo estudiarán.

El profe es muy simpático.

ESCUCHAR 3 🎧 **Escucha otra vez. ¿Verdad o mentira?**

NC 5 *Ejemplo: 1 V*

1 Marisa estudiará historia porque su padre dice que es importante.
2 A Carmen le gustaría estudiar deporte, pero no es muy buena en esa asignatura.
3 Nuria preferiría estudiar matemáticas pero dice que el profe es muy antipático.
4 Alberto estudiará inglés porque es útil.
5 A Eugenio le gustaría estudiar música porque es su asignatura preferida.
6 Pablo no estudiará ciencias porque no le interesan mucho.

HABLAR 4 👥 **Habla con un compañero. ¿Qué estudiarás el año que viene? ¿Por qué? Usa las frases de las actividades 2 y 3 para ayudarte.**

LEER 5 **Lee el chat (página 107). Elena chatea por Internet con su prima Laura. Laura vive en Londres porque su madre es inglesa.**

NC 5

1 What will Laura study? Why?
2 Is there anything she would like to do but can't?
3 Make a note of any differences between British and Spanish schools.

> ### Gramática → p.165
>
> **The conditional**
>
> The conditional is used where in English we use 'would' + verb.
> Me gustaría estudiar música –
> *I would like to study music.*
> Preferiría viajar por el mundo –
> *I would like to travel the world.*
>
> It is formed like the future, with the infinitive, but with different endings:
> **preferir** – *to prefer*
> preferir**ía** – *I would prefer*
> preferir**ías** – *you (s) would prefer*
> preferir**ía** – *he/she/you (formal) would prefer*

Mensajes

Eleniña	Hola, Laura. ¿Qué tal el insti?
Laurita	¡Horrible! Tenemos que escoger las optativas para el año que viene. ¡Es muy difícil!
Eleniña	¿Qué estudiarás?
Laurita	Matemáticas, inglés y ciencias son asignaturas obligatorias. Me gustaría no estudiar inglés – no saco buenas notas.
Eleniña	¿Y las optativas?
Laurita	Español, ¡claro! Soy muy buena en español.
Eleniña	No me digas ...
Laurita	Me gustaría estudiar música, porque mis amigos la estudiarán. Pero papá dice que es más importante estudiar historia o geografía. Me interesa la geografía: el profe es muy simpático.
Eleniña	Tienes suerte. El año que viene estudiaré las mismas asignaturas. No tengo optativas. Seguiré con doce asignaturas.
Laurita	¡Doce! Yo sólo estudiaré ocho ...

LEER 6

¿Qué razones de la actividad 2 son buenas razones para escoger una asignatura? ¿Cuáles son malas?

NC 4–5

Ejemplo: buena – me interesa

? Think

Can you find the Spanish for:
options   really nice
you don't say ...   of course
Remember to make a note of any interesting and unusual vocabulary to use later.

? Think

Can you remember any other differences between Spanish and British schools from *Zoom 1*?

Challenge

Write an email to a friend explaining your study choices for next year (three subjects). Use the future and try to use the conditional. You might also say what you liked studying this year. **NC 5–6**

El Video Reto

VIDEO 7

Mira la primera parte del video y contesta a las preguntas en inglés.

a   What would Roberto like to do next year?
b   What's the problem?

VIDEO 8

Mira el video y completa la tabla.

	Favourite subject	Plan for future	Other information
Girl 1			
Boy 1			

VIDEO 9

• ¿Cuáles son las asignaturas preferidas de los jóvenes de Segovia?
• ¿Qué les gustaría hacer en el futuro?

- Vocabulary: find out and describe how somebody got their dream job
- Grammar: use a variety of tenses (past, present, future)
- Skills: produce a piece of extended writing

Antonio Banderas

José Antonio Domínguez Banderas nació en Málaga el 10 de agosto de 1960. Su madre era maestra y su padre era policía. En el instituto su asignatura preferida era la educación física. Su trabajo de sueño era ser futbolista profesional pero cuando tenía catorce años se rompió el pie.

A los diecinueve años se fue a Madrid, y empezó a ser actor de teatro. Allí le descubrió el famosísimo director de cine español Pedro Almodóvar. Trabajó con Almodóvar durante diez años. En 1992, cuando tenía 32 años, se fue a Hollywood. En la primera película que hizo en lengua inglesa Banderas no hablaba inglés. ¡Aprendió todo el papel fonéticamente! Durante los años siguientes actuó en muchas películas famosas, como *The Mask of Zorro*, y por supuesto *Shrek*.

Vive entre California y España con su mujer Melanie Griffith y su hija Stella. Los dos son famosos por su colaborácion con grupos humanitarios. Es hincha del Real Madrid, y también promociona productos españoles como el vino.

En el futuro, va a trabajar más con la industria del perfume. Seguro que actuará en más películas y quizás le gustaría ganar un premio Oscar.

LEER 1

NC 6–7

¿Verdad o mentira?

1 Antonio Banderas es español.
2 Su trabajo de sueño era ser actor.
3 Su primera película fue en Hollywood.
4 No le gusta mucho el fútbol.
5 En el futuro ganará más Oscars.

maestra – *teacher*
siguiente – *following*
colaboración con grupos humanitarios – *charity work*
hincha – *fan/supporter*

Carlos Sainz

Carlos Sainz Cenamor nació en Madrid el 12 de abril de 1962. En el instituto su asignatura preferida era la educación física. Cuando tenía 16 años fue campeón nacional de squash en España. Estudió dos años derecho en la universidad pero decidió ser piloto de coches de rally. Es muy trabajador.

A los 18 años participó en su primer rally para Ford, y ganó su primer título español en 1987. En 1990, cuando tenía 28 años, ganó su primer título mundial como piloto de Toyota. Ganó muchísimos títulos y premios y fue campeón del mundo dos veces. Todo el mundo le llama *El Matador*.

Con 42 años, se jubiló del deporte, pero un año más tarde, en 2005 conducía otra vez para Citroën. En 2006 condujo en el rally Paris Dakar, y lo ganó en 2010.

Sainz vive todavía en España y está casado con Reyes Vázquez de Castro. Tienen tres hijos, Blanca, Carlos y Ana. Le gusta todo tipo de deporte: el fútbol, el golf, el tenis, el motocross, el esquí y el squash.

En 2013 va a trabajar más para Volkswagen, y seguro que conducirá otra vez. Su hijo, Carlos, también es piloto – de coches de fórmula.

derecho – *law*
piloto de coches – *driver*
jubilarse – *to retire*
se jubiló – *he retired (preterite)*
conducir – *to drive*
condujo – *he drove (preterite)*

 2

NC 6–7

Elige las palabras correctas para terminar las frases.

1 When Sainz was young he played tennis / squash / golf .
2 He began rally driving when he was only 14 / 16 / 18 years old.
3 He won his first world title in 1990 for Volkswagen / Toyota / Ford .
4 He retired in 2004, but won the Dakar rally in 2006 / 2010 / 2011.
5 He's still on the team for Volkswagen / Citroën / Toyota.

 3

NC 5–6

 **Escucha. ¿Hablan de Banderas o de Sainz?**

Ejemplo: 1 Sainz

? Think

The ending **-ísimo** on any adjective makes it **extremely** something:
Estoy **contentísimo** – *I'm extremely happy*
Esta pelicula está es **aburridísima** – *This film is extremely boring*.

As in all adjectives, the ending must agree with the person (masculine, feminine, singular or plural). Find examples in the two texts and work out what they mean.

Gramática → p.161

Check the grammar section at the back of the book to remind you when to use the preterite, imperfect, present, immediate future and future tenses. Find an example of each in these biographies.

Challenge

Interview an older friend, relative, or local celebrity about the work they do. How did they start? What was their first job? What happened next? Is this their dream job? What will they do next? Conduct your interview in English, and write up the biography of your chosen person in Spanish.

NC 6–7

3B.6 Labolengua

Comprender – The future and the conditional

A The future

The future tense is used to talk about **what will happen** in the future. It can also be used to talk about hopes and plans.

Iré a Londres – *I will go to London.*

Estudiaré en la universidad – *I will study at university.*

To form the future, take the infinitive and add the following endings:

volver – *to return*
volver**é** – *I will return*
volver**ás** – *you (s) will return*
volver**á** – *he/she/you (formal) will return*
volver**emos** – *we will return*
volver**éis** – *you (pl) will return*
volver**án** – *they/you (pl formal) will return*

All verbs use these endings, but some have an irregular **stem** – the part the endings attach to.

Future verbs with irregular stems:
decir – diré – *I will say*
haber – habrá – *there will be*
hacer – haré – *I will do*
poder – podré – *I will be able*
poner – pondré – *I will put*
querer – querré – *I will want*
salir – saldré – *I will go out*
tener – tendré – *I will have*
venir – vendré – *I will come*
ver – veré – *I will see*

1 Complete these sentences with the correct part of the verb.

1 Los chicos no _____ (estudiar) inglés el año que viene, porque sacan malas notas.

2 _____ (ayudar) a mi padre en el jardín por la tarde. _____ (ganar) 6€.

3 Juan _____ (ser) astronauta y _____ (viajar) a la luna.

4 Carlos y yo _____ (ser) actores, _____ (ser) muy famosos y _____ (vivir) en Los Ángeles.

B The conditional

The conditional is used where in English we use 'would' + verb.

Me gustaría viajar por el mundo – *I would like to travel the world.*

Sería un buen médico – *I would make a good doctor.*

It is formed like the future, with the infinitive, but with these endings:

estudiar – *to study*
estudiar**ía** – *I would study*
estudiar**ías** – *you (s) would study*
estudiar**ía** – *he/she/you (formal) would study*

The same verbs are irregular in both the future and the conditional, and they use the same stems.

2 Are these sentences in the future or the conditional?

1 Me gustaría ser médico.

2 Recogería mi dormitorio, mamá, pero tengo muchos deberes.

3 Iré con mis amigos al cine la semana que viene.

4 Vendré contigo al partido de fútbol.

Aprender – Checking your work critically

C Improving your written work

To improve your writing in Spanish, there are a number of things to look out for:

- **spelling** – Remembering the rules of pronunciation will help you get your spelling right.
- **verbs** – Have you got the right ending for the right person?
- **tenses** – Past, present, future: are you using the right tense?
- **agreements** – Masculine and feminine, singular and plural: do your adjectives match their nouns?
- **sentence structure** – Have you got your adjectives in the right place?
- **interest** – Have you used a variety of vocabulary, or do you repeat yourself a lot?
- **register** – *Tú* or *usted*, *vosotros* or *ustedes*: are you talking to a friend or formally?

3 How many mistakes can you find in this text? Which of the points above do they match? Can you correct them?

> Me llamo Julia. En el futur me gustaría mucho ser actriz. Soy extrovertido y ambiciosa, y espera ganar un oscar. Viajaré por el mundo, y vivo en Nueva York. Mi preferida asignatura en el instituto es el teatro porque soy muy buena en eso, y es interesante y divertido. No me gustan las ciencias porque no soy buena en ellas y no son interesantes. No me gustaría trabajar en una oficina – en mi opinión sería muy aburrido.

> ¡No es muy interesante!

Hablar – Accents

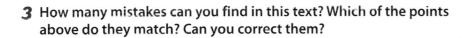

D Using accents when speaking and pronouncing accurately

In *Zoom 1* you learnt how to know where to place the emphasis when speaking. Can you remember the rules?

Especially with verbs, it is very important to emphasise the accented letter; it can completely change the meaning of the word. It also helps you understand what tense is being used. Remember to pronounce every letter in a Spanish word.

traba**jo**   I work (present)   traba**jó** – he worked (preterite)

traba**jé** – I worked (preterite)   trabaja**ré** – I will work (future)

 Listen to them.

4 Add the missing accent, or underline the emphasised letter of these verbs:

viajo *(I – present)*   viajo *(he – preterite)*
ayude *(I – preterite)*   ayudare *(I – future)*

> ¡En el futuro **viajarÉ**!

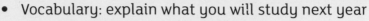

- Vocabulary: explain what you will study next year
- Grammar: practise using the future tense
- Skills: write about future plans

LEER 1

NC 3

Imagina que entrevistas a estas personas cuando eran jóvenes. ¿Qué harán más tarde en la vida? Empareja las dos partes de las frases.

Imagine you are interviewing these people when they were young. What will they do later in life? Match the two halves of the sentences.

Ejemplo: **1** c

1 Ganaré campeonatos de
2 Trabajaré en un
3 Seré una
4 Trabajaré como
5 Seré actriz en

a cantante muy famosa.
b Hollywood.
c baloncesto.
d avión.
e periodista.

LEER 2

Empareja las frases con los dibujos.
Match the sentences with the pictures a–e.

Ejemplo: **1** e

LEER 3

Completa las frases con las palabras de la casilla.
Complete the sentences with one of the words in the box.

NC 3

1 El año que viene estudiaré inglés porque me _____.
2 Juan estudiará música porque sus _____ la estudiarán.
3 Elena estudiará tecnología porque su padre dice que es _____.
4 ¿Estudiarás geografía? El profe es muy _____.
5 Soy _____ en español. Lo estudiaré el año que viene.
6 ¿Estudiarás informática? Es tu _____ preferida, ¿verdad?

> amigos   asignatura   bueno   importante
> interesa   simpático

ESCRIBIR 4

Escribe dos o tres frases para explicar qué estudiarás el año que viene y por qué.

NC 5

Write a couple of sentences explaining what you will study next year and why.

- Vocabulary: understand what qualities are necessary for different jobs; talk about how you earn money now
- Grammar: practise using the future tense
- Skills: find out about some famous Spanish people, past and present

Miguel Indurain

Cristóbal Colón

Salvador Dalí

1 Empareja los anuncios de empleo con las personas.

NC 5

1

Reyes Católicos buscan personas valientes y extrovertidas para viaje en barco muy largo. Viajará durante años, encontrará países nuevos, será muy peligroso. Si tiene éxito, ganará mucho dinero. Tema preferido – la geografía. Fernando e Isabel, Palacio Real

2

El mundo cambiará con su trabajo. La gente nunca verá un reloj sin pensar en usted. Es usted creativo, inteligente, egoísta y completamente distinto a otra gente. Será usted su propio jefe, trabajará solo, pero será muy, muy famoso. Asignatura preferida – el arte.
Los surealistas, C/ Pescado

3

¿Eres ambicioso, trabajador y súper sano? ¿Te mantienes en forma todo el tiempo?
¿Te gusta viajar rápidamente? ¿Te interesaria trabajar al aire libre, con muchas personas pero a la vez solo? No ganarás mucho dinero, pero te conocerá mucha gente.
www.letour.fr

2 Lee los anuncios otra vez y completa la tabla.

NC 5–6

	Persona	Cualidades para el trabajo	En el futuro	Asignatura preferida en el instituto
1	Cristobal Colón	valiente ...	ganará mucho dinero ...	le gustó geografía

3 ¿Cómo ganas dinero? ¿Cuánto te dan? Escribe un párrafo.

NC 4–3

Ejemplo: Ayudo a mi madre cada semana, y me da £10. Paseo al perro y recojo mi dormitorio. También ...

Escuchar

NC 5

Listen and answer the questions:

- How do they earn money?
- How much do they earn?
- What will they be in the future?

Roger

Arancha

José y Conchi

Hablar

NC 5

Take it in turns with a partner to interview each other.
Ask the questions and give answers.

¿Dinero?	¿Opinión?
¿Trabajo?	¿En el futuro?

Leer

NC 5

Read what Eugenia writes. Decide if the sentences are true or false.

1 The English teacher is nice.
2 Eugenia gets good marks in English.
3 She would like to work with children.
4 She would like to look after patients.
5 Her friends will not study history.
6 She is a very talkative person.

Hola, soy Eugenia. El año que viene estudiaré inglés, porque saco buenas notas, y ciencias porque el profe es súper simpático. No estudiaré historia porque mis amigos no la estudiarán. En el futuro iré a la universidad y estudiaré medicina. Sería un buen médico porque me gusta ayudar a la gente, y soy muy comunicativa y trabajadora. No me gustaría ser profesora porque prefiero trabajar con adultos.

Escribir

NC 6

Write an email to your Spanish penfriend explaining what you will study next year and why. What did you like this year? What do you plan to do in the future? Write a short paragraph.

Lo qué haré	**What I will do**
Estaré muy contento/a	I will be very happy
Estudiaré	I will study
Ganaré mucho dinero	I will earn a lot of money
Seré muy famoso/a	I will be very famous
Tendré un buen trabajo	I will have a good job
Volveré a Colombia	I will return to Colombia

Trabajaré como ...	**I'll work as a(n) ...**
actor/actriz	actor
cantante	singer
deportista	sportsperson
director(a) de empresa	managing director
diseñador(a) de videojuegos	video game designer
guía turístico/a	tour guide
informático/a	IT specialist
periodista	reporter
piloto	pilot
ambicioso/a	ambitious
comunicativo/a	good at communicating
organizado/a	organised
serio/a	serious / reliable
trabajador(a)	hard-working
espero trabajar como	I hope to work as
espero ser	I hope to be
al aire libre	outdoors

¿Cómo ganar dinero ahora?	**How can I earn money now?**
dar	to give
ganar	to earn
cada mes	each month
cada semana	each week
mensualmente	monthly
semanalmente	weekly
de 3h a 6h	from 3 to 6
ayudar en casa	to help at home
hacer de canguro	to do babysitting
repartir periódicos	to deliver newspapers

Lo qué estudiaré	**What I will study**
El profe es muy simpático	The teacher is very nice
Es mi asignatura preferida	It's my favourite subject
Soy bueno/a en ...	I'm good at ...
Me interesa	It interests me
Mi padre dice que es importante	My father says it's important
Mis amigos lo estudiarán	My friends will do (study) it
claro	of course
no me digas	you don't say ...
optativas	options
súper simpático	really nice

I can ...

- talk about what I will do in the future
- use the future tense of regular and irregular verbs
- differentiate between the future and the immediate future
- talk about what job I will, would like to, or hope to do in the future
- understand what qualities are necessary for different jobs
- talk about how I earn pocket money now
- talk about choosing options / subjects and give reasons for my choices
- recognise some phrases in the conditional
- find out and describe how somebody got their dream job
- use a variety of tenses (past, present, future)
- do a piece of extended writing
- check work critically
- use accents to pronounce words correctly

4A.1 ¿Cómo es tu mundo?

- Vocabulary: describe environmental problems and their causes
- Grammar: use superlatives (*el/la ... más ...*)
- Skills: give opinions with *para mí, en mi opinión*; understand and use very large numbers

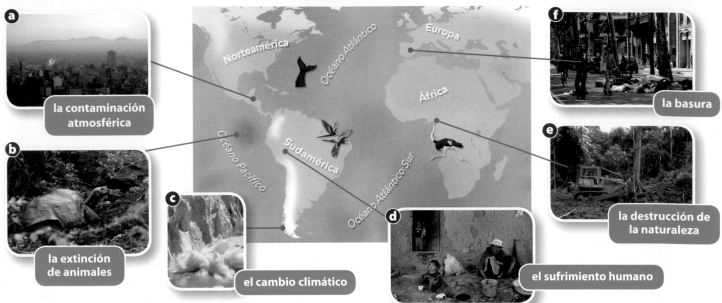

a la contaminación atmosférica

b la extinción de animales

c el cambio climático

d el sufrimiento humano

e la destrucción de la naturaleza

f la basura

ESCUCHAR 1

🎧 **Escucha e identifica de dónde vienen.**

NC 4

1 Conchita	**3** Quidel	**5** Felipe
2 Imasu	**4** Encarna	**6** Sinforosa

100	cien
200	doscientos
500	quinientos
700	setecientos
900	novecientos
1.000	mil
2.000	dos mil
1.000.000	un millón
2.000.000	dos milliones

LEER 2

Empareja las frases de arriba (a–f) con las frases en inglés.

climate change   destruction of nature
extinction of animals   human suffering   pollution   rubbish

ESCUCHAR 3

🎧 **Escucha otra vez e identifica el problema.**

ESCUCHAR 4

🎧 **Escucha otra vez y anota todos los números y, si puedes, lo que significan.**

Ejemplo: 45 (tipos de animales), 2.200 (especies en peligro de extinción) ...

? Think

How would you say and write:
250   575   3,150   4,200   1,600,000
16,000,000   42,800,430?

ESCUCHAR 5

🎧 **Escucha y completa.**

Me llamo Imasu y **1** ▨ de Bolivia. Para **2** ▨ el problema **3** ▨ grave de mi país es el sufrimiento humano.

Imasu

Quidel

Me llamo Quidel y **4** ▨ en Argentina. En mi **5** ▨ el **6** ▨ más grave de mi país es el cambio climático.

Habla con tu compañero.

NC 3–4

Ejemplo: **A** *En mi opinión, el problema más grave en mi país/ mi ciudad es la basura.*
B *Para mí el problema más grave es el sufrimiento humano.*

Lee el reportaje y corrige los errores. Usa tus respuestas de la actividad 4. Copia y completa la tabla.

NC 4–5

? **Think**

How do you say 'the most serious problem'?
What are the two ways of saying 'in my opinion'?

Número en el reportaje	de ...	Número correcto
Ejemplo: 1.000	*tipos de animales en peligro de extinción*	*11.000*

1 En las **Islas Galápagos** el problema más grave es la extinción de animales. En el mundo hay más de 1.000 tipos de animales en peligro de extinción, a causa de la destrucción de sus hábitats.

2 En **Bolivia** el problema más grande es el sufrimiento humano. Casi 700 de personas viven sin agua limpia o electricidad a causa de la pobreza.

3 El problema más grave en **Argentina** es el cambio climático. El agua de los glaciares es necesaria para los 60.000.000 de habitantes de Argentina, pero los glaciares de los Andes son cada vez más pequeños a causa del calentamiento global.

4 En **Madrid** hay mucha basura en la calle porque la gente no usa las papeleras a pesar de que ponen una multa de 570€ por tirar basura.

5 En **Ciudad de Méjico** el problema más grave de los años noventa era la contaminación atmosférica causada por el tráfico y las fábricas. Como resultado, cada año morían 100 personas. Ahora, el aire está mucho más limpio.

6 En **Guinea Ecuatorial**, en África, el problema más grave es la destrucción de la naturaleza. Deforestan más de 5.000 hectáreas de la selva cada año para ganar dinero, y eso es muy destructivo para los animales de la región.

una multa – *a fine*
la selva – *rainforest*

Empareja los dibujos con las frases subrayadas de la actividad 7.

¿Qué significan en inglés? Usa el vocabulario o un diccionario.

Ejemplo: **a** *no usa las papeleras*

a

b

c

d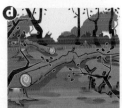

e

f

Challenge

Write a brief report about the environmental problems of your area. Use at least two tenses. If possible, include photos. What's the biggest problem in your opinion? Why? Use activity 7 to help you.

NC 4–6

4A.2 ¿Qué podemos hacer?

- Vocabulary: talk about helping the environment
- Grammar: use expressions to say 'we can', 'we must', 'we have to'; use the imperative
- Skills: carry out and write up a survey

a reciclar

b usar transporte público

c llevar tus propias bolsas al supermercado

d apagar las luces

e ahorrar agua

f plantar árboles

g comprar productos ecológicos

h protestar

 ESCUCHAR 1 🎧 **Escucha y completa.**

NC 4 · *Ejemplo: 1 reciclar*

Es muy importante proteger el medio ambiente, y no es difícil.
En casa se puede **1** *reciclar* las botellas, las latas y el papel
para ayudar a reducir la basura que creamos. Se debe
2 ▨▨▨ las luces cuando salimos de la habitación para ahorrar
energía. En el barrio se puede **3** ▨▨▨ transporte público para
4 ▨▨▨ la contaminación. Cuando vas de compras, debes
5 ▨▨▨ tus propias bolsas al supermercado para no usar bolsas de
plástico. Para ayudar más, se puede **6** ▨▨▨ productos ecológicos.
En el campo hay que **7** ▨▨▨ agua, y para controlar el cambio
climático se puede **8** ▨▨▨ árboles. Finalmente, para educar a la
gente, ¡se puede **9** ▨▨▨ !

 HABLAR 2 👥👥 **¿Cómo ayudar al medio ambiente en la casa, en la calle, en el supermercado y en el campo? Mira las fotos de arriba. Completa las ideas de tu compañero.**

NC 3

Ejemplo: **A** *En la casa ...*
      B *Se puede apagar las luces.*

> ⚙️ **Gramática** → p.167
>
> The following impersonal expressions can be used to say what can or must be done.
> **se puede** – *we can*
> **se debe** – *we must*   + infinitive
> **hay que** – *we have to*
>
> Se puede reciclar – *We can recycle.*
>
> **tener que** – *to have to*
> This one is an ordinary verb that changes:
> Tengo que apagar las luces – *I have to turn the lights out.*
> Tienes que ahorrar agua – *You have to save water.*

Gramática → p.166

The imperative

Remember!

You use this to give instructions, or to tell people what to do.

¡Cierra la puerta! – *Close the door!*

No enciendas la luz – *Don't turn the light on.*

	positive		negative	
	tú	**vosotros**	**tú**	**vosotros**
-ar verbs	ahorr**a** – *save*	ahorr**ad** – *save*	**no** ahorr**es** – *don't save*	**no** ahorr**éis** – *don't save*
-er verbs	com**e** – *eat*	com**ed** – *eat*	**no** com**as** – *don't eat*	**no** com**áis** – *don't eat*
-ir verbs	escrib**e** – *write*	escrib**id** – *write*	**no** escrib**as** – *don't write*	**no** escrib**áis** – *don't write*

Think

What do you notice about the endings for the negative imperative? How does this make it easier to remember?

3

NC 5

Lee la nota de Elena. Busca los imperativos. ¿Tú o vosotros?

Ejemplo: recicla (tú), ...

> Querida familia
>
> ¡Tenemos que ayudar al planeta!
>
> Mamá: ¡recicla todas las botellas y todas las latas! Habrá menos basura.
> Papá: ¡no uses el coche, viaja en autobús! Habrá menos contaminación.
> Roberto y Juan: ¡apagad las luces! Ahorraréis energía. También, chicos, ¡usad la ducha y no os bañéis! Ahorraréis agua.
> Abuela: ¡lleva tus propias bolsas al supermercado! Usarás menos bolsas de plástico. Mamá, abuela: ¡comprad productos ecológicos! Ayudaréis al medio ambiente.
> Abuelo: ¡planta árboles en tu jardín! Ayudarás a prevenir el cambio climático. Todos tenéis que ayudar: ¡protestad! Así educaremos a otra gente.
>
> Abrazos
>
> Elena

4

Lee la carta otra vez. Escribe lo que tienen que hacer los miembros de la familia.

Ejemplo: Mamá tiene que reciclar todas las botellas y latas ...

Challenge

Carry out a survey. Do your friends help the environment? What have they done recently? Write up your results, and say what people must do to help more.

Example: 23 personas no reciclan papel. Se debe reciclar papel. ¡Reciclad papel! Habrá menos basura.

NC 4–6

- Vocabulary: talk about how you look after your world
- Grammar: use negatives
- Skills: reading skills; make and refer to notes

 ESCUCHAR 1 🎧 **Escucha y completa la conversación.**

NC 3–4

> El problema del medio ambiente es que **nadie** cuida del mundo. **No 1** ▒ las botellas y el papel porque en el barrio **no** hay **ningún** contenedor de reciclaje.

 Elena

 Roberto

> Mis amigos **ni 2** ▒ **ni** usan transporte público – van en **3** ▒ a todas partes.

> Es verdad, mis amigos **tampoco** hacen **nada** para ayudar al medio ambiente. **Nunca** llevan sus propias **4** ▒ al supermercado …

 Juan

---

⚙ **Gramática → p.167**

Negatives

You make a sentence negative by putting *no* in front of the verb:
Papá **no** usa transporte público – *Dad doesn't use public transport.*
Learn these other negative expressions as well.

No ayuda **nadie** en proyectos medioambientales – ***Nobody** helps on environmental projects.*
No trabajo **nunca** como voluntario – *I **never** do any charity work.*
Mis amigos **no** hacen **nada** para ayudar – *My friends **don't** do **anything** (do **nothing**) to help.*
No hay **ningún** contenedor de reciclaje en mi barrio – *There are **no** recycling bins in my neighbourhood. (There are **none**.)*
Mamá **ni** compra productos ecológicos **ni** productos de comercio justo – *Mum **neither** buys eco-products **nor** Fairtrade products.*
Yo no los compro **tampoco** – *I don't buy them **either**.*

productos de comercio justo –
Fairtrade products
proyectos medioambientales –
environmental projects
trabajar como voluntario – *to do charity / volunteer work*

 ESCUCHAR 2 🎧 **Escucha y lee la conversación otra vez.**

NC 3–4 Who says …

1 their friends never take their own bags to the supermarket?
2 their friends neither use public transport nor walk?
3 their friends do nothing?
4 no-one looks after the world?
5 there are no recycling bins in the neighbourhood?

En las ciudades y pueblos hay muchos problemas medioambientales. Pero el mayor problema es – ¡la gente! Hay que reciclar cada semana, pero nunca reciclamos nada. Hay que usar el transporte público en vez del coche, pero no vamos en autobús nunca y siempre vamos en coche. Se debe usar la ducha para ahorrar agua, pero nos duchamos raramente y nos bañamos a menudo. Ni compramos productos ecológicos ni llevamos nuestras propias bolsas al supermercado. Se puede trabajar como voluntario para ayudar a otra gente, pero no hay ningún voluntario. También se puede trabajar en proyectos medioambientales pero la gente tampoco trabaja mucho en estos proyectos. ¿Qué se puede hacer para educar a la gente y ayudar más al planeta?

Think

When reading a longer text look for words and phrases you know. Try to get the sense of a whole sentence without worrying about every word. Use the words you know to help you work out the ones you don't.

 Lee el texto y anota todas las expresiones negativas.

Ejemplo: nunca reciclamos nada, ...

 Busca las frases en español. Escríbelas y anota en qué orden se mencionan.

NC 5
- no volunteers
- no recycling
- people don't use own shopping bags
- people not buying eco-products
- taking baths not showers
- too much car use

▶ El Video Reto

 Mira el video y contesta a las preguntas.

a Where do Juan, Roberto and Elena go?
b What do they learn about?
c Note down all the imperatives you hear. What do they mean?
d Which of these negatives do you hear?
  no   nada   nadie   nunca   ningún   tampoco
  ni ... ni

 ¿Verdad o mentira?

a La madre de Elena no usa nunca pesticidas.
b En la huerta no crecen frutas, solamente verduras.
c No es posible reciclar aceite.

 ¿Y tú, qué opinas? ¿Cómo podemos ayudar a proteger el planeta?

el calabacín – *courgette*
el repollo – *cabbage*
los guisantes – *peas*
la mariquita – *ladybird*
crecer – *to grow*
el aceite – *(cooking) oil*

Challenge

Give a report to the class about the state of your school or street. Include two or three tenses. Use notes, for example *instituto – basura – nadie – papeleras: En mi instituto hay mucha basura porque nadie usa nunca las papeleras.* **NC 4–6**

4A.4 Mi mundo familiar

- Vocabulary: talk about your world at home; what you are and aren't allowed to do
- Grammar: use *(no) me permite(n) / (no) puedo*
- Skills: summarise and recount

NC 4

1 Empareja las frases con los dibujos.

Ejemplo: **1 h**

1 llevar lo que quiero
2 poner la música muy alta
3 acostarme cuando quiero
4 tener un trabajo a tiempo parcial
5 tener una televisión en mi dormitorio
6 invitar a mis amigos a mi casa
7 salir cuando quiero
8 tener piercings

2 Escucha. ¿Qué puede hacer Roberto? ¿Es diferente en España y en Colombia? Copia y completa la tabla.

NC 4

	España (tíos)	Colombia (madre)
invitar a mis amigos a mi casa	los fines de semana solamente	cuando quiero
poner la música muy alta		
llevar		
salir		
acostarme		
tener un trabajo a tiempo parcial		
tener una televisión		
tener piercings		

estricto/a – *strict*
indulgente – *lenient*
sereno/a – *laid back*
anticuado/a – *old-fashioned*

⚙ Gramática

***permitir* – to allow (1)**

Mi madre **me permite** – *My mother allows me*
Mis padres **no me permiten** – *My parents don't allow me*
You can also use *puedo* and *no puedo* to say what you are/are not allowed to do.

3 Escribe dos listas. ¿Qué te permiten hacer? ¿Qué no te permiten?

NC 4

Ejemplo: Mis padres me permiten 1 llevar lo que quiero, 2 tener una televisión ...

¿Y tú? ¿Qué puedes hacer? Discute con un compañero.

NC 3–4

Ejemplo: **A** *¿Puedes tener un piercing?*
B *No, mis padres no me permiten.*
A *¿Tus padres te permiten salir cuando quieres?*
B *No, solamente puedo salir los fines de semana.*

 Explica a otra persona.

NC 4

Ejemplo: Megan puede tener un piercing, pero no puede tener una televisión en su dormitorio. Sus padres le permiten salir cuando quiere.

Completa el email con los verbos de la casilla.

NC 4

Ejemplo: 1 puede

Gramática

***permitir* – to allow (2)**

How to say what other people are allowed to do:

Su madre **le** permite – *His/her mother allows **him/her***

Sus padres no **les** permiten – ***Their** parents don't allow **them***

You can also use *puede(n)* and *no puede(n)* to say what other people are allowed to do:
John puede salir cuando quiere pero no puede tener un piercing.

¡Hola, hermanita! ¿Qué tal?

Aquí todo es muy raro. Los tíos son muy diferentes a mamá. Se **1** ▢ hacer una cosa que no se **2** ▢ hacer en Colombia, pero no se puede **3** ▢ otras que mamá permite. Te explico. No **4** ▢ poner la música muy alta, no puedo acostarme cuando quiero, y los tíos no me **5** ▢ tener una televisión en mi dormitorio. Pero me **6** ▢ salir cuando quiero (¡No lo digas a mamá!). En cambio, los tíos solamente nos **7** ▢ invitar a los amigos a casa los fines de semana. ¡En casa invitamos a nuestros amigos todos los días! También **8** ▢ que ayudar en casa más que en Colombia. Juan y yo **9** ▢ que bajar la basura todos los días. **10** ▢ hacer mi cama y recoger el dormitorio, pero la verdad es que lo **11** ▢ raramente … También – ¡qué horror! – los tíos no **12** ▢ lavaplatos. ¡Qué anticuados! Así que Juan, Elena y yo **13** ▢ que lavar los platos cada noche. ¡Imagínate! Soy un desastre porque siempre rompo algo – ¡tres platos y cuatro vasos la semana pasada! No me gusta nada lavar los platos …

Besos

Roberto

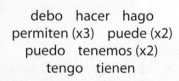

debo   hacer   hago
permiten (x3)   puede (x2)
puedo   tenemos (x2)
tengo   tienen

en cambio – whereas

? Think

Read the email. How do you say:
'It's very strange here'?
'Don't tell mum!'?
'On the other hand'?
Why is Roberto a disaster with the washing up? (Clue: *romper* = to break)

 Escribe un resumen. ¿Qué puede, no puede, debe y tiene que hacer Roberto en Segovia?

NC 4

Ejemplo: Roberto puede salir cuando quiere …

Challenge

Write a few sentences about what you can do at home, what you must do and what you would like to be able to do. You could also write about what you were not allowed to do when you were younger.

NC 4–6

4A.5 ⟫⟫ Tenemos que ayudar ⟫⟫

- Vocabulary: tell others how to care for the environment
- Grammar: use the imperative to write rules
- Skills: speak and write for different audiences – using *tú* and *usted*

Soy Lucía. Soy ecologista en el parque nacional de Doñana. Aquí están las normas del parque: son muy importantes para proteger el medio ambiente.

1 **Recicla latas y papeles.**

2 **No tires basura.**

3 **Ahorra agua.**

4 **No caces animales.**

5 **Utiliza las papeleras.**

6 **Evita hacer ruido.**

7 **No hagas fuego.**

 ESCUCHAR 1 **Escucha las normas de Doñana.**

 LEER 2 **Decide con tu compañero qué significan las normas. Escribe las normas en inglés.**

NC 3–4

Ejemplo: 1 Recycle tins and paper.

 LEER 3 **Empareja las dos partes de las frases.**

NC 4

1 No hacer fuego es muy importante porque
2 Reciclar es muy importante porque
3 No tirar basura es muy importante porque
4 Evitar hacer ruido es muy importante porque
5 Ahorrar agua es muy importante porque
6 No cazar a los animales es muy importante porque
7 Utilizar las papeleras es muy importante porque

a es más limpio.
b es muy peligroso para los animales y los humanos.
c es necesaria para los animales y las plantas.
d es muy sucio.
e están en peligro de extinción.
f protege el planeta.
g no se debe asustar a los animales.

cazar – *to hunt*
evitar – *to avoid*
el ruido – *noise*
el fuego – *fire*
peligroso/a – *dangerous*
sucio/a – *dirty*
asustar – *to frighten*

HABLAR 4

NC 3

Trabaja en un grupo. Pon las normas en orden de importancia.

Ejemplo: **1** *No hagas fuego,* **2** *Utiliza las papeleras ...*

HABLAR 5

NC 4

Presenta tu opinión a la clase.

Ejemplo: Para mí, evitar fuegos es la norma más importante porque son muy peligrosos para los animales y los humanos ...

ESCUCHAR 6

NC 5

🎧 **Escucha. ¿Cuáles son las normas del Demonio del Desastre, y cuáles son normas ecológicas?**

Ejemplo: **1** *No ahorres agua – Demonio del Desastre*

¡SOY EL DEMONIO DEL DESASTRE!

⚙️ **Gramática →** p.166

The imperative (polite form)

When you learnt directions (*Zoom 1*, Unit 2B) you met familiar and polite instructions. Here is how to give polite instructions – using *usted, ustedes* – for all types of verbs.

¡Señor, cierre la puerta, por favor! – *Close the door please, sir.*
Señoras, no enciendan la luz – *Don't turn the light on, ladies.*

	positive		negative	
	usted	ustedes	usted	ustedes
-ar verbs	ahorre – *save*	ahorren – *save*	no ahorre – *don't save*	no ahorren – *don't save*
-er verbs	coma – *eat*	coman – *eat*	no coma – *don't eat*	no coman – *don't eat*
-ir verbs	escriba – *write*	escriban – *write*	no escriba – *don't write*	no escriban – *don't write*

Compare these with the familiar commands on page 119.

? Think

para mí – for me, in my opinion
How would you say 'for us, in our opinion'?

? Think

cazar – to hunt
no caces – don't hunt (*tú*)
no cace – don't hunt (*usted*)
Why do you think the spelling changes?
(Clue: what are the rules of pronunciation in Spanish?)
What other verb used in activity 6 changes in the same way?

LEER 7

👥 **¿Tú, vosotros, usted o ustedes? Trabaja con un compañero y decide.**

Ejemplo: **1** *usted*

1 Ahorre agua.
2 ¡No tiréis basura!
3 Evita hacer ruido.
4 No haga fuego.
5 No cacen animales.
6 Reciclen latas y papeles.
7 Utilicen las papeleras.

Challenge

Draw up rules for your school / home / town, e.g. *No tiréis chicles al suelo* (Don't throw chewing gum on the ground). Which type of instructions would you use? Can you give reasons? For example: *La calle estará muy sucia.*

NC 4–5

Comprender – Negatives and imperatives

A *Nada, nunca, nadie*

You can make a sentence negative by putting *no* in front of the verb:

Me gusta el deporte – *I like sport.*

No me gusta el deporte – *I **don't** like sport.*

To express other negative ideas you use *no* **in front of** the verb plus one of these words **after** it:

No voy **nunca** a la piscina – *I **never** go to the swimming pool.*

La semana pasada **no** compré **nada** en el supermercado – *Last week I **didn't** buy **anything** (I bought **nothing**) in the supermarket.*

Notice how to say 'neither ... nor ...':

No me gustan **ni** el inglés **ni** las ciencias – *I neither like English nor Science.*

nada – *nothing*	no – *no*
nadie – *no-one*	nunca – *never*
ni ... ni ... – *neither ... nor ...*	tampoco – *not ... either*
ningún – *none/not one*	

nada

1 **Make these sentences negative by adding the correct words.**

*Example: **1** Nadie*

1 Todo el mundo estudia español. > ▮▮▮▮ estudia español.

2 Voy a comer un bocadillo o una pizza. > ▮▮▮▮ voy a comer ▮▮▮▮ un bocadillo ▮▮▮▮ una pizza.

3 Siempre vamos de vacaciones a España. > ▮▮▮▮ vamos ▮▮▮▮ de vacaciones a España.

4 Hay mucho que hacer por aquí. > ▮▮▮▮ hay ▮▮▮▮ que hacer por aquí.

5 Mi padre tiene muchos coches. > Mi padre ▮▮▮▮ tiene ▮▮▮▮ coche.

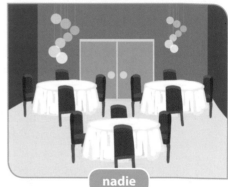

nadie

B *¡No tires chicles al suelo!* – instructions

In Spanish there are lots of different instruction or command forms, where in English we just say 'Do this!' or 'Don't do that!'. You have to pick the right one to use to the right person.

Add the following endings to the stem of the verb:

nunca

	-ar, e.g. ahorrar		-er, e.g. beber		-ir, e.g. subir	
	positive	negative	positive	negative	positive	negative
tú	¡Ahor**ra**! *Save!*	¡No ahor**res**! *Don't save!*	¡Be**be**! *Drink!*	¡No be**bas**! *Don't drink!*	¡Su**be**! *Go up!*	¡No su**bas**! *Don't go up!*
usted	¡Ahor**re**!	¡No ahor**re**!	¡Be**ba**!	¡No be**ba**!	¡Su**ba**!	¡No su**ba**!
vosotros/ as	¡Ahor**rad**!	¡No ahor**réis**!	¡Be**bed**!	¡No be**báis**!	¡Su**bid**!	¡No su**báis**!
ustedes	¡Ahor**ren**!	¡No ahor**ren**!	¡Be**ban**!	¡No be**ban**!	¡Su**ban**!	¡No su**ban**!

2 **Complete these instructions.**

1 ¡(Subir) la escalera! (vosotros)

2 ¡(Reciclar) papel y cartón! (ustedes)

3 ¡No (comer) eso! (usted)

4 ¡No (vivir) aquí! (tú)

5 ¡(Estudiar) más! (vosotros)

Aprender – Writing a formal letter and presenting an argument

C Writing to the local newspaper

If you are writing a formal letter, there are certain things you need to do, just like in English. In this case, Ramón is making a complaint about the state of the streets in Las Palmas. He needs to:

a state what he is writing about
b describe the problem
c state what he would like to happen

> Ramón García
> c/José Franchy y Roca, 56
> 20017 Gran Canaria
>
> Señor Guillermo López
> Director del Diario de las Canarias
> Paseo de las Canteras 143
>
> 22 mayo 2011
>
> Estimado señor
>
> La basura en las calles de Las Palmas <u>presenta un grave problema</u>.
>
> No hay suficientes contenedores para la basura doméstica y la gente deja las bolsas tiradas en la calle. <u>Además</u>, tampoco hay suficientes contenedores de reciclaje y la gente no recicla ni latas, ni cartón, ni plástico y éstos acaban en los contenedores para la basura normal, donde no hay espacio.
>
> <u>En mi opinión, se necesitan</u> más contenedores para la basura normal y para el reciclaje. Así, las calles estarán más limpias y la ciudad será más agradable para los turistas y para los residentes de Las Palmas.
>
> Reciba un cordial saludo
>
> Atentamente
>
> Ramón García

3 Identify parts a, b and c of this letter.

4 How do you say 'Dear Sir' and 'Yours sincerely' in Spanish?

5 How would you address a lady?

6 Write a letter to a paper complaining about the state of your local park; there is a lot of litter, and kids have been lighting fires and making noise late at night. You can use this letter as a model.

Hablar – Appropriate language

D Saying the right thing

As well as remembering to use *tú* or *usted*, it is important to realise that the words you use can sound familiar or polite, just like in English.

So if you are lost, and ask someone your own age the way, you might say *Hola, dime, ¿dónde está ...?* (Hi there, can you tell me, where's the ...?)

But if you ask an older lady it would be more polite to say *Perdone, señora, ¿sabe usted dónde está ...?* (Excuse me, madam, do you know where the ... is?)

7 Familiar or polite? Decide in what situation you might say these things.

1 ¡No comas eso, es mi bocadillo!
2 Lo siento, pero no se permiten perros en el parque.
3 ¡No escribáis en el libro! ¡Escribid en el cuaderno!
4 Perdone, señor, no beba esa Coca-Cola. Es mía.
5 ¡No entres en casa con esos zapatos sucios!
6 Perdone, señora, pero eso no es una buena idea ...

- Vocabulary: talk about environmental problems and their solutions
- Grammar: practise *tú* imperatives
- Skills: write instructions

LEER 1

NC 3

Empareja las fotos con las frases. Completa las frases con las palabras de la casilla.
Match the photos with the sentences. Complete the sentences using the words in the box.

~~basura~~ climático contaminación exterminio naturaleza sufrimiento

*Ejemplo: **1** f, basura*

1 En las calles de mi ciudad, hay mucha ▮▮▮▮▮ .

2 Hay demasiado ▮▮▮▮▮ humano en el mundo.

3 La destrucción de la ▮▮▮▮▮ es un problema en América Latina.

4 En mi opinión, el problema más grave es el ▮▮▮▮▮ de los animales.

5 La ▮▮▮▮▮ atmosférica es un problema grave en algunas ciudades.

6 Para mí, el problema más grave es el cambio ▮▮▮▮▮ .

LEER 2

NC 2

Empareja las instrucciones en español con las en inglés.
Match the Spanish and English instructions.

1 ¡Recicla!
2 ¡Usa la ducha!
3 ¡Protege el medio ambiente!
4 ¡No uses el coche!
5 ¡Protesta contra el calentamiento global!
6 ¡Planta árboles!

a Protect the environment!
b Plant trees!
c Don't use the car!
d Recycle!
e Use the shower!
f Protest against global warming!

ESCRIBIR 3

NC 3

Completa las soluciones a los problemas de la actividad 1.
Complete the solutions to the problems in activity 1.

*Ejemplo: **1** ¡Usa las papeleras!*

1 ¡▮▮▮▮ las papeleras!
2 ¡▮▮▮▮ contra la pobreza!
3 ¡▮▮▮▮ los hábitats!
4 ¡▮▮▮▮ el medio ambiente!
5 ¡No ▮▮▮▮ el coche!
6 ¡▮▮▮▮ árboles!

~~usa~~ protesta proteja (x2) uses planta

- Vocabulary: understand environmental problems and their solutions
- Grammar: practise using polite imperatives
- Skills: summarise a text

LEER 1

NC 4

Completa los textos con las palabras de abajo, y empareja el texto con la foto del problema medioambiental.

contaminación   destrucción de la naturaleza
calentamiento global   cambio climático

el casquete polar – *ice cap*
derretirse – *to melt*
cultivar – *to grow crops*
destruir – *to destroy*
la salud – *health*

1
El ▮▮▮ ya afecta mucho a las regiones polares del mundo. El casquete polar se derrite cada vez más, y el hábitat de animales como el oso polar y los pingüinos desaparecerá.

2
En las regiones más calientes del mundo se nota mucho el efecto del ▮▮▮. En algunos países llueve mucho menos. Es difícil cultivar, y la tierra parece un desierto.

3
El problema de la ▮▮▮ ocurre a menudo en los países pobres. Deforestan las selvas porque los gobiernos necesitan dinero. Eso destruye los hábitats de miles de animales.

4
Es un problema muy grave en las grandes ciudades del mundo, donde hay mucho tráfico, muchas fábricas, y montones de basura. La ▮▮▮ atmosférica causará problemas de salud para sus habitantes.

LEER 2

NC 4

¿Qué describe cada texto? Escribe notas en inglés.

Ejemplo: **1** *polar ice-cap melting – habitats disappearing ...*

ESCRIBIR 3

NC 4–6

Escribe una frase para cada texto.

Ejemplo: **1** *El calentamiento global es un problema en las regiones polares porque desaparece el hábitat de muchos animales.*

ESCRIBIR 4

NC 4–6

Escribe al director de tu instituto sobre un problema medioambiental. ¿Cuál es el problema? ¿Y la causa? ¿Hay una solución?

? Think

Use as many tenses as you can in your writing. In activities 3 and 4, you need to include **two** tenses to achieve a level 5, and **three** tenses for a level 6.

Escuchar

NC 4

Escuchar

Listen and choose the correct picture for each instruction you hear.

a  **b**  **c**  **d**  **e**

Hablar

NC 5

Hablar

Ask your partner what can be done to help the environment, and what they do. Use the pictures if you want to.

¿Qué se puede hacer para ayudar al medio ambiente?

Example: Se puede reciclar botellas y papel.

¿Qué haces tú?

Example: Uso transporte público.

¿Qué harás en el futuro?

Example: Llevaré mis propias bolsas al supermercado.

Leer

NC 4

Leer

Read the text. Note down in Spanish three things we can do to help the environment, and three things we must not do.

No es difícil ayudar a proteger el medio ambiente. Todos podemos usar la ducha o el transporte público. Además es bueno para la salud ir a pie a veces. Es muy importante no contaminar nuestro planeta. No se debe tirar basura al suelo – hay que ponerla en las papeleras. En el campo, hay que proteger la naturaleza. No se deben ni cazar animales en peligro de extinción ni usar mucha agua. ¡Ayude al planeta!

Escribir

NC 5–6

Escribir

Write a short paragraph (about 4 or 5 sentences) about what you are allowed to do at home. Say what you were allowed to do when you were younger and what you will be able to do when you are 18.

¿Cómo es tu mundo?	How's your world?
la basura	rubbish/litter
la contaminación (atmosférica)	(air) pollution
la destrucción de la naturaleza	destruction of nature
la extinción de animales	extinction of animals
el cambio climático	climate change
el sufrimiento humano	human suffering
cien	100
doscientos	200
quinientos	500
setecientos	700
novecientos	900
mil	1,000
un millón	1,000,000
en peligro	in danger
agua limpia	clean water
los glaciares	glaciers
la papelera	litter bin
tirar basura	to throw litter
limpio/a	clean
la selva	the rainforest
ganar dinero	to earn money

¿Qué podemos hacer?	What can we do?
reciclar	to recycle
usar transporte público	to use public transport
llevar tus propias bolsas al supermercado	to take your own bags to the supermarket
apagar las luces	to turn the lights out
ahorrar agua	to save water
plantar árboles	to plant trees
comprar productos ecológicos	to buy eco-products
protestar	to protest
se puede	we can
se debe	we must
hay que	we have to
tener que	to have to
ahorrar	to save
usar	to use
ayudar	to help

Y tú, ¿cuidas del mundo?	And do you look after the world?
no	no
nada	nothing
ningún	none
ni ... ni ...	neither ... nor ...
tampoco	not ... either
nadie	no-one
nunca	never
productos de comercio justo	Fairtrade products

proyectos medioambientales	environmental projects
trabajar como voluntario	to do charity / volunteer work

Mi mundo familiar	My home environment
llevar lo que quiero	to wear what I like
poner la música muy alta	to play music really loudly
acostarme cuando quiero	to go to bed when I want
tener un trabajo a tiempo parcial	to have a part-time job
tener una televisión en mi habitación	to have a TV in my room
invitar a mis amigos a mi casa	to invite my friends to my house
salir cuando quiero	to go out when I want
tener piercings	to have body piercings
estricto/a	strict
indulgente	lenient
guay	cool
sereno/a	laid back
anticuado/a	old-fashioned
permitir	to allow
raro/a	strange
no lo digas	don't tell
en cambio	on the other hand/whereas

Tenemos que ayudar	We have to help
tirar	to throw / drop
cazar	to hunt
evitar	to avoid
el ruido	noise
el fuego	fire
peligroso/a	dangerous
sucio/a	dirty
asustar	to frighten

🎯 I can ...

- ◉ describe problems with the environment and their causes
- ◉ use superlatives (*el/la ... más ...*)
- ◉ give opinions using *para mí, en mi opinión*
- ◉ understand and use very large numbers
- ◉ talk about what we can and have to do to help the environment
- ◉ use expressions to say 'we can', 'we have to', 'we must'.
- ◉ use the imperative
- ◉ use negatives
- ◉ talk about my world at home; what I am and am not allowed to do
- ◉ tell others how to care for the environment
- ◉ write a formal letter and set out an argument

- Vocabulary: give key facts about a country
- Gramática: use comparatives and superlatives
- Skills: carry out research on the internet

 LEER 1 **Lee los expedientes. ¿De qué país se trata?**

EXPEDIENTE 1

Nombre:
Habitantes: 17,1 millones
Capital: Santiago
Extensión: 756.096 km²
Idioma principal: español
Moneda: peso
Exportación: cobre, pescado, fruta, papel, sustancias químicas
Salario mínimo: 258€ por mes

EXPEDIENTE 2

Nombre:
Habitantes: 40,6 millones
Capital: Buenos Aires
Extensión: 2.000.000 km²
Idioma principal: español
Moneda: peso
Exportación: comida y animales vivos, combustibles minerales, cereales, maquinaria
Salario mínimo: 299€ por mes

EXPEDIENTE 3

Nombre:
Habitantes: 29,4 millones
Capital: Lima
Extensión: 1.280.000 km²
Idiomas principales: español, quechua, aymara
Moneda: nuevo sol
Exportación: pescado, cobre, zinc, oro, petróleo crudo y derivados, plomo, café, azúcar, algodón
Salario mínimo: 139€ por mes

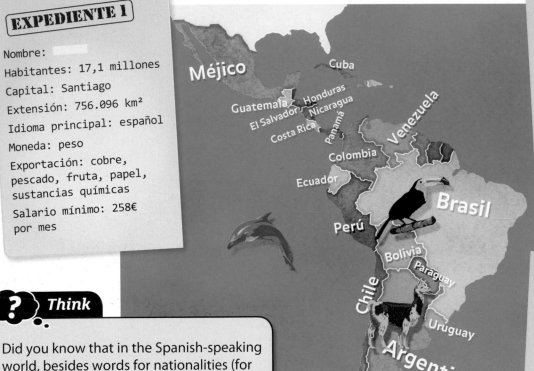

? Think

Did you know that in the Spanish-speaking world, besides words for nationalities (for example *chileno* for someone from Chile), there is a name for the people who live in each and every city?

Roberto is from Cartagena so is *cartaginés* or *cartaginense*. *Madrileños/as* live in Madrid, *segovianos/as* in Segovia.

 LEER 2 **Lee. ¿Verdad o mentira?**

NC 4 *Ejemplo: 1 verdad*

1 Argentina es más grande que Perú.
2 El salario mínimo de los peruanos es más alto que el de los chilenos.
3 Hay menos chilenos que peruanos.
4 Chile es más pequeño que Argentina.
5 Argentina exporta menos productos que Chile.

 LEER 3 **Corrige las frases falsas.**

 Gramática → p.169

Comparatives and superlatives

Remember!
más ... que – *more ... than*
menos ... que – *less ... than*
el/la más ... – *the most ...*
el/la menos ... – *the least ...*

LEER 4

NC 4

Lee el informe de Roberto. Completa el expediente 4 sobre Colombia.

EXPEDIENTE 4

Nombre: Colombia
Habitantes: 46.300
Capital:
Extensión: 1.140.000 km²
Idiomas principales:
Moneda:
Exportación:
Salario mínimo: 207€

EXPEDIENTE 5

Nombre:
Habitantes:
Capital:
Extensión:
Idioma principal:
Moneda:
Exportación:
Salario mínimo:

Gramática → p.169

More comparatives

Remember:

tan *(adjective)* como ... –
as (adjective) as ...

Chile no es **tan grande como** Argentina – *Chile is not as big as Argentina.*

tanto/tanta/tantos/tantas *(noun)* como ... – *as much/many (noun) as ...*

Chile exporta **tantos productos como** Argentina – *Chile exports as many products as Argentina.*

Colombia es el cuarto país más grande de Sudamérica y aunque <u>no es tan grande como Argentina</u>, es más grande que Ecuador, Uruguay o Paraguay.

La capital se encuentra en el interior del país y se llama Bogotá.

Nuestra moneda oficial es el peso colombiano y la lengua oficial y más común es el español. Sin embargo, en Colombia <u>hay tantas lenguas indígenas como en los otros países sudamericanos</u>.

Los colombianos exportan muchos productos al exterior, como por ejemplo petróleo, esmeraldas u oro. También exportan productos químicos, algodón, café, plátanos, azúcar y ganado.

LEER 5

Copia las frases subrayadas. ¿Qué significan en inglés?

ESCUCHAR 6

NC 4

 Escucha y rellena el expediente 5 de arriba.

ESCRIBIR 7

Investigación. Crea tu propio expediente sobre otro país latinoamericano.

 **Think**

Remember to plan your research by making a list of the particular information you need and then be specific with your searches.

 **Challenge**

Prepare an oral presentation about the Spanish-speaking country you chose for activity 7. Try and use present, past and future tenses to reach level 6.

NC 4–6

- Vocabulary: revise describing people
- Grammar: revise use of adjectives and recognise idiomatic uses of *tener*
- Skills: identify false friends

LEER 1

Clasifica las palabras. Escríbelas en la columna adecuada.

Nacionalidad: Es ...	Profesión: Es ...	Descripción (pelo): Tiene el pelo ...	Descripción (ojos): Tiene los ojos ...	Descripción (general): Es ...
cubano/a	cantante	corto	azules	guapo/a

HABLAR 2

¿Quién es quién? Elige un famoso latinoamericano. Adivina el famoso de tu compañero: tu compañero sólo puede responder "sí", "no" o "no sé".

Ejemplo: (Salma Hayek)

A ¿Es cantante?
B No.
A ¿Es hombre?
B No.
A ¿Es guapa?
B Sí. (etc.)

~~guapo/a~~ ~~corto~~ ~~azules~~ actriz rubio ~~cubano/a~~
argentino/a viejo/a verdes hombre actor
mujer largo joven simpático/a ~~cantante~~
moreno mejicano/a ondulado marrones
gris futbolista rizado puertorriqueño/a
castaño escritor(a) negros pintor(a) artista
uruguayo/a productor(a) de cine calvo
pelirrojo blanco negro gris colombiano/a

Shakira; Colombia; cantante

Christina Aguilera; Estados Unidos/ Ecuador (su padre); cantante

Salma Hayek; Méjico; actriz y productora de cine

Lionel Messi; Argentina; futbolista

Frida Kahlo; Méjico; artista/pintora

Gabriel García Márquez; Colombia; escritor/ganador del Premio Nobel

Carlos Tévez; Argentina; futbolista

Gramática → p.158

Adjectives

Remember:
Adjectives must agree with the noun they describe:
un hombre colombian**o** *but* una mujer colombian**a**

Also remember to place them after the noun they describe!

NC 5 **Escucha y lee. Luego completa las frases.**

Consciente de la situación en su país, cuando tenía sólo dieciocho años la simpática cantante colombiana Shakira fundó la Fundación Pies Descalzos. La Fundación se dedica a atender a los niños pobres, particularmente a los niños que tienen que soportar una pobreza extrema.

Actualmente Pies Descalzos apoya a seis colegios colombianos. Más de cinco mil niños asisten a estos colegios donde, además de educación, también reciben comida y apoyo psicológico.

La Fundación de Shakira tiene mucho éxito pero muchos más niños colombianos necesitan ayuda.

1 The singer Shakira founded Barefoot Foundation when she was ...
2 The Foundation takes care of ...
3 At present Barefoot supports ...
4 These schools are attended by more than ...

 Escucha otra vez. ¿Qué significan estas palabras? Utiliza las frases de la actividad 3 para ayudarte.

*Ejemplo: **1** kind/nice (not sympathetic!)*

1 simpática **4** actualmente
2 atender **5** asistir
3 soportar **6** éxito

 Gramática → p.167

Idiomatic uses of *tener*

Remember that when you give your age in Spanish you use the verb *tener* (to have) and not the verb *ser* (to be). There are several common occasions when in English we use the verb 'to be' but in Spanish we use the verb 'to have'. These are known as idiomatic uses of *tener*.

to **be** eighteen = *tener dieciocho años* (literally: to **have** 18 years)

to **be** successful = *tener éxito* (literally: to **have** success)

Find the examples in the text in activity 3 above.

Find more examples of idiomatic uses of *tener* on page 142.

 Escribe seis frases usando las palabras de la actividad 4.

? Think

Beware of false friends! For example:

librería = bookshop (*library* = biblioteca)

embarazada = pregnant (to embarrass – avergonzar)

Which English words do the words in activity 4 resemble?

Challenge

Choose a celebrity from activity 2 and write a detailed description of them. You should include their age, nationality, profession, a physical description, something about his/her personality, a recent success, what they'll do in the future and your opinion of the celebrity. Use past, present and future tenses to reach level 6.

NC 5–6

4B.3 ¡Vamos a celebrar!

- Vocabulary: find out about some Latin American festivals
- Grammar: use *soler* + infinitive when talking about the past
- Skills: pronounce *ñ* correctly

El Día de Todos los Santos

El Día de la Raza

La Fiesta de la Virgen del Carmen

La Semana Santa

Las Fiestas Patrias

ESCUCHAR 1 🎧 **Escucha. ¿En qué orden se mencionan estos festivales latinoamericanos?**

Ejemplo: c, ...

ESCUCHAR 2 🎧 **Escucha otra vez. ¿En qué país o países se celebran? ¿Cuándo?**

Ejemplo: c – Perú, 16 de julio

LEER 3 **Lee y empareja las frases en español con las en inglés.**

NC 4 *Ejemplo: 1 b*

1 La Fiesta de la Virgen del Carmen es una colorida mezcla de ceremonias precolombinas y católicas.
2 En el Día de Todos los Santos se reafirma la vida y se honran los santos y los muertos.
3 En el Día de la Raza se celebra la herencia hispana de América Latina, resultado de la llegada de Cristóbal Colón en 1492.
4 La Semana Santa es el festival católico más importante de Sudamérica donde se celebra el último día de la vida de Jesucristo, su muerte y su resurrección.
5 Las Fiestas Patrias celebran la fecha en que Chile dejó de ser una colonia española y consiguió la independencia.

a It celebrates the Hispanic heritage of Latin America, a result of the arrival of Christopher Columbus in 1492.
b It is a colourful mix of pre-Columbian ceremonies and Catholic religion.
c It is the most important Catholic festival in South America. It celebrates Christ's last day of life, his death and resurrection.
d This celebration is a reaffirmation of life and honours the saints and those who have died.
e It celebrates the country's independence.

> ⚙ **Gramática** → p.167
>
> **Impersonal *se***
>
> *Remember:*
> When the subject of a verb is unspecified (but human), the ending for 'he'/'she' is generally used.
>
> En Latinoamérica **se come** bien – *In Latin America **one** eats well.*

▶ El Video Reto

VIDEO 4

Mira el video y contesta a las preguntas en inglés.

a Juan and Elena suggest two possible activities for their last weekend. What are they?

b Roberto doesn't like the ideas much. Why not? What does he want to do?

c What does Roberto say about travelling?

VIDEO 5

Do you think the festival was a nice way for Roberto to finish his stay in Segovia? Why?

ESCUCHAR 6

🎧 **Lee y escucha a Roberto. ¿Cómo dice …?**

NC 5

1 I used to visit
2 we used to see
3 we used to go for a walk
4 we used to attend

? Think

Remember to get your **ñ**s right: listen to how Roberto pronounces *pequeño* and *niño*. Draw its 'hat' when writing and pronounce it correctly. Other sounds you need to practise are *ll* (as in *Medellín*) and *r* at the beginning of a word (***R**ecuerdo …*).

La Feria de las Flores, Medellín

Recuerdo que cuando era pequeño solía visitar a mis abuelos en Medellín a principios de agosto. En Medellín mis abuelos, mi madre y yo solíamos ir a la Feria de las Flores donde solíamos ver el Desfile de los Silleteros que es un desfile muy bonito y colorido.

A mi madre le gustan mucho las flores, así que durante la feria solíamos pasear por las exposiciones de orquídeas y también solíamos ver los desfiles de autos antiguos ya que a mí me encantan los coches. Además, solíamos asistir a un espectáculo diferente cada noche.

Ahora no suelo ir tan frecuentemente como cuando era niño.

⚙ Gramática → p.166

Soler + infinitive

If you are talking about the past, then you will need the imperfect tense: *I **used to** go to the cinema – **Solía** ir al cine.*

Challenge

Write about a celebration you used to go to when you were little. Do you still go? When will you go again? Include description and past and present opinions.

Example: Cuando era niño solía ir a casa de mis amigos en 'Bonfire Night' …

NC 5–6

- Vocabulary: talk about the importance of language learning
- Grammar: use *lo* + adjective to express opinions
- Skills: use grammar knowledge to eliminate wrong answers in reading tasks

LEER 1

Mira las fotos de los famosos. Todos hablan más de una lengua. Adivina los cuatro que hablan español.

Gwyneth Paltrow

Nick Clegg

Gary Lineker

Arnold Schwarzenegger

Eva Longoria

Emma Watson

LEER 2

Lee. ¿Sabías que ...? Empareja las dos partes de las frases.

Ejemplo: **1 f**

1 Sólo el 6% de la población mundial
2 El 75% de la población mundial
3 El 77% de las compañías británicas dedicadas a la exportación
4 En el Reino Unido, una persona que habla idiomas
5 El español
6 Más de seis millones de británicos

a no habla nada de inglés.
b se habla en veintitrés países.
c gana unas £3000 más al año que una que no los habla.
d pierden contratos porque no pueden hablar idiomas.
e visitan España cada año.
f habla inglés como lengua materna.

? Think

Use your grammar knowledge to help you with this type of exercise. Identify the subject in the sentence in order to work out the likely ending of the verb. This will limit your choices!

Escucha. ¿Por qué estudian otro idioma? Escribe las letras correctas.

NC 4

Ejemplo: **1** c

a It helps your memory.
b It gives you self-confidence.
c It's fun and entertaining.
d It looks good on your CV.
e It shows you have good communication skills.
f It shows respect for other cultures.
g It gives you the ability to communicate with other nationalities.

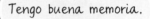

Gramática → p.168

Lo + adjective

Use *lo* + adjective to add variety to your opinions:

Lo difícil de aprender idiomas es la gramática – *The difficult thing* about language learning is grammar.

Lo mejor de Latinoamérica es su diversidad – *The best thing* about Latin America is its diversity.

Lo bueno del Caribe es su clima – *The good thing* about the Caribbean is the weather.

¿Qué dicen los idiomas sobre ti? Lee y empareja las frases con los dibujos.

NC 4

Ejemplo: **1** b

1 Ya sé muchas palabras y cómo escribirlas.
2 Me considero ciudadano del mundo. Quiero ver cómo se vive en otros países y descubrir el resto del planeta.
3 No me preocupo si lo que digo no es perfecto, lo importante es poder comunicarme.
4 No soy una de esas personas que consideran que su manera de pensar es siempre la mejor. La variedad y las diferencias entre países me divierten.

Estoy seguro de mí mismo.

Tengo buena memoria.

a   **b**

En tu opinión, ¿qué es lo mejor/peor de aprender un idioma? Haz una lista.

NC 4

Lo mejor ...   Lo peor ...
Oportunidades de trabajo   Es difícil.

Soy consciente de otras culturas.

Estoy abierto a nuevas experiencias y culturas.

c   **d**

Debate con un compañero:

NC 4

- ¿Es importante aprender idiomas? ¿Por qué?
- ¿Qué es lo mejor de aprender un idioma extranjero?
- ¿Qué dicen los idiomas sobre la persona?

Challenge

Prepare a 60-second video sketch promoting language learning. Be as creative and original as possible. Try to use some of the language you have learnt on these two pages.

NC 4

- Vocabulary: describe people's nationality and personality
- Grammar: revise adjectival agreement
- Skills: sound Spanish when pronouncing cognates

Bolivia

Costa Rica

La República Dominicana

Soy ...
boliviano/a
costarricense
dominicano/a
ecuatoriano/a
hondureño/a
mejicano/a

Ecuador

Honduras

Méjico

Escribe las frases: Es ... / Son ...

*Ejemplo: **a** Son de la República Dominicana. Son dominicanas.*

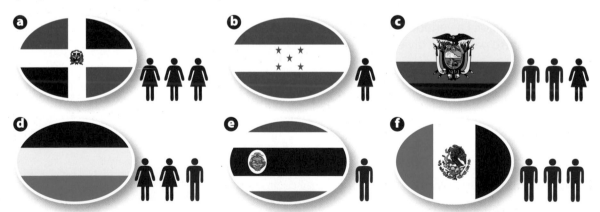

Lee, copia y rellena los espacios.

NC 3 Méjico es un *país* de 1,96 millones de kilómetros cuadrados de _____ donde viven casi 111 millones de _____. La _____ de Méjico es Ciudad de Méjico y su _____ es el español. El peso es la _____ del país y los mejicanos ganan un _____ de al menos 3,25€ por día.

idioma principal   salario mínimo   capital   ~~país~~
habitantes   moneda   extensión

? Think

Remember: in Spanish, nationalities, languages, days of the week and months of the year do not begin with a capital letter unless they are right at the beginning of a sentence!

3 Categoriza los adjetivos. ¿Son positivos o negativos? Adivina su significado.

Positivo	Negativo
ambicioso/a	cruel

~~ambicioso/a~~ conservador(a) ~~cruel~~ honesto/a modesto/a introvertido/a extrovertido/a generoso/a responsable moderno/a inteligente popular serio/a agresivo/a violento/a adorable

4 Escribe otros seis o más adjetivos de personalidad en tu lista.

5 🎧 Escucha y escoge la respuesta correcta.

NC 5

1 Salma Hayek es una actriz
  a chilena.
  b boliviana.
  c mejicana.
2 Nació el
  a tres de agosto.
  b dos de septiembre.
  c doce de septiembre.
3 Su madre era
  a cantante de ópera.
  b secretaria.
  c profesora de música.

4 De joven Salma solía practicar
  a el baloncesto.
  b la gimnasia.
  c la natación.
5 Ahora es la actriz mejicana
  a menos famosa del mundo.
  b más famosa del mundo.
  c más cara del mundo.
6 Salma Hayek es
  a bonita, audaz y simpática.
  b alegre, profesional y audaz.
  c bonita, audaz e inteligente.

6 👥 Imagina que eres Salma Hayek. Contesta a las preguntas.

NC 5

A ¿Dónde naciste? ¿Cuál es tu nacionalidad?
B Nací en … Soy …
A ¿En qué trabaja(ba) tu madre?
B Mi madre es/era …
A ¿Qué solías hacer cuando eras más joven?
B Solía …
A ¿Cómo te describirías?
B En mi opinión soy …

 **Challenge**

Use your partner's answers to activity 7 to write a passage about him/her. Include at least two tenses.

NC 5

7 👥 Entrevista a tu compañero utilizando las preguntas de la actividad 6. Toma notas de sus respuestas.

NC 5

4B.6 Labolengua

Comprender – Comparatives and superlatives, *tener* and *soler*

A Comparatives and superlatives

When you're talking about one thing, it's 'easy' – *fácil* (adjective):
La tarea es fácil – The task is easy.

When you're comparing it to something else, it's 'easier than' – ***más** fácil **que*** (comparative): *La tarea 2 es más fácil que la 3* – Task 2 is easier than 3.

Or you can also say 'it's less complicated than' – ***menos** complicado **que*** (comparative): *El ejercicio 3 es menos complicado que el ejercicio 2* – Exercise 3 is less complicated than exercise 2.

At times you want to say that something is 'the most/ the least' (superlative): the easiest = *el/la más fácil*. *La tarea 4 es la más fácil* – Task 4 is the easiest.

1 **Look at the outfits. Write sentences about them using the structures given. You may want to use the adjectives in the box.**

Example: El traje cubano es menos extravagante que el traje peruano.

traje mejicano

traje peruano

traje cubano

1 Cuban, less ... than
2 Mexican, more ... than
3 Peruvian, more ... than
4 Cuban, the most ...
5 Mexican, the least ...
6 Peruvian, the most ...

moderno colorido
extravagante elegante
divertido cómodo

B Idiomatic uses of *tener*

Besides when expressing your age, e.g. *tengo catorce años*, there are many occasions where in English we use the verb 'to be' + adjective and in Spanish we use the verb *tener* + noun. Here are some common examples:

tener hambre/sed – *to be hungry/thirsty*	tener calor/frío – *to be hot/cold*
tener éxito – *to be successful*	tener miedo – *to be scared*
tener razón – *to be right*	tener suerte – *to be lucky*

2 **Write the correct word.**

1 Jorge _____ doce años. *Jorge is 12 years old.*
2 Llevo la chaqueta porque _____ frío. *I am wearing my jacket because I am cold.*
3 Bebo agua porque tengo _____. *I drink water because I am thirsty.*
4 Tiene salud, dinero y amor; tiene mucha _____. *He has health, money and love; he is very lucky.*
5 Es muy inteligente, siempre tiene _____. *He is very intelligent, he is always right.*
6 Tengo _____ de las arañas. *I am scared of spiders.*

C *Soler* + infinitive

The structure *soler* + infinitive is used to refer to what is **usually** done or, when used in the imperfect, what one **used to** do in the past.

Suelo ir a Argentina en verano – *I usually go to Argentina in summer*.

Imperfect:

solía	solíamos
solías	solíais
solía	solían

Solía ir a Argentina en verano – *I used to go to Argentina in summer*.

3 Write these sentences in the imperfect.

1 Suelo celebrar las Navidades en Méjico.
2 Solemos ir en coche.
3 Mi abuela suele cocinar mucha comida.
4 En Navidad suele hacer bastante calor.
5 Solemos comer excesivamente.

Aprender – Vocabulary learning

D False friends

Amongst the hundreds of cognates which do have the same meaning in English and Spanish, there are some you must watch out for because they have totally different meanings.

4 Write what these Spanish words look like. Then look them up in a dictionary and write the correct translation.

	It looks like	It means
Example: pariente	*parent*	*relative*

carpeta   codo   contestar   éxito
ganga   molestar   revolver
ropa   suceso

Hablar – Pronunciation

E The sounds *ll, ñ* and *r/rr*

Sounds that don't exist in your own language can be tricky to pronounce.

ll   The pronunciation of the Spanish *ll* can vary widely from region to region. In some regions it is pronounced like the 'y' in the word 'yes' and in some Latin American countries like the 'j' in 'Jamie'.

ñ   The Spanish *ñ* is pronounced like the 'ny' in the word 'canyon'.

r/rr   Generally the single 'r' doesn't cause problems as it is similar to the English 'r'. However, when a single 'r' is found at the beginning of a word or after an 'l', 'n' or 's', then you will need to roll it as if it were an 'rr'.

5 Practise pronouncing these words. Listen and check your pronunciation.

1 llora (*he cries*), llave (*key*), llueve (*it rains*), llama (*he calls*), lleno (*full*)
2 niño (*boy*), año (*year*), uña (*nail*), baño (*bath*), araña (*spider*)
3 raro (*strange*), Enrique, rico (*rich*), roto (*broken*), carro (*cart*)
4 El perro de San Roque no tiene rabo porque Ramón Rodríguez se lo ha cortado.

- Vocabulary: learn more about the Spanish-speaking world
- Grammar: use comparatives
- Skills: work out the meaning of unfamiliar vocabulary

 Mira las fotos de las actrices de 'Betty la Fea' y lee las frases. ¿Qué opinas?
Look at the photos and read the sentences. What is your opinion?

Ana Ortiz

América Ferrera

1 América Ferrera es más guapa que Ana Ortiz.
2 América Ferrera es más alta que Ana Ortiz.
3 Ana Ortiz es más delgada que América Ferrera.
4 Ana Ortiz es más simpática que América Ferrera.
5 Ana Ortiz es más inteligente que América Ferrera.

 Escribe las frases de otra manera.
Rewrite the sentences without changing their meaning.

NC 3

Ejemplo: 1 Ana Ortiz es menos guapa que América Ferrera.

 ¿Cuál es el origen de los sombreros mejicanos?
Lee y contesta a las preguntas.

NC 5

Where do Mexican sombreros come from? Read and answer the questions.

1 Why was work in the Mexican fields so hard?
2 Why did the labourers wear a straw hat?
3 Who started to wear the wide-brimmed straw hats?
4 Why are they called 'sombreros'?

 Escribe frases comparando estos sombreros.

NC 3

Write a few sentences comparing these hats.

original   elegante   práctico   cómodo

Ejemplo: El sombrero mejicano es más/menos … que el sombrero inglés.

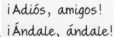

¡Buenos días, amigos!
El trabajo en los campos soleados de Méjico y del sur de los Estados Unidos solía ser muy duro porque hacía mucho sol. Había pocos árboles y había muy poca protección natural del sol. Para protegerse del sol, los trabajadores llevaban un sombrero de paja. En estos climas cálidos, los trabajadores mestizos empezaron a hacer sombreros de ala ancha. La palabra "sombrero" tiene su origen en la palabra "sombra" porque con sus sombreros de ala ancha, los mestizos llevaban su propio pedacito de sombra.
¡Adiós, amigos!
¡Ándale, ándale!

- Vocabulary: describe someone in detail
- Grammar: use comparatives; use the preterite
- Skills: complete gap-fill exercises

1 ESCRIBIR

NC 3

¿Qué sabes de estos dos futbolistas latinoamericanos? Compáralos utilizando los adjetivos de la casilla.

> guapo   alto   bajo   rápido   dotado (*gifted*)

Ejemplo: Messi es más guapo que Rodríguez.

Lionel Messi

Maxi Rodríguez

2 LEER

NC 5

Lee el artículo sobre Maxi Rodríguez y completa su línea cronológica con la información del texto.

Ejemplo: 1981   Nació .

_____ La carrera futbolística de Rodríguez empezó.

2002 _____

2003 _____

2005 _____

2007 _____

_____ Se traspasó al Liverpool.

Maximiliano Rubén Rodríguez *"La Fiera"*

Es un futbolista de mucho éxito. Nació el dos de enero de 1981 en Rosario, Santa Fe. Rodríguez apendió a jugar al fútbol en Argentina y su carrera comenzó en 1999 en Argentina con el Newell's Old Boys. Se trasladó a España en el 2002 y jugó en La Liga con RCD Espanyol durante 3 años. En 2005 se trasladó al Atlético de Madrid por 5 millones de euros. En 2007 fue el capitán del equipo después de la partida de Fernando Torres al Liverpool.

En enero de 2010 Rodríguez se traspasó gratis al Liverpool por tres años y medio. Llevaba la camiseta número 17 pero ahora lleva la número 11. Hasta el momento ha marcado 13 goles con el Liverpool.

También juega para su equipo nacional de Argentina. Su debut fue en 2003 contra Japón.

¡Será un jugador importante para sus equipos en el futuro!

3 LEER

NC 4–5

Copia y completa las frases sobre Maxi Rodríguez con las palabras de la casilla.

1 El _____ Maxi Rodríquez juega para el _____ desde 2010 y para el equipo nacional de _____ desde 2003.

2 En el 2002 Rodríguez _____ a España para jugar con el RCD Espanyol.

3 La carrera de "La Fiera" _____ en Argentina en 1999.

4 El traspaso de Rodríguez no _____ nada al Liverpool.

> futbolista   costó   Liverpool   Argentina   RCD Espanyol
> comenzó   fue   costó

? Think

When attempting a gap fill exercise with a bank of words, don't try to complete it in order. It is much easier if you fill the gaps you know and use elimination techniques for those you are not sure about.

4 ESCRIBIR

NC 4–5

Escribe una descripción completa de Maxi Rodríguez.

NC 5

🎧 Escuchar

Listen to the information about the Dominican Republic and answer the questions in English.

1 What is the size of the Dominican Republic?
2 Where is the Dominican Republic located?
3 Mention two facts about its capital.
4 How many inhabitants are there in the country?
5 What kind of tourist would enjoy going there?

NC 4–6

Hablar

Prepare a 90-second presentation about a period of time in your life when you were younger. You can choose up to 15 words from your presentation to have with you during your test. Include:

- What you used to do, when, where and who with
- If you enjoyed it and why
- If you would like to do it again in the future
- If you do something similar/different now

NC 6

Leer

Read the passage. True or false?

1 Joanna wants to travel in the future.
2 She thinks everyone speaks English.
3 Joanna used to practise new words with her uncle.
4 She thinks she can earn the same amount if she speaks a foreign language.
5 Joanna will spend three weeks with her father next year.

Joanna

> Estudio español y francés porque pienso que en el futuro me van a ser útiles porque quiero viajar. Hay personas que dicen que no es necesario aprender otra lengua porque se habla inglés en todo el mundo pero no es verdad. Mi padre es chileno y cuando era pequeña solía ir de vacaciones a un pueblecito llamado Los Dominicanos en Chile y allí la gente no habla inglés. Solía aprender dos o tres palabras nuevas cada día y solía practicarlas por la noche con mi abuelo. Yo creo que aprender idiomas es muy importante para poder encontrar un buen trabajo y ganar más dinero. El próximo año voy a pasar tres meses en Chile con mi padre así que voy a poder practicar español.

Escribir

Imagine you are a Spanish teacher. Write an article for the school magazine about language learning. You may want to include:

NC 5–6

- An introduction and description of yourself
- What languages you speak
- Why you think learning languages is important
- Where did you go on holiday this year?
- Your plans for your next holiday – will you go somewhere where you speak the language?

Países de habla hispana	Spanish-speaking countries
el expediente	profile
el idioma principal	main language
la moneda	currency
la exportación	exports
el chileno/la chilena	Chilean
el peruano/la peruana	Peruvian
desgraciadamente	unfortunately
màs ... que	more ... than
menos ... que	less ... than
tan ... como	as ... as
tanto ... como	as much/many ... as

Sabor latino	Latin flavour
el/la actriz	actor/actress
el/la cantante	singer
un hombre	a man
la pobreza	poverty
argentino/a	Argentinian
colombiano/a	Colombian
cubano/a	Cuban
simpático/a	nice/kind
atender	to take care of / look after
soportar	to suffer
actualmente	at present
asistir	to attend
tener éxito	to be successful

¡Vamos a celebrar!	Let's celebrate!
colorido/a	colourful
los santos	the saints
los muertos	the dead
el Festival de las Velas	Festival of the Candles
el Día de la Raza	the Day of the Race
el Día de Todos los Santos	All Saints' Day
solía visitar	I/He/She used to visit
solía quedarme	I used to stay
solía venir	I/He/She used to come
solíamos ver	we used to see
solíamos asistir	we used to attend
no suelo ir	I don't usually go

Lo mejor de los idiomas	The best thing about languages
la población mundial	the world's population
la lengua materna	mother tongue
otro idioma	another language
estoy seguro/a de mí mismo	I am confident
soy consciente de otras culturas	I am aware of other cultures
estoy abierto/a a nuevas experiencias	I am open to new experiences

Hispanoamericanos	Spanish-speaking Americans
Soy ...	I am ...
boliviano/a	Bolivian
costarricense	Costa Rican
dominicano/a	Dominican
ecuatoriano/a	Ecuadorian
hondureño/a	Honduran
Nací en ...	I was born in ...
¿Qué solías hacer?	What did you used to do?

I can ...

- ● talk about Spanish-speaking countries, their people and festivals
- ● give key facts about a country I have researched
- ● describe myself and other people
- ● talk about the importance of language learning
- ● use *tener* in some of its idiomatic uses
- ● use comparatives and superlatives
- ● use *soler* + infinitive when talking about the past
- ● identify common false friends

Leer 0

¡Saludos! Soy Nicolás, y soy de Santa Cruz. Santa Cruz está en el norte de Tenerife, una de las islas Canarias. Aquí estamos muy lejos de España.

Vivo con mi familia – es una familia muy grande. Tengo tres hermanos y dos hermanas, y vivimos también con mis abuelos. ¡Menos mal que nuestra casa es muy grande!

Normalmente me llevo muy bien con mi familia. Todos somos extrovertidos y alegres. Mi hermano Raúl es muy divertido, aunque a veces es un poco tonto, pero también me ayuda mucho.

Mi madre es muy organizada, y un poco estricta. ¡Creo que es necesario con una familia tan grande! Mi padre es más desordenado. Mi madre dice que es imposible.

No me caen muy bien mis hermanas pequeñas. Solamente tienen tres y cinco años, y son un poco pesadas. Pero son muy niñas.

¿Y yo? Inteligente, ¡claro! Soy paciente y flexible, pero a veces testarudo.

¡Hola! Me llamo Jacinta y soy de Ciudad Rodrigo. Vivo con mi madre y mis abuelos, porque mis padres están divorciados. Estoy muy triste porque mi padre no vive con nosotros, pero le visito todos los sábados.

Mi padre es simpático, pero muy organizado y bastante estricto conmigo. Es muy inteligente, es profesor de universidad.

Mi madre es muy flexible y desordenada. ¡Yo soy más organizada que ella, y mi abuela es un desastre! Mi madre es simpática pero también es impaciente y testaruda.

Mi abuelo es muy paciente, ¡menos mal! Siempre está contento.

Yo no estoy siempre contenta. Soy bastante tímida y estudiosa. Quiero ser profesora como mi padre.

Lee los textos y contesta a las preguntas.

Who ...

1 has a father who is a university lecturer?
2 has a disastrously disorganised grandmother?
3 has a strict mother?
4 has three brothers and two sisters?

5 is usually patient and easy-going, but can be stubborn?
6 is shy and studious?
7 has an impatient mother?
8 has, according to their mother, an impossible father?

NC 4

Dos ciudades Patrimonio de la Humanidad

Segovia

Segovia, que está a unos noventa kilómetros de la capital Madrid, es la ciudad donde vivo. Es una ciudad histórica, no muy grande pero declarada Patrimonio de la Humanidad.

En Segovia se puede visitar muchos monumentos. El más famoso es el Acueducto, una impresionante obra de ingeniería romana del siglo I.

Además hay el Alcázar, una fortaleza de estilo gótico del siglo XII que se encuentra estratégicamente ubicada sobre una roca.

El tercer monumento más distintivo de la ciudad es la Catedral. Fue edificada en la parte más alta de Segovia, lo que acentúa aún más su majestuosidad.

En cuanto a la gastronomía no hace falta decir que el plato más famoso es el cochinillo de Segovia.

Las fiestas de San Juan y San Pedro, que se celebran del 23 al 29 de junio, son las más tradicionales.

LEER 1

Lee los textos. Busca seis palabras que son similares a palabras inglesas.

Ejemplo: histórico – historic

LEER 2

NC 5

Contesta a las preguntas.
Which of the two cities ...

1 is by the sea?
2 has a Roman aqueduct?
3 has ancient walls around it?
4 serves a traditional dish of suckling pig?
5 was attacked by Francis Drake?

LEER 3

NC 5

What do the two cities have in common?

Cartagena

Mi ciudad, la histórica Cartagena de Indias, está situada en la costa norte de Colombia a orillas del mar Caribe. Es un destino turístico muy popular.

El asentamiento original fue creado 4.000 años antes de Cristo pero la ciudad actual fue fundada en 1533 por los españoles. También ha sido designada como Patrimonio de la Humanidad por la UNESCO.

Tiene muchos monumentos importantes como el Castillo de San Felipe que el famoso pirata inglés Francisco Drake atacó en 1586. Hay varios conventos que ahora son hoteles muy bonitos y de mucho lujo. Lo que más me gusta de mi ciudad son las murallas antiguas desde donde puedo ver el mar y la puesta del sol.

¡Buscamos diseñadores nuevos!

¿Quieres ganar un premio?

Los equipos deportivos del pueblo de San Antonio necesitan uniformes nuevos. Vamos a hacer un concurso para buscar diseñadores nuevos y jóvenes. Si tienes imaginación y creatividad, haz un diseño para tu equipo favorito. ¡Puedes ganar billetes para los juegos y competiciones del equipo para ti y un amigo, para un año entero!

Necesitamos –

Equipo de fútbol
Los jugadores llevan camisas, pantalones cortos y chándales para el entrenamiento. Los colores del equipo son azul y rojo.

Equipo de baile (hombres y mujeres)
Los bailarines necesitan ropa de entrenamiento como mallas, medias, tutús etcétera. La tela sintética es muy importante. Prefieren colores neutros como negro, blanco y gris.

Equipo de piragüismo
Trajes de neopreno, zapatillas, chalecos de salvavida – todo lo necesario para este deporte emocionante y rápido. No hay colores preferidos – ¡a tu gusto!

Equipo de tenis
Los hombres y las mujeres del equipo necesitan pantalones cortos y camisetas, aunque algunas mujeres prefieren vestidos. También llevan sudadera. De color buscamos algo nuevo y un poco diferente.

Equipo de esquí
El equipo de esquí es muy importante en San Antonio, y gana muchos premios. Buscamos un diseño con colores muy vivos para las chaquetas y los pantalones acolchados.

 LEER 1

Contesta a las preguntas.

1 What do they need in San Antonio?
2 What are they looking for?
3 What will the lucky winner get in return?
4 What are the different teams you will be designing for?

 LEER 2

¿Verdad o mentira?

1 Los colores del equipo de fútbol son negro y blanco.
2 El equipo de esquí necesita chándales para el entrenamiento.

3 Solamente hay mujeres en el equipo de baile.
4 No hay colores preferidos para el equipo de piragüismo.
5 Necesitan vestidos y pantalones cortos para el equipo de tenis.

 ESCRIBIR 3

NC 4

Escribe y diseña.
Draw a design and write about it. Choose one of the teams, design their new team outfit, and then write a description in Spanish. Try and write four sentences describing the style of the clothing you have chosen.

Carnaval en Colombia

A mí me encantan las fiestas de Carnaval. Se celebran por toda la costa norte de Colombia pero las más famosas y las mejores son las de Barranquilla. Siempre hay procesiones increíbles y todos nos ponemos trajes típicos y salimos a bailar. También se ponen disfraces de diablos o de reyes del Congo. Llevamos máscaras de animales fabulosos. Lo más importante es divertirse.

El año pasado fui con mis primos, ¡y pasamos los cuatro días de ataque! Llegamos de Cartagena el sábado por la mañana y fuimos directos a buscar el mejor sitio para ver pasar la procesión de la Batalla de Flores cuando salen la Reina y todos los grupos de baile folklórico.

Había miles de personas en la calle principal, niños y adultos, todos muy alegres. Hizo mucho calor pero no nos importaba porque lo pasamos bomba. Comimos unas empanadas deliciosas y otras cosas fritas y bebimos cantidad de gaseosa y limonada.

Por la noche fuimos a escuchar a los mejores grupos de música y a unos cantantes fenomenales.

Nos quedamos bailando y cantando hasta las tres de la mañana. Así lo pasamos cada día hasta el martes por la tarde cuando celebramos con Joselito, el símbolo histórico que significa el final de la alegría de carnaval y el comienzo del festival religioso de la Cuaresma.

LEER 1 — Read Roberto's account and find:

1 five verbs in the preterite tense
2 two verbs in the imperfect tense
3 four adjectives describing the scene.

LEER 2 — Busca las frases en español.

1 the most famous and best
2 the most important thing is to enjoy yourself
3 there were thousands of people
4 at night
5 the religious festival of Lent

LEER 3 — Contesta a las preguntas.

NC 5

1 Where is the best Carnival held, according to Roberto?

2 Name three things you can see there.
3 How long does it last?
4 What was the weather like the last time Roberto was there?
5 Mention three things he did.
6 What time did he go to bed on the first night?

ESCRIBIR 4 — Escribe cinco preguntas sobre el texto. Contesta a las preguntas de tu compañero.

ESCRIBIR 5 — Escribe sobre una fiesta similar.

NC 5

Write about a similar festival (imaginary or real) you went to or took part in this or last year.

Leer 2B

¿Cuánto sabes?

Empareja las preguntas en español con las en inglés.

Ejemplo: 1 c

1 ¿Cuándo abrió el Museo Nacional del Prado?
2 ¿Madrid está tan al norte como qué ciudad estadounidense?
3 En el atentado terrorista del 2004, ¿cuánta gente murió en las tres estaciones?
4 ¿Cuántas habitaciones tiene el Palacio Real?
5 ¿Cómo se llama la gente que vive en Madrid?
6 Madrid tiene tres equipos de fútbol: el Real Madrid, el Atlético de Madrid y ¿qué otro?
7 ¿Cómo se llama el aeropuerto de Madrid?
8 Entre las capitales europeas, ¿por qué destaca Madrid?
9 ¿Dónde está el Kilómetro Cero, donde las carreteras radiales empiezan?
10 ¿Quién es el mayor rival del Real Madrid?

a Amongst the European capitals, what does Madrid stand out for?
b How many people died in the three stations, in the terrorist attack of 2004?
c When did the national museum El Prado open?
d What is Madrid's airport called?
e What are people from Madrid called?
f Who is Real Madrid's biggest rival?
g Madrid has three football teams: Real Madrid, Atlético de Madrid and which other?
h Madrid is as far north as which American city?
i How many rooms does the Spanish Royal Palace have?
j Where is Km 0, where the national roads of Spain start from?

How many questions can you answer without help?

¿Cómo se dice en español?

Ejemplo: as far north as – tan al norte como

1 terrorist attack
2 football team
3 stands out
4 roads

Empareja las respuestas con las preguntas de la actividad 1.

Ejemplo: 1 1819

191 el Barça 1819 Barajas
madrileños   Es la capital a más altitud
más o menos 2.800   el Rayo Vallecano
La Puerta del Sol   Nueva York

Mi deporte favorito

Noelia

El deporte que más me gusta y que siempre he practicado desde niña es el alpinismo. Aquí en los Picos de Europa en el norte de España salía con mis padres todos los fines de semana y ahora que soy mayor suelo salir con un grupo del club local. Durante el invierno tenemos que llevar ropa térmica porque hace mucho frío, sobre todo en lo alto de las montañas donde cae mucha nieve. Estoy practicando mucho porque me gustaría ser como mi ídolo Araceli Segarra que subió el Everest en 2007.

Nico

Para mí la locura total es el kitesurf que practicamos aquí en Tarifa en la punta más al sur de España; es fenomenal. Me flipa la sensación de libertad cuando el viento me empuja hacia arriba como una cometa con mi tabla de surf. A veces no se puede salir porque hace demasiado viento y entonces paso el día practicando con los patines.

Nati

Paso todo mi tiempo libre practicando el baloncesto. Lo mejor de este deporte es que lo puedes hacer tanto si llueve como si hace sol. Aquí en Barcelona hay varios equipos buenísimos que tienen academias para jóvenes y que nos animan a imitar a las estrellas como Pau Gasol o Cindy Lima.

Sebas

Tengo varios ídolos a quienes me gustaría imitar, por ejemplo Dani Pedrosa o Jorge Lorenzo. El problema de mi deporte favorito es que cuesta bastante y sólo se puede practicar en un circuito especial. Mi padre también es un fanático del motociclismo así que me llevó a ver el campeonato del mundo aquí en Valencia.

LEER 1 **Lee los textos y busca las frases en español.**

1 now that I'm older
2 on top of the mountains
3 the southern tip of Spain
4 flying like a kite
5 the best thing … is
6 they encourage us
7 it costs a lot
8 world championships

LEER 2 👥 **Escribe una lista de las nuevas palabras.**
List the new words. Which can you guess? Which do you need to check in a dictionary? Compare your list with a partner.

LEER 3 **Busca las expresiones del tiempo.**
How many expressions to do with the weather can you find?

ESCRIBIR 4 **¿Qué haces si llueve? ¿Y si hace sol, viento o nieva?**
Write what activities you do in different weather.

LEER 5 **Identifica los tiempos de los verbos.**
How many different tenses can you find? Write all the verbs down and say what they mean.

NC 6

ESCRIBIR 6 👥 **Escribe seis preguntas sobre los textos. Contesta a las preguntas de tu compañero.**

¿Qué estudiará Laura el año que viene?

Laura, la prima de Elena y Juan, es española pero vive y estudia en Londres.

Laura

> El año que viene tengo que estudiar inglés, matemáticas y ciencias porque son obligatorias.
>
> Para las asignaturas optativas me gustaría estudiar arte, música y teatro porque son mis asignaturas preferidas, y mis amigos las estudiarán. En el futuro me gustaría ser actiz o cantante, pero no sé si es posible.

> Es muy importante estudiar lenguas modernas como francés para comunicarse bien en el mundo. También la informática es necesaria hoy en día. En mi opinión es más importante estudiar historia y geografía que arte o música. En el futuro Laura debe ser profesora o traductora – son trabajos buenos.

El padre de Laura

La profesora de Laura ha escrito unos consejos en español para sus padres.

matemáticas	Laura va bien y saca buenas notas. No tendrá problemas.
ciencias	Laura hace lo mínimo posible. El año que viene tendrá que trabajar con más esfuerzo.
historia	Saca malas notas, y hace lo mínimo. ¡Mi consejo es no estudiar historia el año que viene!
informática	Laura no va muy bien en informática, pero es una asignatura muy importante en el mundo moderno. Sería mejor estudiarla, pero no es esencial. Es posible practicarla en el tiempo libre.
español	¡Claro que Laura es una estudiante fenomenal en español! Debe estudiarlo: será fácil para ella.
francés	También va muy bien en francés – otra posibilidad para el año que viene.
música	Laura tiene un talento fenomenal en música. Toca la guitarra y la flauta de maravilla, canta muy bien, escribe música. Debe estudiarla el año que viene.
teatro	También tiene un talento dramático muy impresionante. Seguro que en el futuro Laura será actriz o música con mucho éxito. Debe seguir con sus estudios. ¡Es muy importante!

LEER 1
NC 6

Lee lo que dicen Laura y su padre. Contesta a las preguntas.

1. What would Laura like to study next year?
2. What does her father want her to study?
3. What would Laura like to be in the future?
4. What does her father consider a good job?

LEER 2
NC 6

¿Verdad o mentira?
According to Laura's teacher:

1. Laura will struggle with science next year.
2. Laura should choose history – she's really good at it.
3. It's essential to study ICT.
4. She's not doing so well in French.
5. Laura is a talented musician.
6. Laura could have a great future as an actress or musician.

Animales en peligro en América Latina

La ardilla, tan común en el Reino Unido, está en peligro de extinción en América Latina. Las ardillas grises son las únicas que habitan en la península de Yucatán.

Son de tamaño mediano, tienen la espalda gris y el estómago de color rojizo, viven en las costas y en las partes altas del sur de Méjico. Normalmente viven en los bosques tropicales y sólo

bajan de los árboles para buscar comida o agua o para cambiar de árbol.

Nacen en las partes más altas de los árboles y pueden reproducirse durante todo el año. Tienen de dos a seis crías. Las ardillas comen plantas, insectos, huevos de aves y pequeños reptiles, pero están en peligro a causa de la invasión del hombre en su hábitat, y de la caza deportiva.

Unos pescadores, aparentemente envenenaron y mataron a más de quince delfines rosados en una laguna de la Amazonia del Perú, porque los delfines pueden romper sus redes de pesca. Descubrieron los cuerpos, adultos y jóvenes, flotando en la laguna al noroeste del país. Parece que los delfines comieron pescado envenenado con fosforados o pesticidas. Es un crimen en Perú atentar contra la vida de estos animales en peligro de extinción.

El delfín rosado habita el río Amazonas y sus afluentes de la Guayana, Venezuela, Colombia, Ecuador, Perú, Bolivia y Brasil.

 LEER 1

NC 7

Read the reports and decide if the following statements are about the Mexican squirrels or the Amazon dolphins.

1 They are in danger because of humans invading their habitat.
2 Some of these animals were poisoned.
3 These animals are hunted for sport.
4 It's a crime to kill these animals according to the law of that country.

 LEER 2

NC 7

Completa las frases.

1 The squirrels live in ...
2 They leave the trees to ...
3 The squirrels have ... babies at a time.
4 The poisoned dolphins were in the country of ...
5 They were probably killed because ...
6 They were found ...

rojizo – *reddish*
el bosque – *forest*
la cría – *young*
el pescador – *fisherman*
envenenado – *poisoned*
la red – *net*
el afluente – *tributary*

El Día de la Raza

El doce de octubre se celebra en las Américas el día de la llegada de Cristóbal Colón en 1492.

Cristóbal Colón nació en Génova en Italia y era el mayor de cinco hermanos. No se sabe si navegaba de España a China para demostrar que la Tierra no era plana o si sólo quería encontrar una ruta más corta cuando el doce de octubre de 1492 su pequeña flota de tres barcos, la Pinta, la Niña y la Santa María, llegó a una isla, ahora llamada Las Bahamas. De Las Bahamas Colón fue a Cuba, después a La República Dominicana y luego a Haití antes de volver a España para contar sus aventuras.

Cristóbal Colón era cristiano y quería contar la historia de Cristo a la gente de aquellas tierras lejanas. También buscaba riqueza para él y para España. Durante su vida Cristóbal Colón hizo cuatro expediciones a Latinoamérica. Después de su tercer viaje fue nombrado Gobernador General de las nuevas colonias.

Actualmente, más de quinientos años más tarde, entre otros países, Argentina, Chile, Costa Rica, Ecuador, Honduras, Méjico, Uruguay y Venezuela celebran en octubre el Día de la Raza; para celebrar la sociedad multicultural y multiétnica que ha resultado de la colonización española de las Américas.

 LEER 1

Contesta a las preguntas.

 NC 7

1 What is celebrated on the 12th October?
2 How many siblings did Columbus have?
3 When did he arrive in the Americas for the first time?
4 How did he get there?
5 What did he do after visiting Haiti?
6 What did Columbus want to do in the Americas? (two things)
7 How many times did he go to the Americas?
8 What happened after his third voyage?
9 What does *El Día de la Raza* celebrate?

 LEER 2

Lee el texto. ¿Cómo se dice en español?

1 the day of Columbus' arrival
2 he was the eldest of five children
3 the world was not flat
4 his small fleet of three ships
5 now called the Bahamas
6 to recount his adventures
7 to people of those faraway lands
8 after his third trip
9 at present
10 more than 500 years later

Gramática

Introduction

In order to speak or write correctly in a language, we need to know the grammar basics behind the construction of sentences. The ability to identify patterns and to understand and apply grammar rules in Spanish allows you to use the language to say what you want to say.

In this section you will find a summary of the main grammar points covered by this book with some activities to check that you have understood and can use the language accurately.

Grammar index

Glossary of terms

noun *un sustantivo* – a person, animal, object, place or thing

Pablo *navega por* **internet** *en el* **ordenador** *de su* **dormitorio**.

determiner *un determinante* = a little word before a noun to introduce it or modify it

un *perro,* **unos** *CDs,* **la** *casa,* **mi** *hermano*

singular *el singular* = one of something

un *gato,* **la** *cocina*

plural *el plural* = two or more of something

unos *gatos,* **las** *serpientes,* **tres** *elefantes*

pronoun *un pronombre* – a little word used to replace a noun or a name

Él *juega al fútbol.* **Ellas** *van al cine.*

verb *un verbo* = a 'doing' or 'being' word

Hablo *español.* **Estudias** *francés.* **Somos** *deportistas.* **Van** *al cine.* **Odio** *la lectura.*

tense *el tiempo verbal* = tells you when the action takes place

Normalmente **voy** *en autobús. Ayer* **fui** *a pie. Mañana* **voy a ir** *en coche.*

adjective *un adjetivo* = a describing word

Mi madre es **simpática**. *La cocina es* **grande**.

adverb *un adverbio* = a word that modifies or qualifies a verb or adjective

Hizo los deberes **rápidamente**. *Tenía un coche* **muy** *rápido.*

preposition *una preposición* = tells you the position of someone or something

El cine está **delante** *del restaurante. El perro está* **en** *el jardín.*

Gramática

1 Nouns and determiners

1.1 Nouns

All nouns in Spanish are either masculine or feminine. Most nouns ending in **o** are masculine and most ending in **a** are feminine.

libro → masculine   *biblioteca* → feminine

1.2 Making the plural

Add an **-s** to nouns ending in a vowel and **-es** to words ending in a consonant.

un perro → *dos perros*
un profesor → *dos profesores*

1.3 Determiners (the, a, an, some)

Determiners in Spanish change depending on the gender (masculine/feminine) and number (singular/plural) of the noun they precede.

the (definite article):

	masculine	feminine
singular	el	la
plural	los	las

a/an/some (indefinite article):

	masculine	feminine
singular	un	una
plural	unos	unas

When you learn a new noun, it is a good idea to learn it together with the determiner, particularly if it doesn't end in **-o** or **-a**; so that you know whether it is masculine or feminine.

the tree → **el** *árbol*   **the** trees → **los** *árboles*
a tree → **un** *árbol*   **some** trees → **unos** *árboles*

the flower → **la** *flor*   **the** flowers → **las** *flores*
a flower → **una** *flor*   **some** flowers → **unas** *flores*

A Copy and complete the table. Follow the example.

m.	f.	the (definite article)		a/an/some (indefinite article)		
		singular	plural	singular	plural	
	✓	la manzana	las manzanas	una manzana	unas manzanas	apple/apples

perro   casa   hotel   lápiz   araña   canción
jardín   piscina   animal

2 Adjectives

Adjectives are words we use to describe nouns.
In Spanish:
- They generally go after the noun: the white house → *la casa blanca*
- They always match the gender and number of the noun they describe:
  un *perro negro* **but** *una rata negra*
  un *gato blanco* **but** *unos gatos blancos*

To make the feminine of adjectives:

If the masc. ends in:	The feminine form:	
-o	changes to -a	**un** libro roj**o** → **una** revist**a** roj**a**
-l, -s, -e, -n (except nationalities)	There is no change	**un** balón gri**s** → **una** pelot**a** gri**s** *but* **un** chico inglé**s** → **una** chic**a** ingle**sa**
-r	Add an -a	**un** niño hablador → **una** niñ**a** hablador**a**
-a (some exceptions like *rosa*)	There is no change	**un** joven deportista → un**a** joven deportista

To make the plural of adjectives follow the same rules as for making the plural of nouns: add **-s** to adjectives ending in a vowel and **-es** to adjectives ending in consonants.

black	masculine	feminine
singular	negro	negra
plural	negros	negras

charming	masculine	feminine
singular	encantador	encantadora
plural	encantadores	encantadoras

B How would you say these in Spanish?

1. a green coat – *un abrigo verde*
2. the blue hats
3. a white dress
4. the red t-shirts
5. (some) yellow socks
6. the brown boots
7. the black trousers
8. a pink shirt

3 Demonstrative adjectives

The function of demonstrative adjectives is to point at something: this, that, these and those.

Demonstrative adjectives always precede the noun and agree with it in gender and number.

Whereas in English we have only two demonstrative adjectives ('this' and 'that'), Spanish has three: *este*, *ese* and *aquel*.

this/these	masculine	feminine
singular	este	esta
plural	estos	estas

that/those	masculine	feminine
singular	ese	esa
plural	esos	esas

that over there/ those over there	masculine	feminine
singular	aquel	aquella
plural	aquellos	aquellas

Examples:
est**e** zapat**o** → *this shoe*, est**a** camis**a** → *this shirt*

C Tell the shop assistant which item from this shop window you want using demonstrative adjectives. Think about how close the item is to you.

1 the purple sandals – *Quiero aquellas sandalias moradas.*
2 the yellow t-shirt
3 the blue jeans
4 the red sandals
5 the purple skirt
6 the black handbag
7 the brown shoes
8 the white sandals

Rebajas del 50%
vaqueros
faldas
camisetas
bolsos
zapatos
sandalias

---

4 Possessives

4.1 The possessive of nouns

Beware! In Spanish, English structures such as 'my father's car' which have an apostrophe ('s), do not exist.

To show who or what something or someone belongs to use **de** (of) with the noun.

*el coche **de** mi padre* → the car **of** my father → my father's car

 Note that **de** + **el** = **del** → *el comedor **del** instituto*

4.2 Possessive adjectives

Possessive adjectives show who or what something belongs to (my school, your books, his family etc.).

They come before the noun they describe and like all adjectives, they have to match the noun they describe.

		singular (one thing *owned*)	plural (two or more things *owned*)
singular (1 owner)	my	mi	mis
	your	tu	tus
	his/her/your (formal)	su	sus
plural (2 or more owners)	our	nuestro (*what is owned is masculine*) nuestra (*what is owned is feminine*)	nuestros (*what is owned is masculine*) nuestras (*what is owned is feminine*)
	your (plural)	vuestro (*what is owned is masculine*) vuestra (*what is owned is feminine*)	vuestros (*what is owned is masculine*) vuestras (*what is owned is feminine*)
	their/your (formal plural)	su	sus

For example:

My father is taller than your mother. → *Mi padre es más alto que tu madre.*

Our mother speaks to your brothers. → *Nuestra **madre** habla con tu**s** hermano**s**.*

D Translate into Spanish.

1 your (plural) parents – *vuestros padres*
2 his house
3 her cousins
4 my friends
5 your (sing.) grandfather
6 our mother

---

5 Prepositions

Prepositions are words that specify time, direction or place.

a → at *Empieza **a** las tres.* → It starts **at** three.

de → from *Viene **de** la piscina.* → He comes **from** the swimming pool.

en → in *José está **en** el instituto.* → José is **in** school.

⚠ Note that in Spanish, prepositions are generally followed by the definite article:

*a + el = **al*** → *Voy **a** la piscina* **but** *Voy **al** instituto*

*de + el = **del*** → *Vengo **de** la piscina* **but** *Vengo **del** instituto*

5.1 Simple prepositions

These consist of one word only: *a* (at, to), *de* (of, from), *sobre* (on), *en* (in), *entre* (between), etc.

*Los deberes están **sobre** la mesa.* → The homework is **on** the table.

5.2 Compound prepositions

These require more than one word in order to be grammatically correct. In Spanish, most prepositions of place are compound prepositions because they require *de*:

delante de → in front of *al lado de* → next to
detrás de → behind *a la derecha de* → to the right of
enfrente de → opposite *a la izquierda de* → to the left of
debajo de → under

E Where is Don Quijote?

Example: **1** Don Quijote está sobre el (*or* encima del) coche.

❶ ❷ ❸

❹ ❺ ❻

5.3 Personal *a*

The personal *a* needs to be used after certain verbs if the object of the verb is a person. You do not use it when talking about things. For example:

*Voy a ver **a** mi amigo* – I'm going to see my friend.

In the sentence above 'my friend' is the object of the verb and is a person so we need to use the personal *a*.

But:
Voy a ver una película – I'm going to see a film
'A film' is not a person so we do not need the *a*.

The personal *a* in Spanish has no real translation in English.

6 Pronouns

6.1 Subject pronouns

The subject of a sentence tells you who or what is doing the action. We use subject pronouns to replace nouns or names and avoid repetition:

Anna is washing her hair; **she** will call you back in a while.
The exam was difficult. **It** was very long too.

Singular (subject is on his/her/ its own)	I	yo
	you	tú
	he/she/it	él/ella/-
Plural (action is done by two or more subjects)	we	nosotros/nosotras
	you	vosotros/vosotras
	they	ellos/ellas

⚠ • In Spanish we don't have 'it' because all nouns are either masculine or feminine.
  • Use masculine pronouns to refer to masculine subjects and feminine to refer to feminine subjects. When talking about a mixed group, use the masculine even when masculine is a minority within the group.

6.2 Relative pronouns

Relative pronouns in English are *which, that, who, whom* and *whose*. They are used to refer to something in a sentence that has already been mentioned. In Spanish the most common relative pronoun is *que*. You can use it to refer to things or people:

*El libro **que** pertenece a mi hermano* – The book **that** belongs to my brother
*El hombre **que** viste ayer es de Madrid* – The man **that/who** you saw yesterday is from Madrid.

When you are referring to a concept, you use *lo que*:

Lo que *más me gusta de Madrid es el estadio Bernabéu* – **What** I like most in Madrid is the Bernabeu stadium.

7 Verbs

7.1 The infinitive

The infinitive is the original form of a verb and often the only one you will find in the dictionary.

In English the infinitive form is the one that has 'to' in front: to cook, to read, to write, etc. In Spanish infinitives end in *-ar, -er* or *-ir*: *cocinar, leer, escribir*.

Spanish infinitives are made of a stem + an ending.

stem	ending
estudi	*-ar*
com	*-er*
viv	*-ir*

The infinitive of a verb is extremely important as it is your starting point if you are to use verbs correctly.

7.2 Present tense

The present tense describes actions which take place regularly or are taking place at this moment in time:

I go to school (every day) / **I am going** to school (right now)

Unlike English, in Spanish you have a different ending for each subject pronoun. This means that subject pronouns can and most often are omitted without the sentence becoming unclear.

Present tense: regular verbs

	hablar (to speak)	comer (to eat)	vivir (to live)
(yo)	habl**o** (I speak)	com**o** (I eat)	viv**o** (I live)
(tú)	habl**as** (you speak)	com**es** (you eat)	viv**es** (you live)
(él/ella/Ud.*)	habl**a** (he/she/It/you speak[s])	com**e** (he/she/it/you eat[s])	viv**e** (he/she/it/you live[s])
(nosotros/as)	habl**amos** (we speak)	com**emos** (we eat)	viv**imos** (we live)
(vosotros/as)	habl**áis** (you [plural] speak)	com**éis** (you [plural] eat)	viv**ís** (you [plural] live)
(ellos/as/Uds.*)	habl**an** (they/you speak)	com**en** (they/you eat)	viv**en** (they/you live)

* *Ud.* (*Usted*) and *Uds.* (*Ustedes*) are polite forms used when speaking to someone older that you need or want to show respect to. They take the third person endings, singular or plural.

Regular verbs follow a clear pattern so you only need to know one verb of each ending (*-ar, -er, -ir*). In order to work out any regular verb, follow these simple 1, 2, 3 rules:

1. Identify which column you need according to the ending of the infinitive of your new verb (*-ar, -er* or *-ir*).
2. Identify which row you need by working out you who is talking or being talked about (I, you, he/she/it, we, you, they).
3. Remove the ending of your new verb and replace it with the new ending found where your column and row meet.

For 'they work' you need the infinitive 'to work' → *trabajar*.

1. *Trabajar* will follow the same pattern as *hablar* as it is an *-ar* verb.
2. You will need the last row as it is the one referring to 'they' (*ellos*).
3. They work → (*ellos*) *trabaj+an* → *trabajan*

 Beware! Irregular verbs don't follow a given pattern and so they need to be learnt in full. Here are some examples:

Gramática

Present tense: irregular verbs

ser to be (permanent)	estar to be (temporary or location)	hacer (to do/to make	tener (to have)	ir (to go)
soy	estoy	hago	tengo	voy
eres	estás	haces	tienes	vas
es	está	hace	tiene	va
somos	estamos	hacemos	tenemos	vamos
sois	estáis	hacéis	tenéis	vais
son	están	hacen	tienen	van

F How would you say in Spanish ...?

1 we finish – *terminamos*
2 he admits
3 you (sing.) go
4 they open
5 I believe
6 we read
7 you (plural) open
8 she has

abrir (*to open*)   admitir (*to admit*)   ir (*to go*)
leer (*to read*)   tener (*to have*)

7.3 The present continuous

The present continuous tense is used to say **what you are doing** or **what is happening** at the moment.

The present continuous is used in Spanish in the same way as it is in English.

It is formed with the present tense of *estar* (to be) plus the verb of action with its ending changed to *-ando* for *-ar* verbs and *-iendo* for *-er* and *-ir* verbs. This is like the English ending *-ing*.

*¿Qué está pas**ando**?* – What is happen**ing**?
*Estoy com**iendo** la cena* – I am eat**ing** my dinner.

There are, however, some verbs that break the rule and should be learned. They include *dormir* and *leer*.

*Papá está durm**iendo** en su cama.*
*Estoy ley**endo** mi novela favorita.*

You can see that in the present continuous of *dormir*, the 'o' changes to a 'u'. In the present continuous of *leer* the 'i' in *-iendo* changes to a 'y'.

7.4 Stem-changing verbs (or radical-changing verbs)

A small number of verbs follow the rules of regular verbs but there is also a change in the stem in the present tense.

jugar (to play) → *ju**e**go* (I play)
*pref**e**rir* (to prefer) → *pref**ie**ro* (I prefer)

When a verb is stem-changing, you need to remember the pattern 1, 2, 3, 6 as these persons change.

Common changes include **e** to **ie** (*pref**e**rir* → *pref**ie**ro*), **o** to **ue** (*p**o**der* → *p**ue**do*) and **e** to **i** (*p**e**dir* → *p**i**do*). You can also use the 'boot strategy' as all persons whose stem changes are in the boot:

jugar
singular   *plural*

(1) ju**e**go   (4) jugamos
(2) ju**e**gas   (5) jugáis
(3) ju**e**ga   (6) ju**e**gan

pref**e**rir
singular   *plural*

(1) pref**ie**ro   (4) preferimos
(2) pref**ie**res (5) preferís
(3) pref**ie**re   (6) pref**ie**ren

G Complete these sentences with the verbs in the box.

1 El director almuerza a las dos.
The headteacher has lunch at two.
2 _____ cuando _____ que se olvidó los deberes en casa. *He is lying when he says that he left his homework at home.*
3 En la cantina del instituto no _____ patatas fritas. *In the college canteen they don't serve chips.*
4 _____ al golf los domingos. *I play golf on Sundays.*
5 Siempre _____ en aerolíneas de bajo coste.
We always fly with budget airlines.

almorzar (o → ue) – *to have lunch*
decir (e → i) – *to say*
jugar (u → ue) – *to play*
mentir (e → ie) – *to lie*
servir (e → i) – *to serve*
volar (o → ue) – *to fly*

7.5 Preterite (past tense)

We use the preterite tense to describe completed actions that have already happened and so are in the past.

I **studied** for my exam. I **ate** chips.

In English one form of the verb suits all pronouns: I talked, you talked, he/she/it talked, we talked, you (plural) talked, they talked. Once again, this doesn't happen in Spanish and each subject pronoun has its own ending.

Preterite (past) tense: regular verbs

	hablar (to speak)	comer (to eat)	vivir (to live)
(yo)	hablé (I spoke)	comí (I ate)	viví (I lived)
(tú)	hablaste (you spoke)	comiste (you ate)	viviste (you lived)
(él/ella/Ud.)	habló (he/she/it/you spoke)	comió (he/she/it/you ate)	vivió (he/she/it/you lived)
(nosotros/as)	hablamos (we spoke)	comimos (we ate)	vivimos (we lived)
(vosotros/as)	hablasteis (you [plural] spoke)	comisteis (you [plural] ate)	vivisteis (you [plural] lived)
(ellos/as/Uds.)	hablaron (they/you spoke)	comieron (they ate)	vivieron (they/you lived)

You can work out the ending you need by following the same 1, 2, 3 rules as for the present tense of regular verbs but make sure that you are using a preterite tense table!

Preterite (past) tense: irregular verbs

ser	estar	hacer	tener	ir	dar
fui	estuve	hice	tuve	fui	di
fuiste	estuviste	hiciste	tuviste	fuiste	diste
fue	estuvo	hizo	tuvo	fue	dio
fuimos	estuvimos	hicimos	tuvimos	fuimos	dimos
fuisteis	estuvisteis	hicisteis	tuvisteis	fuisteis	disteis
fueron	estuvieron	hicieron	tuvieron	fueron	dieron

H Complete the sentences with the correct form of the preterite.

1 Mi madre cocinó paella el martes pasado. (cocinar)
2 Yo _____ Harry Potter en el cine con mi hermano. (ver)
3 Lena _____ una sorpresa a sus padres ayer. (dar)
4 Vosotros _____ al tenis durante las vacaciones. (jugar)
5 Tú no _____ bien porque _____ demasiada gaseosa durante la fiesta. (dormir, beber)
6 Carolina _____ los deberes a las ocho. (terminar)
7 Carlos y Sofía _____ idiomas en el instituto. (estudiar)
8 Los chicos _____ al parque a jugar al fútbol. (ir)

7.6 Imperfect (past tense)

The imperfect tense is used to express actions repeated over an indefinite period of time with an ambiguous beginning and end: 'I used to go shopping on Tuesdays'. (We don't know when the action started or if this person still goes shopping on Tuesdays.) It is also used to express what someone 'was doing' and/or to set the scene: 'I was studying all the time'.

Imperfect tense: regular verbs

-ar	-er/-ir
hablar	comer
hablaba	comía
hablabas	comías
hablaba	comía
hablábamos	comíamos
hablabais	comíais
hablaban	comían

There are only three verbs that are irregular in the imperfect tense.

Imperfect tense: irregular verbs

ir	ser	ver
iba	era	veía
ibas	eras	veías
iba	era	veía
íbamos	éramos	veíamos
ibais	erais	veíais
iban	eran	veían

I Write in Spanish using the imperfect.

1 it was raining – *llovía*
2 I used to wear
3 we used to have
4 he was using
5 they used to work
6 I was buying
7 we used to eat
8 we were making

comprar usar hacer tener llevar comer
llover trabajar

7.7 Preterite v imperfect

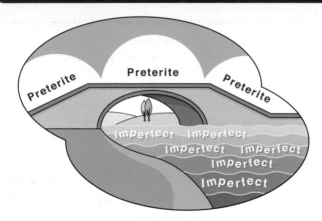

Where there is more than one past tense verb in a sentence, the action which went on for a longer time will need the imperfect and another action that interrupted it, or happened in the middle of it, will need the preterite. The imperfect action will have started before the preterite's and is likely to continue afterwards. The imperfect action sets the scene for the preterite.

Mientras estaba en la cocina sonó el teléfono → While I was in the kitchen the phone rang.

Llovía mucho cuando ocurrió el accidente → It was raining heavily when the accident happened.

J Preterite or imperfect? Rewrite the sentences with the correct verbs.

Example: 1 ***Estaba*** *en la fiesta cuando me* ***llamaste***.

1 Estuve/Estaba en la fiesta cuando me llamaste/llamabas.
2 La película terminó/terminaba mientras hablamos/hablábamos por teléfono.
3 Hicimos/Hacíamos los deberes cuando papá llegó/llegaba.
4 Estuve/Estaba enfermo cuando empezaron/empezaban las vacaciones.
5 Llevé/Llevaba una falda roja cuando fueron/iban de compras.
6 Llamé/Llamaba a mi madre mientras esperé/esperaba el autobús.

7.8 Immediate future

The immediate future means '**going to do** something', e.g. '**I am going to go** to the cinema'.

To form the immediate future use the following formula:

present tense of verb to go (*ir*) + *a* + infinitive form of the verb

Examples:

Voy a hablar/comer/salir …	I am going to speak/eat/go out …
Vas a hablar/comer/salir …	You are going to speak/eat/go out …
Va a hablar/comer/salir …	He/she is going to speak/eat/go out …
Vamos a hablar/comer/salir …	We are going to speak/eat/go out …
Vais a hablar/comer/salir …	You (plural) are going to speak/eat/go out …
Van a hablar/comer/salir …	They are going to speak/eat/go out …

K Rewrite these sentences in the immediate future.

1 Viajamos por Madrid en metro. – *Vamos a viajar por Madrid en metro.*
2 Como en el restaurante del museo.
3 Alquilan una bicicleta para visitar el parque.
4 Compra recuerdos en el Rastro.
5 Va a la capital el fin de semana.

7.9 Future tense

To say what one **will** do in the future we use the future tense. Unlike other tenses, the future tense adds endings on to the infinitive, so you don't remove the -*ar*, -*er* or -*ir*.

The following endings are added:

viajar (to travel)
viajar**é** (I will travel)
viajar**ás** (you will travel)
viajar**á** (he/she will travel)
viajar**emos** (we will travel)
viajar**éis** (you [plural] will travel)
viajar**án** (they will travel)

A few verbs are irregular in the future tense. The endings remain the same but it is the stem that changes:

Future tense: Irregular verbs

hacer *(to do)*	poder *(to be able)*	salir *(to go out)*	tener *(to have)*
haré, harás, etc.	podré, podrás, etc.	saldré, saldrás, etc.	tendré, tendrás, etc.

L Translate into Spanish.

1 I will go to university – *Iré a la universidad.*
2 I will make a lot of friends.
3 My parents will win the lottery.
4 I will travel the world.
5 I will have a well paid job.
6 My father will buy a Ferrari.
7 We will live at the coast.
8 I will be rich and famous.

7.10 Conditional tense

The conditional is also a future tense and it is used to express what one **would** do: 'I **would live** in New York.'

To form the conditional add the following endings to the full infinitive: -*ía*, -*ías*, -*ía*, -*íamos*, -*íais*, -*ían*.

ir (to go)
Iría   iríamos
irías   iríais
iría   irían

Verbs that are irregular in the future tense are also irregular in the conditional and use the same stem: *haría* (I would do), *podría* (I would be able), *saldría* (I would go out), *tendría* (I would have).

M You have been granted five wishes. Write a sentence for each of the verbs in the box.

Example: Sería muy guapa.

> ser   tener   hacer   comprar   ir

7.11 Reflexive verbs

When you look up a reflexive verb in a dictionary you will find its infinitive has -**se** at the end: *llamarse, ponerse, vestirse*.

The -*se* needs to be removed from the end and brought to the front of the verb as a reflexive pronoun which will take a different form for each subject pronoun: *me, te, se, nos, os, se*.

You then work out the ending of the verb as you would if it was any other verb.

Remember to use the correct endings for the tense you want.

levantarse – *to get up*

present	preterite	future
me levant**o**	**me** levant**é**	**me** levantar**é**
I get up	*I got up*	*I will get up*
te levant**as**	**te** levant**aste**	**te** levantar**ás**
you get up	*you got up*	*you will get up*
se levant**a**	**se** levant**ó**	**se** levantar**á**
he/she gets up	*he/she got up*	*he/she will get up*
nos levant**amos**	**nos** levant**amos**	**nos** levantar**emos**
we get up	*we got up*	*we will get up*
os levant**áis**	**os** levant**asteis**	**os** levantar**éis**
you (plural) get up	*you (plural) got up*	*you (plural) will get up*
se levant**an**	**se** levant**aron**	**se** levantar**án**
they get up	*they got up*	*they will get up*

Gramática

In the case of the immediate future you can place the pronoun either at the beginning – **Me** *voy a levantar* – or at the end following the infinitive ending: *Voy a levantar***me**.

 Beware! Some reflexive verbs are stem-changing: *acostarse – me ac***ue***sto, despertarse – me desp***ie***rto.*

N **Use the verbs in the box to translate these phrases.**

1 he got angry – *se enojó*
2 she worries
3 we are going to bed
4 I will shave
5 you (sing.) put make-up on (yesterday)
6 we have a shower
7 I get up
8 she woke up

acostarse	afeitarse	despertarse	ducharse
to go to bed	*to shave*	*to wake up*	*to have a shower*
enojarse	levantarse	maquillarse	preocuparse
to get angry	*to get up*	*to put make-up on*	*to worry*

7.12 Imperative

The imperative is used when you are telling somebody to do something or giving them an order.

The Spanish imperative exists for five different grammatical people: *tú, usted, nosotros, vosotros* and *ustedes*. The *nosotros* form is less commonly used than the others.

 Positive and negative commands have different endings for the informal forms.

To form the imperative:
Take the *-ar, -er* or *-ir* ending and replace it with the relevant ending from the table:

	-ar e.g. *hablar*		-er e.g. *comer*		-ir e.g. *escribir*	
	positive	negative	positive	negative	positive	negative
tú	¡Habl**a**!	¡No habl**es**!	¡Com**e**!	¡No com**as**!	¡Escrib**e**!	¡No escrib**as**!
usted	¡Habl**e**!	¡No habl**e**!	¡Com**a**!	¡No com**a**!	¡Escrib**a**!	¡No escrib**a**!
vosotros/as	¡Habl**ad**!	¡No habl**éis**!	¡Com**ed**!	¡No com**áis**!	¡Escrib**id**!	¡No escrib**áis**!
ustedes	¡Habl**en**!	¡No habl**en**!	¡Com**an**!	¡No com**an**!	¡Escrib**an**!	¡No escrib**an**!

O **Write the correct form of the imperative to complete these sentences.**

1 ¡ Ahorra el dinero para las vacaciones! (ahorrar, tú)
2 En España, ¡ la capital! (visitar, vosotros)
3 No en taxi, el metro es más barato. (viajar, vosotros)
4 ¡ comida típica! (comer, vosotros)
5 No su pasaporte. (olvidar, ustedes)

7.13 The verb *soler*

The structure *soler* + infinitive is very common in Spanish. The verb *soler* is only used in the present and imperfect. In the present it translates as 'usually' and in the imperfect as 'used to':
Solemos *ir al cine los lunes* → We usually go to the cinema on Mondays.
En verano **solíamos** *ir a la costa* → In the summer we used to go to the coast.

 Beware! *Soler* is a stem-changing verb: *o* → *ue* (*s***o***ler* → *s***ue***lo*)

P **Answer the questions using the structure *soler* + infinitive.**

1 ¿Cómo vas al instituto? *Suelo ir al instituto en autobús.*
2 ¿Qué desayunas normalmente?
3 ¿Qué haces después del instituto?
4 ¿A qué hora sueles acostarte?
5 Cuando eras pequeño/a, ¿qué solías ver en la tele?
6 En primaria, ¿qué solíais hacer por las mañanas?

7.14 Impersonal *se*

Where in English we use expressions such as 'one does ...', or 'you/we/they do ...' to make general statements or express rules or duties, in Spanish we often use the impersonal *se*.
The impersonal *se* is formed with *se* + third person singular of the verb:
*En España **se come** mucho marisco* → In Spain they eat a lot of seafood. (general statement)
***No se puede** fumar en las discotecas* → One/You can't smoke in clubs. (rule)
***Se debe** respetar las reglas* → One/We should respect the rules. (duty)

7.15 *Hay que* and *tener que*

To express obligation in Spanish use the expressions *hay que* + infinitive or *tener que* + infinitive.
Similarly to the impersonal *se*, *hay que* + infinitive is an impersonal expression:
***Hay que** ser tolerante* → One/We must be tolerant.
In the structure *tener que* + infinitive remember to conjugate the verb *tener*:
***Tengo que** hacer los deberes* → I have to do my homework.
***Tuvimos que** comprar comida* → We had to buy food.

Q What do these sentences mean in English?

1 No se debe fumar – *One/You must not smoke.*
2 No se puede fumar.
3 Tenemos que cuidar el medio ambiente.
4 Hay que reciclar.
5 Tendrían que reciclar la basura.
6 Aquí se vive bien.

7.16 Idiomatic uses of *tener*

There are a number of occasions where in English we use 'to be' + adjective and in Spanish we use *tener* + noun. We call these idiomatic uses of *tener*.

Here are some examples you may be familiar with:

tener ... años	to be ... years old
tener calor	to be hot
tener frío	to be cold
tener éxito	to be successful
tener hambre	to be hungry
tener sed	to be thirsty
tener miedo	to be scared
tener razón	to be right
tener suerte	to be lucky

8 Negatives

To make a sentence negative, place the word **no** before the verb:
Tengo hermanos → *No tengo hermanos.*

When the answer to a question is negative, the word *no* appears twice:
¿Tienes animales? No, no tengo animales.

Other negative words:
nunca – never
nada – nothing
nadie – no one
ningún – none, not one
ni ... ni – neither ... nor
tampoco – not ... either

 Beware! Unlike English, Spanish uses a double negative:
No** vienes **nunca – You never come (literally: You don't come never).
***No** tengo **nada** que hacer* – I have nothing to do (literally: I don't have nothing to do).

R Complete the sentences with the appropriate negative word.

1 Luisa no hizo los deberes.
2 Pepa no hizo   .
3 No tienen   ordenador   consola de videojuegos.
4 No vi   león en el zoo.
5 No fue   a la clase de español.
6 No voy   en autobús.
7 No vamos a comprar   .
8 En la clase de historia   habla   .

9 Direct object pronouns

We use direct object pronouns to replace the direct object in order to avoid repetition. The direct object is the thing that the action in the sentence is happening to:

George bought a t-shirt → 'George' is the subject
→ 'bought' is the verb
→ 'a t-shirt' is the direct object

The direct object is often the answer to the question 'What?': What did he buy? A t-shirt.

	masculine	feminine
singular	lo	la
plural	los	las

Gramática

Direct object pronouns must agree in gender and number with the object they replace.
They usually precede the verb.

*Compra **unos pantalones** → **Los** compra.*
He buys some trousers → He buys them.

When the verb is an infinitive or an imperative, the pronoun is usually added to the end of the verb.

*Voy a comprar **el coche** → Voy a comprar**lo**.*

> **S** **Identify and replace the direct objects in these sentences.**
>
> 1 Compro **flores** para mi madre – ***Las** compro para mi madre.*
> 2 Comí los mangos ayer.
> 3 Escribo un email.
> 4 Vendí mi coche a un amigo.
> 5 Compraré la camiseta azul.
> 6 Marisa no entiende inglés.

10 Asking questions

In Spanish there is no difference in the word order of statements and questions. For this reason it is important that:

- When writing, in addition to the question mark at the end, you must also write an upside down question mark at the beginning of your question: ¿ ... ?
- When speaking, you make your voice go up at the end of the sentence:

Statement:
You like animals.
Te gustan los animales. →

Question:
Do you like animals?
¿Te gustan los animales? →

All Spanish question words have accents:

¿Quién/Quiénes ...? Who ...?	*¿Cuándo ...?* When ...?
¿Qué ...? What ...?	*¿Cuánto/cuánta/cuántos/cuántas ...?* How much/How many ...?
¿Cuál/Cuáles ...? Which ...?	
¿Dónde ...? Where ...?	*¿Cómo ...?* How/What is it like?
¿Adónde ...? Where (to) ...?	*¿Por qué ...?* Why ...?

> **T** **Complete the questions with an appropriate question word.**
>
> 1 ¿ Quién va a venir a la fiesta?
> 2 ¿ _____ es tu cumpleaños?
> 3 ¿ _____ años tienes?
> 4 ¿ _____ es tu casa?
> 5 ¿ _____ está tu instituto?
> 6 ¿ _____ te gusta el fútbol?

11 Opinions

11.1 *Gustar*

Opinions such as *me gusta* or *me interesa* don't end in an **o** for the present tense when talking about 'myself' because they actually translate as 'it pleases me' and 'it interests me'. Effectively the ending matches 'it' (third person singular). This is why when what you like is plural, e.g. *las matemáticas*, we say *me gust**an*** ('they please me').

The same thing occurs in the past tenses so you need to use the ending of the third person singular or plural according to what it is you liked, e.g. *Me gust**ó** la playa* (I liked the beach) but *Me gust**aron** los museos* (I liked the museums).

When you talk about other people's likes and dislikes the pronoun changes: *me, te, le, nos, os, les*.

Example: *te gusta(n)* → you like (it/they please(s) you), *nos gusta(n)* → we like (it/they please(s) us).

When the opinion is followed by a noun, the definite article is needed:

- *Me gustan **las** ciencias. No me gusta **el** fútbol.*

When the opinion is followed by a verb, you must use its infinitive form:

- *Me gusta cocin**ar**. Me gusta aprend**er** idiomas.*

> **U** **How do you say in Spanish ...?**
>
> 1 He likes chips – *Le gustan las patatas fritas.*
> 2 I am interested in culture.
> 3 We loved the film.
> 4 They like art.
> 5 I didn't like the food.
> 6 I don't like the noise.

11.2 *Lo + adjective*

You can use *lo* plus an adjective to give your opinion about something. For example:

***Lo mejor** de Madrid es el Palacio Real* – The best thing about Madrid is the Royal Palace.
***Lo mejor** de viajar es conocer otras culturas* – The best thing about travelling is getting to know other cultures.
***Lo difícil** de hablar español es la pronunciación* – The difficult thing about speaking Spanish is the pronunciation.
***Lo bueno** de España es la comida* – The good thing about Spain is the food.

12 Comparative and superlative

In order to make comparisons in Spanish you will need to use:

- *más/menos* + adjective or noun + *que* ... → more/less ... than ...

  *El zumo es **más sano que** una gaseosa.* Juice is healthier than a fizzy drink.

  *En Lérida hay **menos turismo que** en Tarragona.* In Lérida there is less tourism than in Tarragona.

- *tan* + adjective + *como* ... → as ... as ...

  *El examen de ciencias fue **tan difícil como** el de historia.* The science exam was as difficult as the history one.

- *tanto/tanta/tantos/tantas* + noun + *como* – as much/ many ... as

  *En Mijas no hay **tantas tiendas como** en Málaga.* In Mijas there aren't as many shops as in Málaga.

- *el/la/los/las más/menos* + adjective → the most/least ...

  *Alicia es **la menos deportista** del grupo.* Alicia is the least sporty of the group.

⚠ Remember that there are some common irregular comparatives and superlatives:

bueno → *mejor que, el/la mejor*

malo → *peor que, el/la peor*

viejo (referring to people) → *mayor que, el/la mayor*

joven → *menor que, el/la menor*

> **V** **Compare the two neighbourhoods. Write at least six sentences. Use the words in the box.**
>
> *Example: El barrio A tiene menos tráfico que el barrio B.*
>
> turistas   tiendas   tráfico   limpio   verde   tranquilo

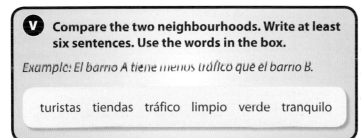

13 Adverbs

Adverbs are words that describe or modify verbs. Most Spanish adverbs are formed by adding **-mente** to the feminine singular form of the adjective.

	adjective		adverb	
	masculine	**feminine**		
fast	rápido	rápida	rápidamente	quickly
generous	generoso	generosa	generosamente	generously
difficult	difícil	difícil	difícilmente	with difficulty
affectionate	cariñoso	cariñosa	cariñosamente	affectionately

⚠ *Bastante* (quite), *demasiado* (too), *mucho* (a lot), *muy* (very), *nunca* (never), *poco* (little) and *siempre* (always) are common adverbs that don't follow the pattern.

> **W** **Complete these sentences with the adverb which comes from the adjective in brackets.**
>
> 1 Cantaba *felizmente* en la ducha. (feliz)
>   *He was singing happily in the shower.*
> 2 Era una persona _____ maravillosa. (verdadero)
>   *He was a truly marvellous person.*
> 3 _____ el perro murió después del accidente. (triste)
>   *Sadly the dog died after the accident.*
> 4 Terminaron sus tareas _____. (rápido)
>   *They finished their tasks quickly.*

Glosario

A

abierto/a *adj* open
el abrazo *nm* hug
abrigar *vb* to protect
abrir *vb* to open
los abuelos *nmpl* grandparents
acogedor(a) *adj* welcoming
acolchado/a *adj* padded
acostarse *vb* to go to bed
la actriz *nf* actress
actuar *vb* to act
el acuario *nm* aquarium
el acueducto *nm* aqueduct
además *adv* besides
adivinar *vb* to guess
¿adónde? *adv* where (to)?
las afueras *nfpl* outskirts
agradable *adj* pleasant
le agradezco (from **agradecer**) I'm grateful
agradecer *vb* to be grateful
ahora *adv* now
el aire *nm* **libre** outdoors
aislado/a *adj* isolated
el ajedrez *nm* chess
la ala *nf* brim (of hat)
la aldea *nf* village
alegremente *adv* happily
algo *pron* something
el algodón *nm* cotton
alguno/a *adj* some
algún tipo de some kind of
allí *adv* there
almorzar *vb* to have (for) lunch
alrededor de *prep* around
amarillo/a *adj* yellow
americano/a *adj* American
el amigo *nm* friend

ancho/a *adj* baggy, wide
los animales salvajes *nmpl* wild animals
el año *nm* year
antiguo/a *adj* old
anual *adj* annual
aparecer *vb* to appear
aplastar *vb* to roll out
apoyar *vb* to support
aprender *vb* to learn
apresuradamente *adv* hastily
aquel/aquella *adj* that (far away)
aquí *adv* here
aquí tienes here you are
el árbol *nm* tree
el arroz *nm* rice
asado/a *adj* roast
asegurar *vb* to secure
la asignatura *nf* subject
atado (from **atar**) tied
atar *vb* to tie
atender *vb* to attend to
audaz *adj* bold
el aula *nf* classroom
aunque *conj* although
australiano/a *adj* Australian
el autocar *nm* coach
autoguiado/a *adj* self-guided (tour)
el ave *nf* bird
ayer *adv* yesterday
ayudar *vb* to help
el azúcar *nm* sugar
azul *adj* blue

B

bailar *vb* to dance
el baile *nm* dance
bajar *vb* to go down
el baloncesto *nm* basketball
el barrio *nm* district

bastante *adv* quite
los bastones de senderismo *nmpl* hiking poles
la batería *nf* drums
beber *vb* to drink
los besos *nmpl* kisses
los besotes *nmpl* kisses
la bicicleta *nf* bicycle
el billete *nm* **sencillo** single ticket
blanco/a *adj* white
bobo/a *adj* silly
el bocadillo *nm* sandwich
el bolso *nm* (hand) bag
bonito/a *adj* pretty
las botas *nfpl* **de vaquero** cowboy boots
la botella *nf* bottle
británico/a *adj* British
bueno/a *adj* good
buscar *vb* to look for

C

los caballeros *nmpl* men
a caballo on horseback
los cabezudos *nmpl* big-headed carnival figures
el cacao *nm* cocoa
cada *adj* each
el café *nm* coffee
el calentamiento *nm* **global** global warming
caliente *adj* hot
calvo/a *adj* bald
la camarera *nf* waitress
el camarero *nm* waiter
cambiar *vb* to change
caminar *vb* to travel
la camisa *nf* shirt
la camiseta *nf* T-shirt
el campo *nm* country
la canción *nf* song
cansado/a *adj* tired
el/la cantante *nm/f* singer
cantar *vb* to sing

caro/a *adj* expensive
la carrera *nf* career
el cartón *nm* cardboard
la casa *nf* house
casado/a *adj* married
castaño/a *adj* chestnut(-coloured)
castigar *vb* to punish
los castillos de arena *nmpl* sandcastles
castizo/a *adj* traditional
celebrar *vb* to celebrate
cenar *vb* to have dinner
cercano/a *adj* near
el cerdo *nm* pork
cerrado (*from* **cerrar**) closed
cerrar *vb* to close
el chándal *nm* tracksuit
charlar *vb* to chat
la charlatana *nf* chatterbox
la chica *nf* girl
el chicle *nm* chewing gum
el chico *nm* boy
chileno/a *adj* Chilean
los chistes *nmpl* jokes
el chorizo *nm* spicy sausage
chulo/a *adj* cool
las ciencias *nfpl* science
por ciento per cent
cincuenta fifty
el cine *nm* cinema
la ciudad *nf* city
el ciudadano (del mundo) citizen (of the world)
claro que of course
el cobre *nm* copper
el coche *nm* car
el cochinillo *nm* suckling pig
la cocina *nf* kitchen
cocinar *vb* to cook
el codo *nf* elbow
coger *vb* to take

la **colección** *nf* collection

el **colegio** *nm* school

colgante *adj* hanging

los **columpios** *nmpl* swings

comer *vb* to eat

cómico/a *adj* funny

la **comida** *nf* meal

comiendo (from **comer**) eating

como *prep* like, the same as

¿cómo? *adv* how?

cómodo/a *adj* comfortable

el **compañero** *nm* partner

la **compañía** *nf* company

competitivo/a *adj* competitive

completamente *adv* completely

comprar *vb* to buy

las **compras** *nfpl* shopping

la **comunidad** *nf* community

con *prep* with

el **concierto** *nm* concert

el **conejo** *nm* rabbit

conmigo *pron* with me

conocer *vb* to know

conocido/a *adj* well-known

conseguir *vb* to achieve

conservador(a) *adj* conservative

construido/a *adj* built

contar *vb* to tell

el **contenedor** *nm* container

contestar *vb* to answer

contratar *vb* to hire

la **corbata** *nf* tie

correr *vb* to run

cortar *vb* to cut (down)

costoso/a *adj* expensive

crecer *vb* to increase

creer *vb* to believe

no **creo** (from **creer**) I don't think so

cruzar *vb* to cross

el **cuaderno** *nm* exercise book

cuadrado/a *adj* squared

cuando *conj* when

¿cuánto? *adv* how much/many?

cuarenta forty

el **cuarto** *nm* **de baño** bathroom

cuarto/a *adj* fourth

el **cuchillo** *nm* knife

la **cuenta** *nf* account

el **cuidado** *nm* care

cuidadosamente *adv* carefully

el **cumpleaños** *nm* birthday

cumplir *vb* to reach (age)

D

la **danza** *nf* **folklórica** folk dancing

dar *vb* to give

dar *vb* **un paseo** to go for a walk

dar *vb* **una vuelta** to go for a stroll

los **deberes** *nmpl* homework

decidir *vb* to decide

décimo/a *adj* tenth

decir *vb* to say

los **dedos** *nmpl* fingers

el **delantero** *nm* forward (in football)

delgado/a *adj* slim

demasiado *adv* too much

el **deporte** *nm* sport

los **deportes acuáticos** *nmpl* water sports

el/la **deportista** *nm/f* sportsman/woman

deprimido/a *adj* depressed

desafortunada- mente *adv* unfortunately

desaparecer *vb* to disappear

la **desaparición** *nf* disappearance

desayunar *vb* to have breakfast

descansar *vb* to rest

la **descripción** *nf* description

descubrir *vb* to discover

desde *prep* from

el **desfile** *nm* procession

desgraciadamente *adv* unfortunately

el **desierto** *nm* desert

desordenado/a *adj* messy

después *adv* later, then

después de *prep* after

detallado/a *adj* detailed

di (from **dar**) I gave

el **día** *nm* day

dibujar *vb* to draw

difícil *adj* difficult

el **dinero** *nm* money

la **dirección** *nf* direction/address

dirigir *vb* to direct

el **diseñador** designer

los **disfraces** *nmpl* costumes

el **disfraz** *nm* disguise

disfrutar *vb* to enjoy

divertirse *vb* to have a good time

la **docena** *nf* dozen

el **domingo** *nm* Sunday

donde *conj* where

dormir *vb* to sleep

el **dormitorio** *nm* bedroom

la **ducha** *nf* shower

ducharse *vb* to have a shower

dulce *adj* soft

durante *prep* for, during

E

ecológico/a *adj* eco-friendly

ecuatoriano/a *adj* Ecuadorian

la **edad** *f* age

el **ejercicio** *nm* exercise

el **embajador** *nm* ambassador

sin **embargo** however

la **emoción** *nf* emotion

la **empanada** *nf* pie

empezar *vb* to begin

encontrar *vb* to find

encontrarse *vb* to meet

enfadado/a *adj* annoyed

enfermo/a *adj* sick

la **ensalada** *nf* salad

entonces *adv* then

la **entrada** *nf* (entrance) ticket

la **época** *nf* time

equilibrado/a *adj* balanced

el **equipo** *nm* team

era (from **ser**) it was

Escocia *nf* Scotland

escoger *vb* to choose

escribir *vb* to write

el/la **escritor(a)** *nm/f* writer

escuchando (from **escuchar**) listening (to)

escuchar *vb* to listen to

la **escultura** *nf* sculpture

ese/a *adj* that (close)

la **esmeralda** *nf* emerald

a **eso de** *adv* about

la **espalda** *nf* back

español(a) *adj* Spanish

especializado/a *adj* specialised

específico/a *adj* specific

Glosario

los **espectadores** *nmpl* spectators
esperar *vb* to hope
el **esquí** *nm* skiing
esquiar *vb* to ski
la **estación** *nf* station
estar *vb* to be
este/a *adj* this
el **estilo** *nm* style
estrecho/a *adj* tight
la **estrella** *nf* star
estricto/a *adj* strict
estuve (from **estar**) I was
europeo/a *adj* European
extenderse *vb* to extend

F

la **fábrica** *nf* factory
fácil *adj* easy
la **falda** *nf* skirt
la **familia** *nf* family
famoso/a *adj* famous
me **fastidia** it annoys me
favorito/a *adj* favourite
la **fecha** *nf* date
feo/a *adj* ugly
la **feria** *nf* fair
la **fiesta** *nf* party, festival
por **fin** finally
el **fin de semana** *nm* weekend
me **flipa(n)** I'm mad about
la **flor** *nf* flower
frecuentemente *adv* often
freír *vb* to fry
fresco/a *adj* fresh
frito/a *adj* fried
las **frutas** *nfpl* fruit
fuerte *adj* strong
fui (from **ir**) I went
fui (from **ser**) I was
el **fútbol** *nm* football

G

las **gafas de sol** *nfpl* sunglasses
la **galleta** *nf* biscuit

las **gambas** *nfpl* prawns
el **ganado** *nm* cattle
ganar *vb* to earn
la **gente** *nf* people
los **gigantes** *nmpl* giants
grabar *vb* to record
los **grados** *nmpl* degrees
la **gran tirolina** *nf* zip-lining
grande *adj* big
gratis *adj* free
gris *adj* grey
el **grupo** *nm* group
los **guantes** *nmpl* gloves
guapo/a *adj* pretty
guay *adj* cool
la **guitarra** *nf* guitar
me **gusta(n)** I like
no me **gusta(n) nada** … I don't like … at all

H

haber *vb* to have
el **habitante** *nm* inhabitant
habitual *adj* usual
hablar *vb* to speak
hacer *vb* to do/make
haciendo (from **hacer**) doing
hago (from **hacer**) I do
el **hambre** *nf* hunger
hasta *prep* until
hay (from **haber**) there is/are
el **helado** *nm* ice-cream
la **herencia** *nf* heritage
la **hermana** *nf* sister
el **hermano** *nm* brother
hice (from **hacer**) I did
la **hija** *nf* daughter
el **hijo** *nm* son
el/la **hincha** *nm/f* fan
el **hogar** *nm* home
el **hombre** *nm* man
la **hora** *nf* hour
el **horario** *nm* timetable

hospedarse *vb* to stay
hoy *adv* today
el **huevo** *nm* egg

I

la **ilustración** *nf* illustration
impermeable *adj* waterproof
inaugurar *vb* to open
incluso *prep* including
incómodo/a *adj* uncomfortable
increíble *adj* incredible
indígena *adj* indigenous
infantil *adj* children's
el **infierno** *nm* hell
la **información** *nf* information
inglés *adj* English
inmaduro/a *adj* immature
la **insolación** *nf* sunstroke
el **insti(tuto)** *nm* school
insuficiente *adj* inadequate
interesante *adj* interesting
ir *vb* (**de paseo**) to go (for a walk)
la **izquierda** *nf* left

J

el **jefe** *nm* boss
joven *adj* young
los **jóvenes** *nmpl* young people
el **jueves** *nm* Thursday
el **jugador** *nm* player
jugar *vb* to play
los **juguetes** *nmpl* toys
juntos *adv* together

L

el **lago** *nm* lake
el **lápiz** *nm* pencil
largo/a *adj* long
la **lata** *nf* tin

el **lavaplatos** *nm* dishwasher
la **leche** *nf* milk
leer *vb* to read
lejos *adv* far
la **lengua** *nf* **materna** mother tongue
lentamente *adv* slowly
el **león** *nm* lion
levantarse *vb* to get up
libre *adj* free
la **librería** *nf* bookshop
el **libro** *nm* book
ligero/a *adj* light
la **limonada** *nf* lemonade
limpiar *vb* to clean
limpio/a *adj* clean
la **línea** *nf* line
lírico/a *adj* lyrical
el **litoral** *nm* coastline
llamarse *vb* to be called
la **llegada** *nf* arrival
llegar *vb* to arrive
llegué (from **llegar**) I arrived
lleno/a *adj* full of
llover *vb* to rain
el **logotipo** *nm* logo
luego *adv* then
el **lugar** *nm* place
el **lunes** *nm* Monday

M

la **madrastra** *nf* stepmother
la **madre** *nf* mother
maduro/a *adj* ripe
la **maestra** *nf* (female) schoolteacher
el **maíz** *nm* corn
mal *adj* bad
malsano/a *adj* unhealthy
mañana *adv* tomorrow
la **mañana** *nf* morning
la **manera** *nf* way
la **mantequilla** *nf* butter
la **manzana** *nf* apple

la **maquinaria** *nf* machinery

el **mar** *nm* sea

maravilloso/a *adj* wonderful

mareado/a *adj* seasick

el **marido** *nm* husband

marrón *adj* brown

el **martes** *nm* Tuesday

más *adv* more

a **más tardar** *adv* at the latest

mediano/a *adj* average

las **medias** *nfpl* tights

el **medio ambiente** *nm* environment

el **medio** *nm* half

medioambiental *adj* environmental

el **mediodía** *nm* midday

el **medio-hermano** *nm* half-brother

medir *vb* to measure

mejor *adv* better

el **melón** *nm* melon

menos *adv* less

el **mensaje** *nm* message

mensual *adj* monthly

mensualmente *adv* monthly

la **mentira** *nf* lie

a **menudo** *adv* often

merendar *vb* to have tea/a snack

la **mermelada** *nf* jam

el **mes** *nm* month

mestizo/a *adj* mixed-race

la **mezcla** *nf* mixture

mezclar *vb* to mix

sin **miedo** *adj* fearless

el **miércoles** *nm* Wednesday

la **minifalda** *nf* mini-skirt

mirar *vb* to look at

mismo/a *adj* same

la **mochila** *nf* rucksack

la **moda** *nf* fashion

la **modelo** *nf* model

moderno/a *adj* modern

la **mojarra** *nf* type of fish (sea bream)

me **mola** it's great

montar *vb* to ride

moreno/a *adj* dark(-haired)

morir *vb* to die

mostrar *vb* to show

mover *vb* to move

mucho/a *adj* a lot of

muchas veces often

los **muebles** *nmpl* furniture

la **muerte** *nf* death

la **mujer** *nf* woman, wife

multicolor *adj* multi-coloured

multitudinario/a *adj* huge (concert)

el **mundo** *nm* world

el **muñeco** *nm* doll

el **museo** *nm* museum

la **música** *nf* music

muy *adv* very

N

nacer *vb* to be born

nacido/a *adj* born

nació (from **nacer**) was born

nada *pron* nothing

nadar *vb* to swim

la **naranja** *nf* orange

la **nave** *nf* **espacial** spaceship

negro/a *adj* black

la **nieve** *nf* snow

el **niño** *nm* child

los **niños** *nmpl* children

el **nivel** *nm* level

la **noche** *nf* night

el **nombre** *nm* name

normalmente *adv* usually

noveno/a *adj* ninth

noventa ninety

nuevo/a *adj* new

nunca *adv* never

O

la **obra** *nf* work

ochenta eighty

el **ocio** *nm* leisure

octavo/a *adj* eighth

odiar *vb* to hate

ofrecer *vb* to offer

las **olas** *nfpl* waves

ondulado/a *adj* wavy

el **ordenador** *nm* computer

el **oro** *nm* gold

la **orquídea** *nf* orchid

el **oso** *nm* bear

otro/a *adj* another

P

el **padrastro** *nm* stepfather

el **padre** *nm* father

pagar *vb* to pay

el **país** *nm* country

la **paja** *nf* straw

el **papel** *nm* role

para *prep* in order to

la **parada** *nf* stop

parar *vb* to stop

parecer *vb* to seem

el **parque** *nm* park

el **partido** *nm* game

el **pasado** *nm* past

pasado/a *adj* last

pasar *vb* to spend

pasar *vb* **un rato** to spend time

pasear *vb* to walk

las **patatas** *nfpl* **fritas** chips, crisps

el **pedacito** *nm* small piece

pedir *vb* to ask for

pegar *vb* to hit (a ball)

peinarse *vb* to comb your hair

la **película** *nf* film

el **peligro** *nm* danger

pelirrojo/a *adj* red-haired

el **pelo** *nm* hair

la **peluquería** *nf* hairdresser's

pensar *vb* to think

lo **peor** the worst

pequeño/a *adj* small

perder *vb* to miss

perdonar *vb* to forgive

perfectamente *adv* perfectly

el **periódico** *nm* newspaper

pero *conj* but

el **perro** *nm* dog

peruano/a *adj* Peruvian

el **pescado** *nm* fish

los **pesos** *nmpl* weights

el **petróleo** *nm* oil

pidiendo (from **pedir**) asking for

el **pimiento** *nm* pepper

la **piña** *nf* pineapple

el/la **pintor(a)** *nm/f* painter

la **piscina** *nf* swimming pool

el **piso** *nm* floor

los **plátanos** *nmpl* bananas

el **plato** *nm* dish

la **playa** *nf* beach

el **plomo** *nm* lead

pobre *adj* poor

la **pobreza** *nf* poverty

poco a poco gradually

poco/a *adj* little

poder *vb* to be able

el **polideportivo** *nm* sports centre

poner *vb* to put

porque *conj* because

practicar *vb* to go in for (sport)

el **precio** *nm* price

precioso/a *adj* pretty

preferido/a *adj* favourite

preferir *vb* to prefer

el **premio** *nm* prize

preocuparse *vb* to worry

el/la **primo/a** *nm/f* cousin

a **principios de** *adv* at the beginning of

probar *vb* to try (taste)

la **procesión** *nf* procession

Glosario

prometer *vb* to promise
pronto *adv* soon
propio/a *adj* own
protegido/a *adj* protected
próximo/a *adj* next
el **proyecto** *nm* project
el **pueblo** *nm* town
puedes (from **poder**) you can
puertorriqueño/a *adj* Puerto Rican
la **punta** *nf* tip
en **punto** *adv* exactly
el **punto** *nm* dot
puse (from **poner**) I put

Q

¿qué? *adv* what?
que viene next
¡qué asco! how horrible!
¡qué lástima! what a pity!
¡qué vergüenza! what a shame!
quedar *vb* to suit; to be (situated)
quedarse *vb* to stay
querer *vb* to want
quiero (from **querer**) I want
quinto/a *adj* fifth
el **quiosco** *nm* kiosk
quise (from **querer**) I wanted
quizás *adv* perhaps

R

rápido/a *adj* quick
con **rayas (blancas)** (white) striped
la **receta** *nf* recipe
recibir *vb* to receive
recientemente *adv* recently
recoger *vb* to clean up
recordar *vb* to remember

el **recorrido** *nm* journey
la **red** *nf* network
las **redes** *nfpl* **sociales** social networks
redondo/a *adj* round
regalar *vb* to give as a gift
el **regalo** *nm* present
el **regreso** *nm* return
regular *adj* average
relajado/a *adj* relaxed
relajarse *vb* to relax
rellenar *vb* to fill
el **reloj** *nm* clock, watch
repartir *vb* to distribute
repetir *vb* to repeat
respirar *vb* to breathe
la **revista** *nf* magazine
rico/a *adj* rich/delicious
ridículo/a *adj* ridiculous
rítmico/a *adj* rhythmic(al)
el **ritmo** *nm* rhythm
rizado/a *adj* curly
rodeado/a (por) *adj* encircled (by)
el **rodillo** *nm* rolling pin
rojo/a *adj* red
romper *vb* to break
rosa *adj* pink
rubio/a *adj* blond
las **ruedas** *nfpl* wheels
ruidosamente *adv* loudly
ruidoso/a *adj* noisy
la **ruta** *nf* route

S

el **sábado** *nm* Saturday
sabroso/a *adj* tasty
sacar *vb* to pull out
sacar *vb* **fotos** to take photos
el **salario** *nm* salary
salgo (from **salir**) I go out

salir *vb* to go out
el **salón** *nm* living room
saltar *vb* to jump
el **salto** *nm* jump
saludable *adj* healthy
el **sancocho** *nm* dish (stew)
los **santos** *nmpl* saints
en **seguida** *adv* straight away
seguir *vb* to follow
segundo/a *adj* second
seguro/a *adj* sure, safe
la **selva** *nf* tropical forest
la **semana** *nf* week
semanal *adj* weekly
semanalmente *adv* weekly
el **senderismo** *nm* hiking
las **señoras** *nfpl* women
sensacional *adj* sensational
sentado/a *adj* seated
sentir *vb* to be sorry
séptimo/a *adj* seventh
ser *vb* to be
la **serie** *nf* series
serio/a *adj* serious
la **serranía** *nf* mountains
sexto/a *adj* sixth
siempre *adv* always
lo **siento** (from **sentir**) I'm sorry
la **sierra** *nf* mountain range
sigue (from **seguir**) continue
simpático/a *adj* nice, kind
sintético/a *adj* synthetic
sobre todo especially
sobresaliente *adj* outstanding
el **sol** *nm* sun
sólo *adv* only

solo/a *adj* alone
la **sombra** *nf* shade
el **sondeo** *nm* survey
soportar *vb* to stand (endure)
soy (from **ser**) I am
suave *adj* soft
subir *vb* to climb
sudamericano/a *adj* South American
sueles ir you usually go
el **suelo** *nm* floor
el **sueño** *nm* dream
la **suerte** *nf* (good) luck
por **supuesto** of course
el **sur** *nm* south
las **sustancias** *nfpl* **químicas** chemicals

T

también *adv* also
tan *adv* so
la **tarde** *nf* evening
la **taza** *nf* cup
la **telenovela** *nf* soap opera
temblando (from **temblar**) trembling
temblar *vb* to tremble
temprano *adv* early
tener que *vb* to have to
tener *vb* to have
tener *vb* **miedo** to be afraid
tercero/a *adj* third
testarudo/a *adj* stubborn
el **tiempo** *nm* weather
a **tiempo parcial** part-time
la **tienda** *nf* **de electrodomésticos** household appliances shop
la **tierra** *nf* earth
el **tío** *nm* uncle
típico/a *adj* typical
tirar *vb* to throw

el **tiro con arco** *nm* archery

el **título** *nm* title

el **tobogán** *nm* slide

tocar *vb* to play (instrument), to touch

por **todas partes** *adv* everywhere

todavía *adv* still

todo/a *adj* all

tomar *vb* to take

los **tomates** *nmpl* tomatoes

torcer *vb* to turn

el **toro** *nm* bull

el **trabajador** *nm* worker

trabajar *vb* to work

tradicional *adj* traditional

traer *vb* to bring

el **traje** *nm* **de baño** swimsuit

el **tratamiento** *nm* treatment

tratar *vb* to deal with

el **trayecto** *nm* journey

treinta thirty

tristemente *adv* sadly

el **tubo** *nm* tube

tuerce (from **torcer**) turn

tuve (from **tener**) I had

U

último/a *adj* last

el **uniforme** *nm* uniform

uruguayo/a *adj* Uruguayan

usar *vb* to use

útil *adj* useful

utilizarse *vb* to be used

las **uvas** *nfpl* grapes

V

las **vacaciones** *nfpl* holidays

valiente *adj* brave

los **vaqueros** *nmpl* jeans

la **variedad** *nf* variety

el **vaso** *nm* glass

a **veces** *adv* sometimes

el **vecino** *nm* neighbour

ver *vb* to see

ver *vb* **la tele** to watch TV

el **verano** *nm* summer

la **verdad** *nf* truth

verde *adj* green

las **verduras** *nfpl* vegetables

verificar *vb* to check

vestirse *vb* to get dressed

la **vez** *nf* time

vi (from **ver**) I saw

viajar *vb* to travel

el **viajero** *nm* traveller

la **vida** *nf* life

los **videojuegos** *nmpl* video games

viejo/a *adj* old

el **viernes** *nm* Friday

el **viñedo** *nm* vineyard

el **vino** *nm* wine

la **vista** *nf* view

vivir *vb* to live

vivo/a *adj* bright

volver *vb* to return

Z

la **zapatería** *nf* shoe shop

los **zapatos** *nmpl* shoes

el **zumo** *nm* juice

OXFORD
UNIVERSITY PRESS

Great Clarendon Street, Oxford OX2 6DP

Oxford University Press is a department of the University of Oxford.

It furthers the University's objective of excellence in research, scholarship, and education by publishing worldwide in
Oxford New York Auckland Cape Town Dar es Salaam Hong Kong
Karachi Kuala Lumpur Madrid Melbourne Mexico City Nairobi
New Delhi Shanghai Taipei Toronto

With offices in
Argentina Austria Brazil Chile Czech Republic France Greece
Guatemala Hungary Italy Japan South Korea Poland Portugal
Singapore Switzerland Thailand Turkey Ukraine Vietnam

Oxford is a registered trade mark of Oxford University Press
in the UK and in certain other countries

British Library Cataloguing in Publication Data

Data available

ISBN 978 019 912762 7

10 9 8

Printed in China by Leo Paper Products Ltd.

Paper used in the production of this book is a natural, recyclable product made from wood grown in sustainable forests. The manufacturing process conforms to the environmental regulations of the country of origin.

Acknowledgements

The publishers would like to thank the following for permission to reproduce photographs: **p.4**: Leam David; **p.4**: Tomas Sereda/Shutterstock; **p.9**: Monart Design/Fotolia; **p.9**: Istockphoto/Thinkstock; **p.9**: Jack Hollingsworth/ Photodisc/Thinkstock; **p.12**: Luckyphoto/Shutterstock; **p.18**: Rubberball/ Alamy; **p.18**: Marko Tomicic/Shutterstock; **p.18**: Layland Masuda/Shutterstock; **p.18**: Alexandrenunes/Shutterstock; **p.28**: Pres Panayotov/Shutterstock.Com; **p.28**: Shutterstock/Gkuna; **p.28**: Ta_Samaya/Dreamstime; **p.28**: Istockphoto/ Thinkstock; **p.28**: Botond/Dreamstime; **p.28**: Justin Black/Dreamstime; **p.28**: Petrenko Andriy/Shutterstock; **p.33**: Radius Images/Alamy; **p.33**: Catchlight Visual Services/Alamy/Photolibrary; **p.34**: Glowimages/Alamy/Photolibrary; **p.36**: Gulei Ivan/Shutterstock; **p.36**: Karkas/Shutterstock; **p.36**: Karkas/ Shutterstock; **p.36**: Ugorenkov Aleksandr/Shutterstock; **p.36**: Kadroff/ Shutterstock; **p.36**: Vereshchagin Dmitry/Shutterstock; **p.36**: Ecco/Shutterstock; **p.36**: Sergios/Shutterstock; **p.39**: Pictorial Press Ltd/Alamy; **p.39**: Bettmann/ Corbis; **p.39**: Mauro Carraro/Rex Features; **p.40**: Angela Cantó Soto; **p.42**: Heng Kong Chen/Istockphoto; **p.42**: Despotovic Dusko/Corbis Sygma; **p.42**: Susana Vera/Reuters/Corbis; **p.42**: Jbor/Shutterstock; **p.42**: Jbor/Shutterstock; **p.42**: Alex Segre/Alamy; **p.43**: Laura Gangi Pond/Shutterstock; **p.43**: Tao Images Limited/Alamy; **p.43**: Tupungato/Shutterstock; **p.43**: Juanmonino/Istockphoto; **p.44**: Juan Medina/Reuters/Corbis; **p.44**: Vitalii Nesterchuk/Shutterstock; **p.44**: Stockphoto4u/istockphoto.com; **p.44**: Ilja Mašík/Shutterstock; **p.44**: Supri Suharjoto/Shutterstock; **p.44**: Ivanova Inga/Shutterstock; **p.54**: Compuinfoto/ Fotolia; **p.54**: Emilio Ereza/Alamy/Photolibrary; **p.54**: Dumont Bildarchiv/Dpa Picture Alliance; **p.54**: Emilio Ereza/Alamy/Photolibrary; **p.54**: Peter Horree/ Alamy; **p.56**: Bob Thomas/Photographer's Choice/Getty Images; **p.56**: Corbis; **p.56**: Luigi Roscia/Dreamstime; **p.56**: The Print Collector/Getty Images; **p.56**: Sandimako/Shutterstock; **p.56**: Dmitriy Shironosov/Shutterstock; **p.58**: Bjanka Kadic/Alamy/Photolibrary; **p.58**: Agencia Efe/Rex Features; **p.58**: American Images Inc/Getty Images; **p.58**: Sitges' Council; **p.65**: Erik Pendzich/Rex/Rex Features; **p.65**: Rangizzz/Shutterstock; **p.66**: Jarno Gonzalez Zarraonandia/ Shutterstock; **p.68**: Dpa Picture Alliance; **p.68**: María Galán/Photolibrary; **p.68**: Solodovnikova Elena/Shutterstock; **p.68**: Rafal Olkis/Shutterstock; **p.68**: Ungor/Fotolia; **p.68**: Peter Titmuss/Alamy; **p.69**: Forget Patrick/Sagaphoto.Com/ Alamy; **p.70**: Rob Wilson/Shutterstock; **p.70**: Alexandra Gnatush/Fotolia; **p.70**: Peter Horree/Alamy/Photolibrary; **p.70**: Jlimages/Alamy/Photolibrary; **p.70**: Tupungato/Shutterstock; **p.70**: Vaju Ariel/Shutterstock; **p.71**: Chris Rout/Alamy/

Photolibrary; **p.71**: Big Cheese/Photolibrary; **p.72**: Alberto Paredes/Alamy/ Photolibrary; **p.73**: Madrid Guide; **p.73**: Faberfoto/Shutterstock; **p.81**: Arco Images Gmbh/Dpa Picture Alliance; **p.87**: Goodshoot/Thinkstock; **p.87**: Angela Cantó Soto; **p.89**: Sipa Press/Rex Features; **p.91**: Chrislofoto/Shutterstock; **p.91**: Mana Photo/Shutterstock; **p.91**: Sue Mcdonald/Shutterstock; **p.91**: Oliveromg/ Shutterstock; **p.93**: Creatista/Shutterstock; **p.96**: Harry Page/Rex Features; **p.97**: Sportgraphic/Shutterstock.Com; **p.98**: Sabri Deniz Kizil/Shutterstock; **p.100**: Dpa Picture Alliance; **p.103**: Matt Antonino/Shutterstock; **p.103**: Mircea Bezergheanu/Shutterstock; **p.103**: Istockphoto/Thinkstock; **p.103**: Bill Bachmann/Alamy/Photolibrary; **p.104**: Jack Hollingsworth/Thinkstock; **p.104**: Pt Images/Shutterstock; **p.105**: Luckyraccoon/Shutterstock; **p.108**: Kpa Honorar & Belege/Dpa Picture Alliance; **p.108**: C.Paramount/Everett/Rex Features; **p.109**: Ker Robertson/Getty Images Sport; **p.109**: Dpa Picture Alliance; **p.109**: Katyart/ Shutterstock; **p.113**: Pascal Rondeau/Getty Images Sport; **p.113**: Photos.Com/ Thinkstock; **p.113**: Lebrecht Music & Arts Photo Library/Photographers Direct; **p.113**: Francesco81/Shutterstock; **p.114**: Jupiterimages/Pixland/Thinkstock; **p.114**: Todd Warnock/Lifesize/Thinkstock; **p.114**: George Doyle/Thinkstock; **p.116**: Tatiana Edrenkina/Shutterstock; **p.116**: Istockphoto/Thinkstock; **p.116**: Balance/Photoshot/Dpa Picture Alliance; **p.116**: Jenny Leonard/Istock; **p.116**: Psd Photography/Shutterstock; **p.116**: Sean Sprague/Photolibrary; **p.116**: Ralf Heinze/Photolibrary; **p.116**: Jason Stitt/Shutterstock; **p.118**: Frances Fruit/Dreamstime; **p.118**: Tupungato/Dreamstime; **p.118**: Rubberball/Alamy; **p.118**: Elena Elisseeva/Shutterstock; **p.118**: Lyf1/Shutterstock; **p.118**: Dpa Picture Alliance; **p.118**: Destiny Vispro/Shutterstock; **p.118**: Jesus_Cabrera/ Demotix/Demotix/Corbis; **p.119**: Bruce Rolff/Shutterstock; **p.121**: Sylwia Blaszczyszyn/Dreamstime; **p.124**: Bill Bachmann/Alamy/Photolibrary; **p.124**: Nhpa/Photoshot/Dpa Picture Alliance; **p.128**: Psd Photography/Shutterstock; **p.128**: Balance/Photoshot/Dpa Picture Alliance; **p.128**: jleonard/istockphoto; **p.128**: Sean Sprague/Photolibrary; **p.128**: Istockphoto/Thinkstock; **p.128**: Tatiana Edrenkina/Shutterstock; **p.129**: Sima/Shutterstock; **p.129**: Volodymyr Goinyk/Shutterstock; **p.129**: Zhan Tian/Istock; **p.129**: Lafoto/Shutterstock; **p.130**: Andrey Arkusha/Shuttertock; **p.130**: Agnieszka Pastuszak – Maksim/ Dreamstime; **p.130**: Andrey Arkusha/Shuttertock; **p.133**: Oup; **p.134**: Vipflash/Shutterstock.Com; **p.134**: Joe Seer/Shutterstock.Com; **p.134**: Joe Seer/ Shutterstock.Com; **p.134**: Sportgraphic/Shutterstock.Com; **p.134**: Bettmann/ Corbis; **p.134**: Ulf Andersen/Getty Images; **p.134**: Allstar Picture Library/Alamy; **p.135**: Afp/Getty Images; **p.136**: Tipograffias/Shutterstock.Com; **p.136**: Bao Feifei/Xinhua Press/Corbis; **p.136**: Darrell Gulin/Corbis; **p.136**: Robert Harding World Imagery/Corbis; **p.136**: Js Photo/Alamy; **p.137**: Victor Chavez/Getty Images; **p.138**: Helga Esteb/Shutterstock.Com; **p.138**: Mark Makela/In Pictures/ Corbis; **p.138**: Allstar Picture Library/Alamy; **p.138**: Helga Esteb/Shutterstock. Com; **p.138**: Dfree/Shutterstock.Com; **p.138**: Kristin Callahan/Rex Features; **p.141**: Allstar Picture Library/Alamy; **p.144**: Leon/Retna Ltd./Corbis; **p.144**: Rune Hellestad/Corbis; **p.144**: C.Abc/Everett/Rex Features; **p.145**: Sportgraphic/ Shutterstock.Com; **p.145**: Clive Mason/Staff/Getty Images; **p.146**: Elena Elisseeva/Shutterstock; **p.146**: Hola Images/Alamy; **p.148**: Francesco Ridolfi/ Dreamstime; **p.148**: Christopher Meder – Photography/Shutterstock; **p.149**: Janos Csernoch/Alamy/Photolibrary; **p.150**: Supri Suharjoto/Shutterstock; **p.150**: Ivanova Inga/Shutterstock; **p.150**: Oleg Zabielin/Shutterstock; **p.150**: Ilja Mašík/Shutterstock; **p.151**: Jan Sochor/Alamy/Photolibrary; **p.151**: Max Blain/Shutterstock; **p.152**: Derek Punaro/Dreamstime; **p.152**: Tp/Alamy; **p.152**: Dpa Picture Alliance; **p.152**: Dpa Picture Alliance; **p.153**: Tony West/ Alamy/Photolibrary **p.153**: Fotoandrea/Shutterstock; **p.153**: Blend Images/ Alamy/Photolibrary; **p.153**: Sw Productions/Photolibrary; **p.154**: Chepe Nicoli/ Shutterstock; **p.154**: Elena Elisseeva/Shutterstock; **p.155**: Peter Scoones/Science Photo Library; **p.155**: Gregory Ochocki/Science Photo Library; **p.156**: L. Prang & Co./Popular Graphic Arts/Library Of Congress; **p.156**: Maxym/Shutterstock.

All other photography contributed by Ángela Cantó Soto.

Illustrations by Caron Painter, John Hallett, Martin Sanders, Q2A Media, Theresa Tibbetts, Paul Daviz, Javier Joaquin and Stuart Holmes.

Cover illustration by: Oxford Designers & Illustrators

The authors and publisher would like to thank the following people for their help and advice: Michelle Armstrong (editor), Karen Sherwood (course consultant), Julie Green (course consultant), Jaime Veiga-Perez (language consultant).

Audio recordings produced by Colette Thomson for Footstep Productions Ltd; Andrew Garratt (engineer).

Video shot on location in Segovia with grateful thanks to Colette Thomson (producer, director, writer) for Footstep Productions Ltd. Ángela Cantó Soto (location manager); Pablo Vega (cameraman); José Ignacio Arrufat and Adrián Povedo (sound). Actors: Helena Martín Arribas (Elena), Adrián Moreno (Roberto), Juan Horcajo Collazo (Juan).

Every effort has been made to contact copyright holders of material reproduced in this book. If notified, the publishers will be pleased to rectify any errors or omissions at the earliest opportunity.